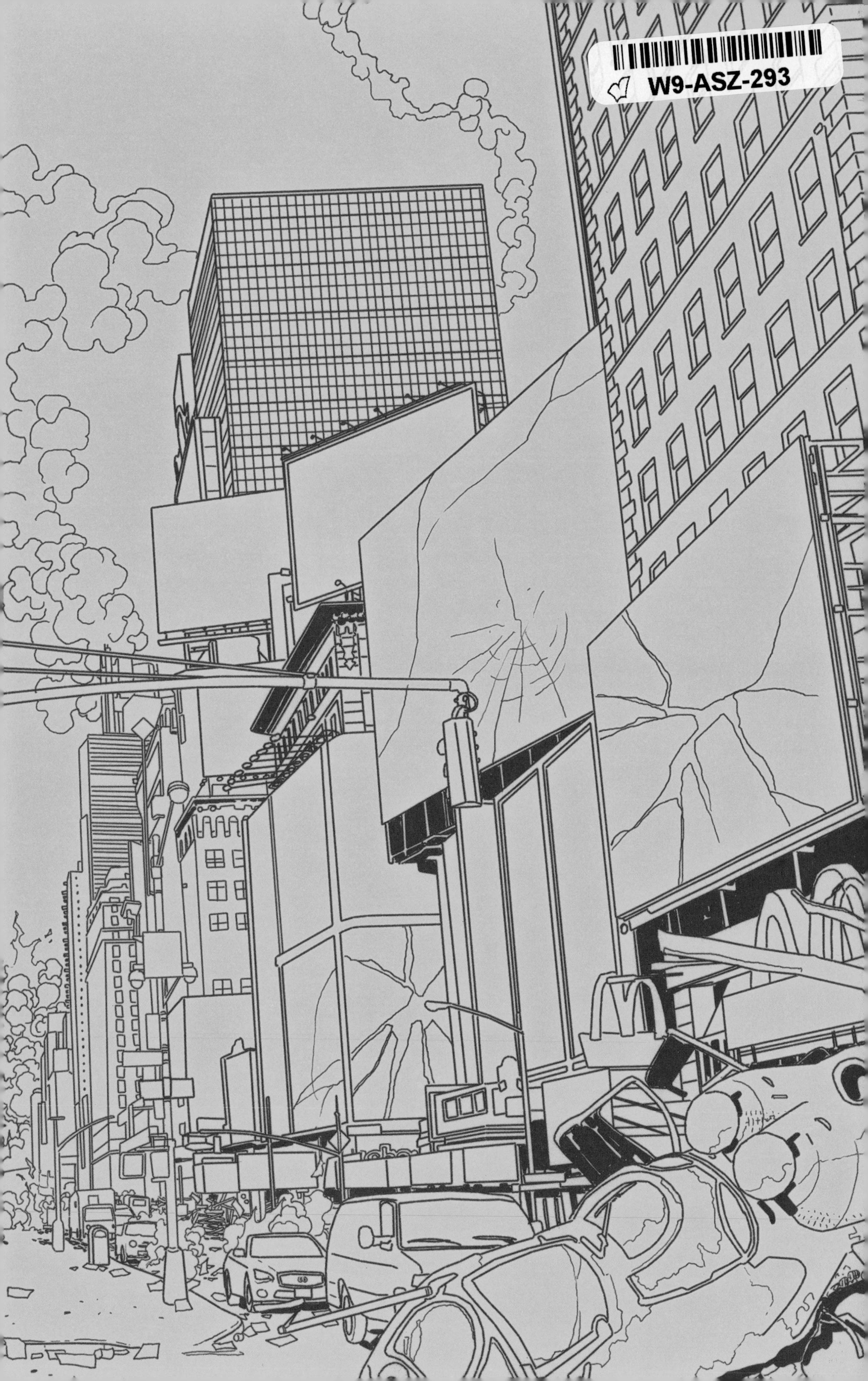

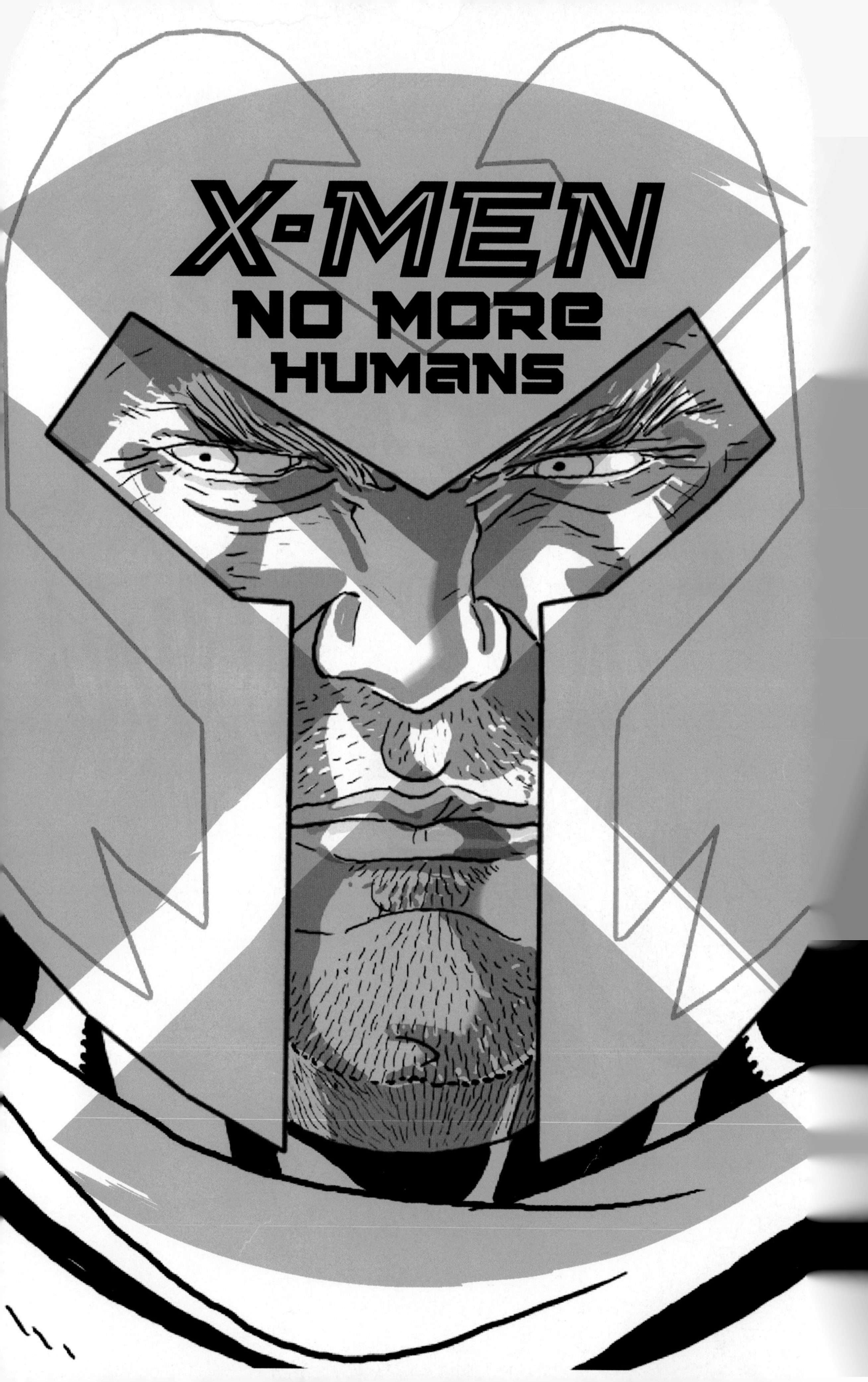
X-MEN
NO MORE HUMANS

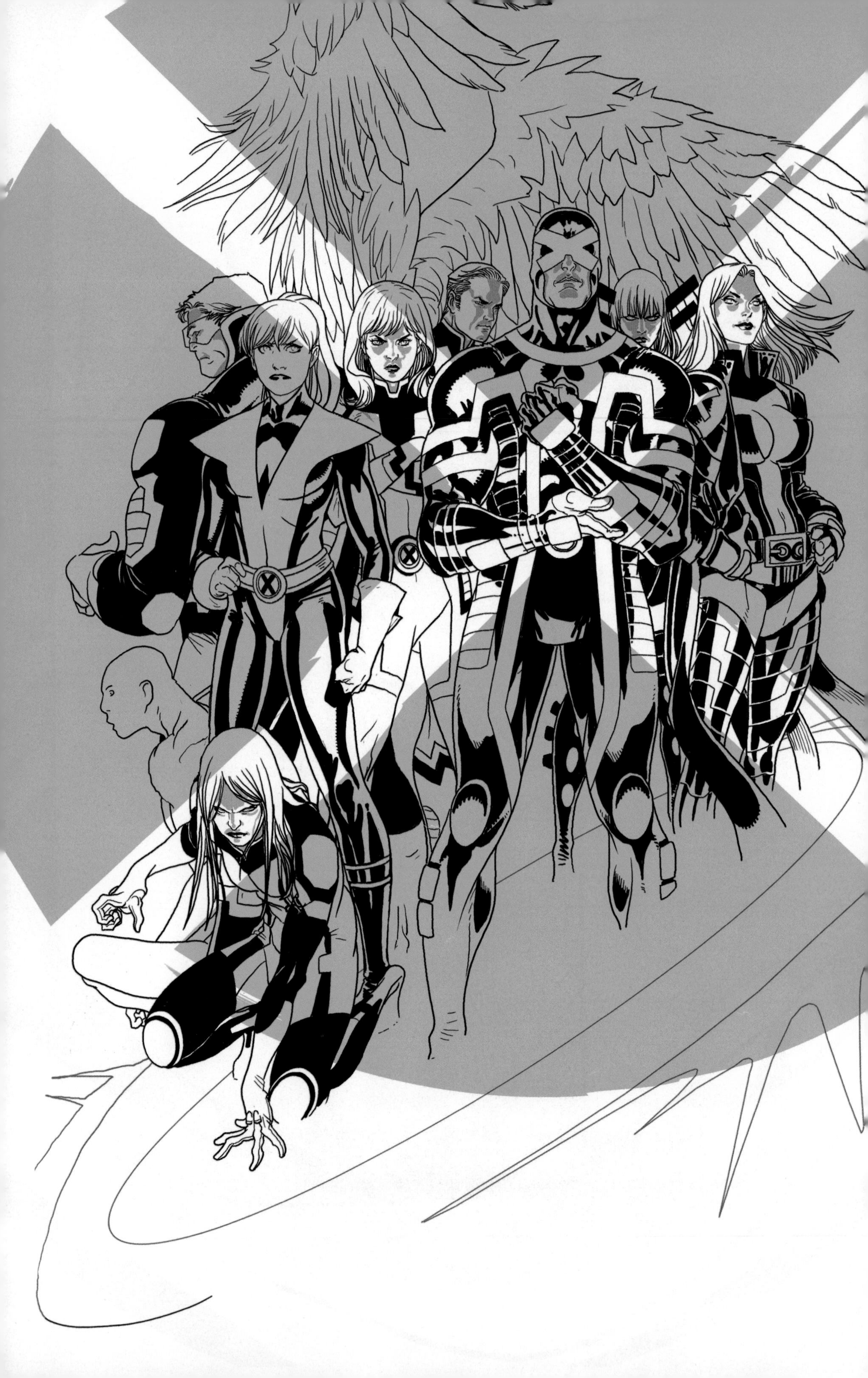

X-MEN
NO MORE HUMANS

MIKE CAREY WRITER
SALVADOR LARROCA ARTIST
JUSTIN PONSOR COLOR ARTIST
WITH MATT MILLA, JEROMY COX AND GURU-EFX

VC'S CORY PETIT LETTERER
SALVADOR LARROCA COVER ARTIST
XANDER JAROWEY ASSISTANT EDITOR
NICK LOWE EDITOR

JENNIFER GRÜNWALD COLLECTION EDITOR
ALEX STARBUCK ASSOCIATE MANAGING EDITOR
MARK D. BEAZLEY EDITOR, SPECIAL PROJECTS
JEFF YOUNGQUIST SENIOR EDITOR, SPECIAL PROJECTS
DAVID GABRIEL SVP PRINT, SALES & MARKETING
JARED K. FLETCHER BOOK DESIGNER

AXEL ALONSO EDITOR IN CHIEF
JOE QUESADA CHIEF CREATIVE OFFICER
DAN BUCKLEY PUBLISHER
ALAN FINE EXECUTIVE PRODUCER

X-MEN: NO MORE HUMANS. FIRST PRINTING 2014. ISBN# 978-0-7851-5402-0. PUBLISHED BY MARVEL WORLDWIDE, INC., A SUBSIDIARY OF MARVEL ENTERTAINMENT, LLC. OFFICE OF PUBLICATION: 135 WEST 50TH STREET, NEW YORK, NY 10020. COPYRIGHT © 2014 MARVEL CHARACTERS, INC. ALL RIGHTS RESERVED. ALL CHARACTERS FEATURED IN THIS ISSUE AND THE DISTINCTIVE NAMES AND LIKENESSES THEREOF, AND ALL RELATED INDICIA ARE TRADEMARKS OF MARVEL CHARACTERS, INC. NO SIMILARITY BETWEEN ANY OF THE NAMES, CHARACTERS, PERSONS, AND/OR INSTITUTIONS IN THIS MAGAZINE WITH THOSE OF ANY LIVING OR DEAD PERSON OR INSTITUTION IS INTENDED, AND ANY SUCH SIMILARITY WHICH MAY EXIST IS PURELY COINCIDENTAL. **PRINTED IN THE U.S.A.** ALAN FINE, EVP - OFFICE OF THE PRESIDENT, MARVEL WORLDWIDE, INC. AND EVP & CMO MARVEL CHARACTERS B.V.; DAN BUCKLEY, PUBLISHER & PRESIDENT - PRINT, ANIMATION & DIGITAL DIVISIONS; JOE QUESADA, CHIEF CREATIVE OFFICER; TOM BREVOORT, SVP OF PUBLISHING; DAVID BOGART, SVP OF OPERATIONS & PROCUREMENT, PUBLISHING; C.B. CEBULSKI, SVP OF CREATOR & CONTENT DEVELOPMENT; DAVID GABRIEL, SVP PRINT, SALES & MARKETING; JIM O'KEEFE, VP OF OPERATIONS & LOGISTICS; DAN CARR, EXECUTIVE DIRECTOR OF PUBLISHING TECHNOLOGY; SUSAN CRESPI, EDITORIAL OPERATIONS MANAGER; ALEX MORALES, PUBLISHING OPERATIONS MANAGER; STAN LEE, CHAIRMAN EMERITUS. FOR INFORMATION REGARDING ADVERTISING IN MARVEL COMICS OR ON MARVEL.COM, PLEASE CONTACT NIZA DISLA, DIRECTOR OF MARVEL PARTNERSHIPS, AT NDISLA@MARVEL.COM. FOR MARVEL SUBSCRIPTION INQUIRIES, PLEASE CALL 800-217-9158. MANUFACTURED BETWEEN 2/7/2014 AND 3/24/2014 BY WORZALLA PUBLISHING CO., STEVENS POINT, WI, USA.

10 9 8 7 6 5 4 3 2 1

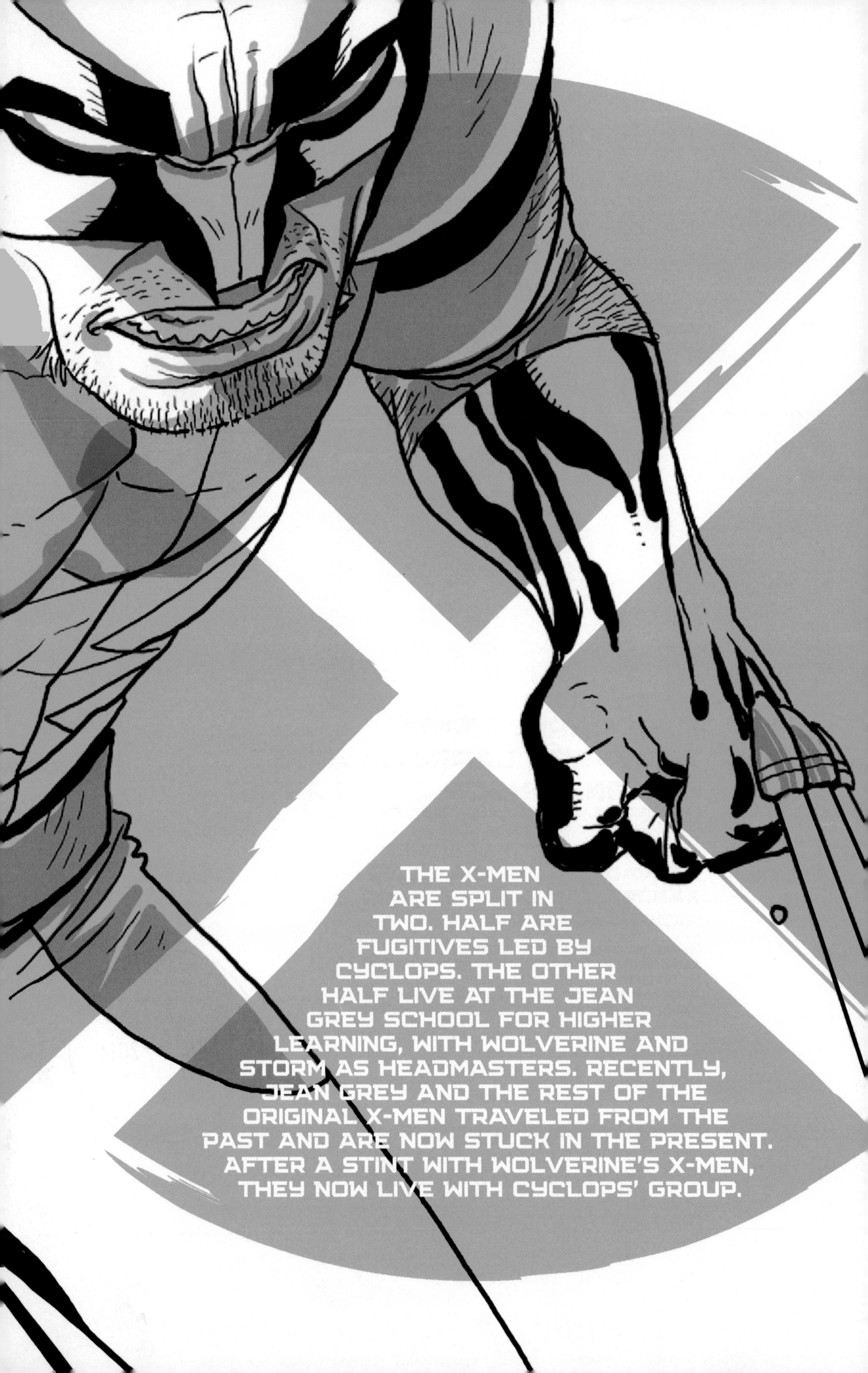
THE X-MEN ARE SPLIT IN TWO. HALF ARE FUGITIVES LED BY CYCLOPS. THE OTHER HALF LIVE AT THE JEAN GREY SCHOOL FOR HIGHER LEARNING, WITH WOLVERINE AND STORM AS HEADMASTERS. RECENTLY, JEAN GREY AND THE REST OF THE ORIGINAL X-MEN TRAVELED FROM THE PAST AND ARE NOW STUCK IN THE PRESENT. AFTER A STINT WITH WOLVERINE'S X-MEN, THEY NOW LIVE WITH CYCLOPS' GROUP.

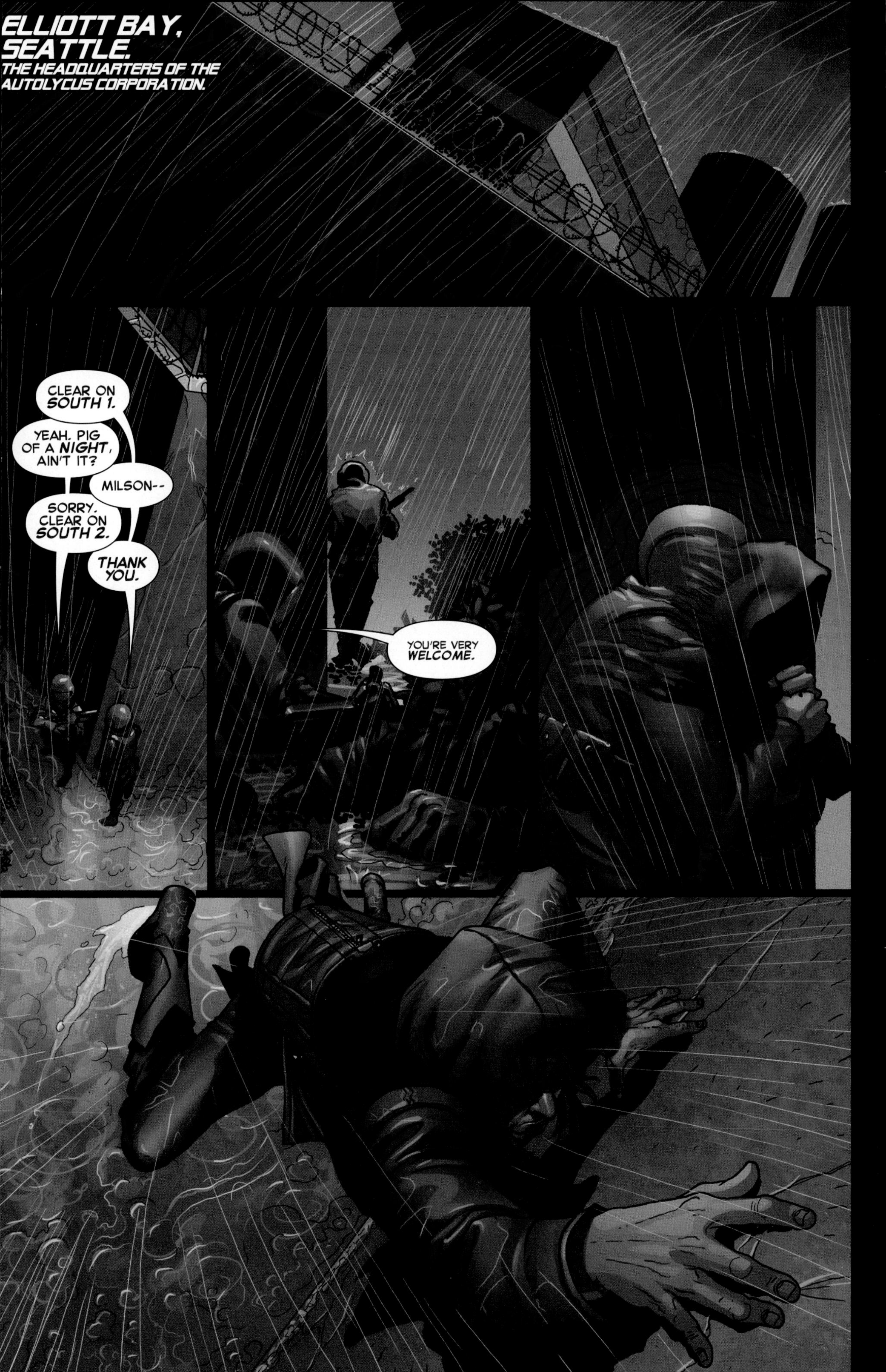
ELLIOTT BAY, SEATTLE.
THE HEADQUARTERS OF THE AUTOLYCUS CORPORATION.
CLEAR ON SOUTH 1.
YEAH. PIG OF A NIGHT, AIN'T IT?
MILSON--
SORRY. CLEAR ON SOUTH 2.
THANK YOU.
YOU'RE VERY WELCOME.

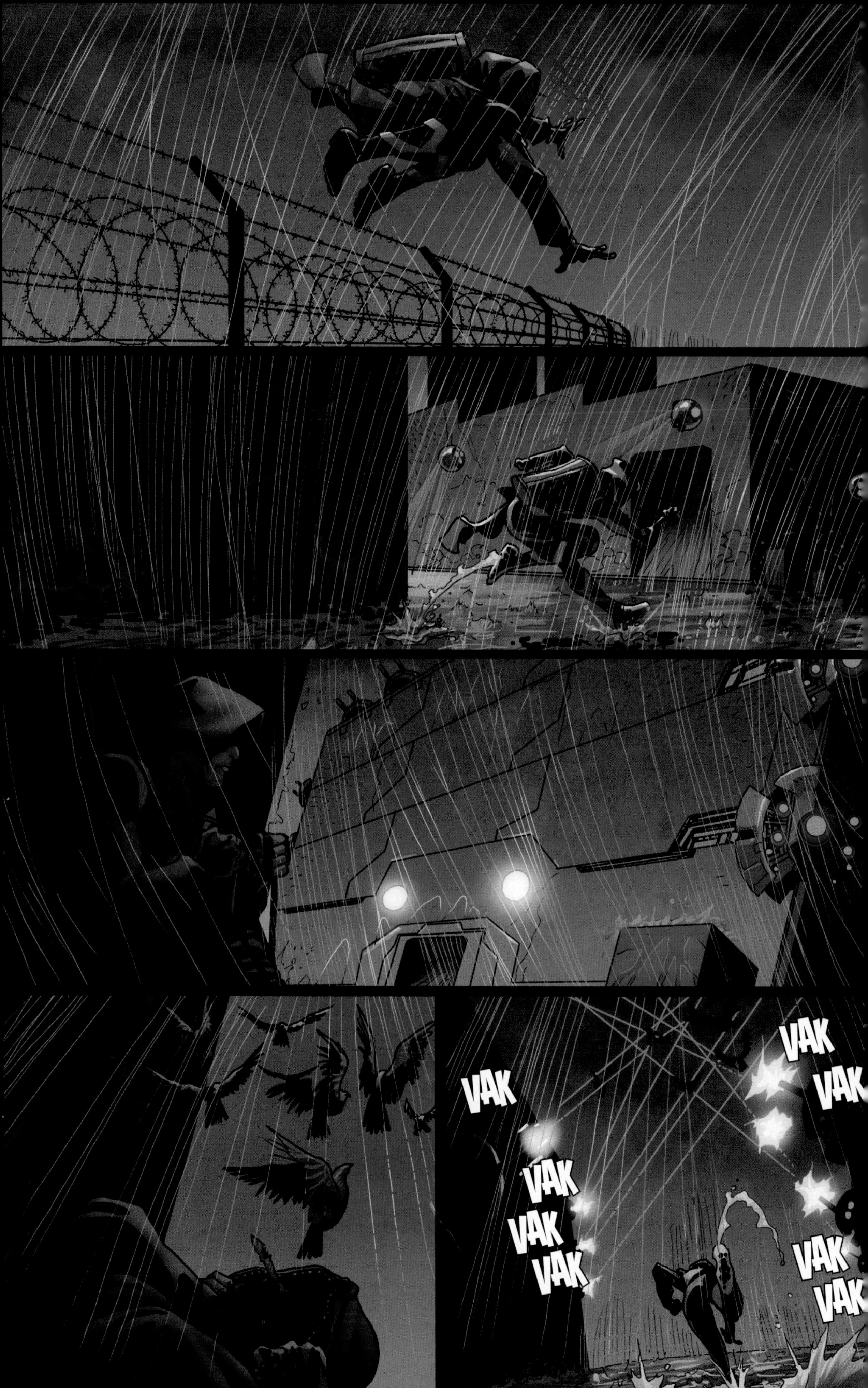
VAK
VAK
VAK
VAK
VAK
VAK
VAK
VAK

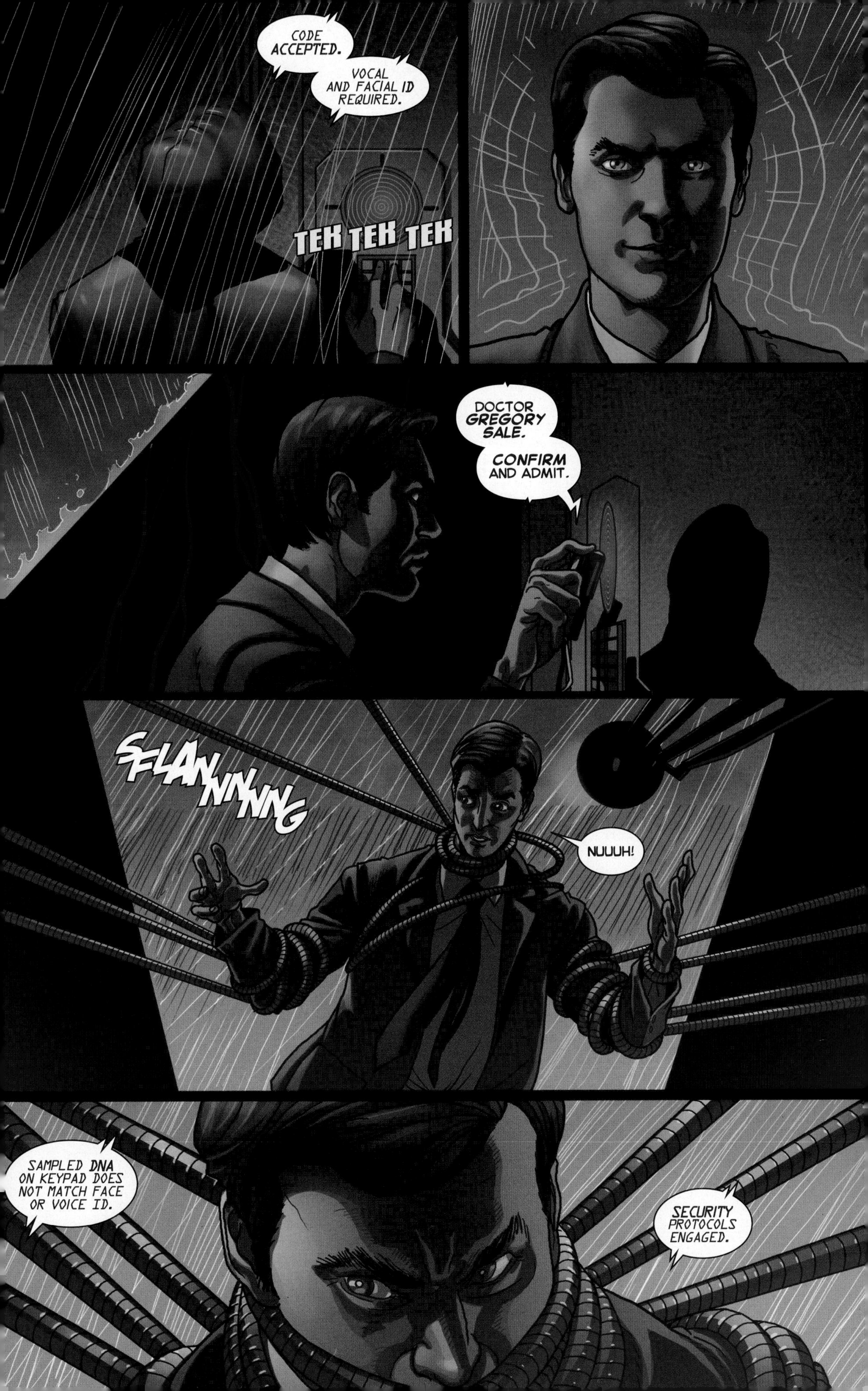

CODE ACCEPTED.
VOCAL AND FACIAL ID REQUIRED.
TEK TEK TEK
DOCTOR GREGORY SALE.
CONFIRM AND ADMIT.
SFLANNNNNG
NUUUH!
SAMPLED DNA ON KEYPAD DOES NOT MATCH FACE OR VOICE ID.
SECURITY PROTOCOLS ENGAGED.

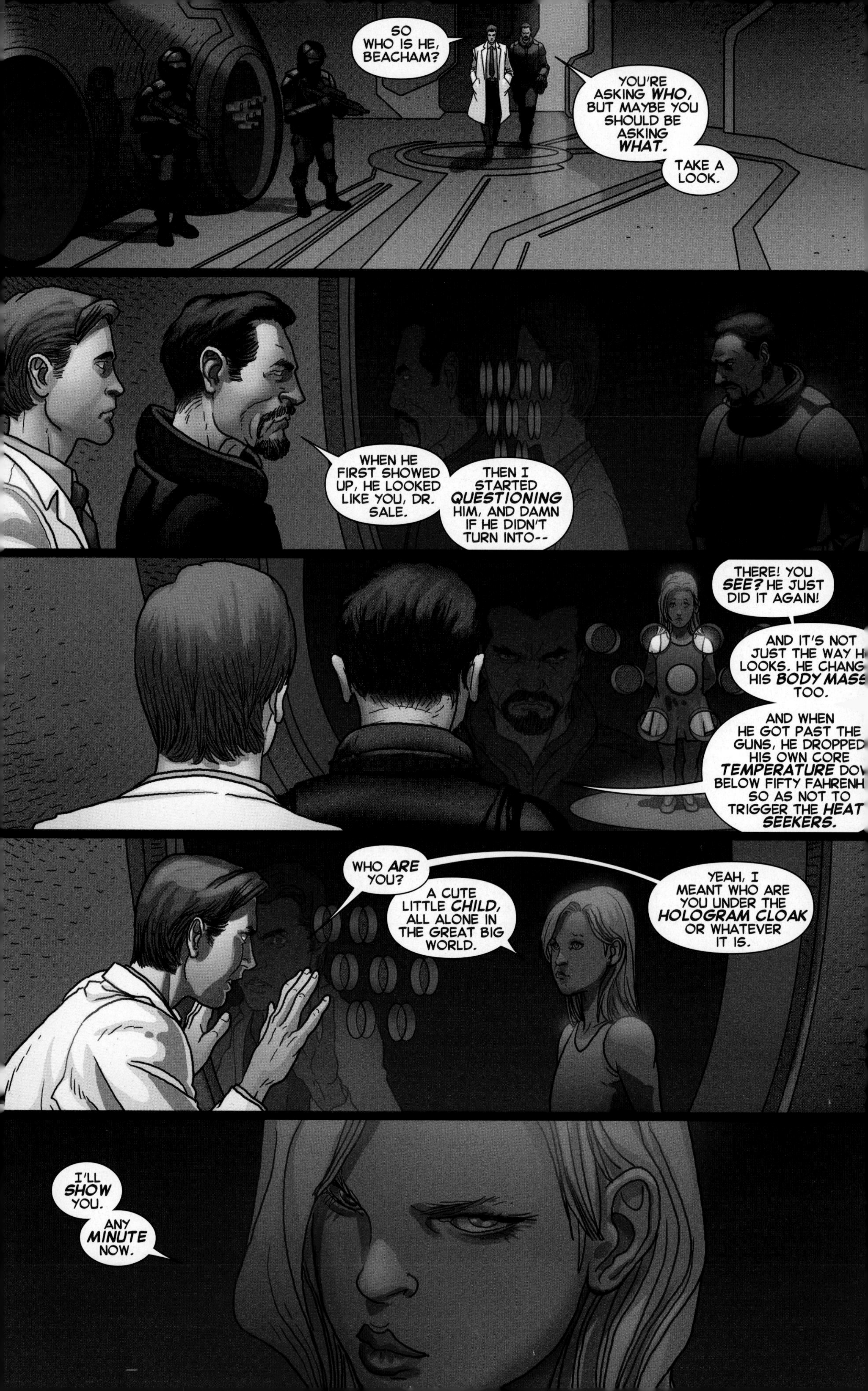
SO WHO IS HE, BEACHAM?
YOU'RE ASKING WHO, BUT MAYBE YOU SHOULD BE ASKING WHAT.
TAKE A LOOK.
WHEN HE FIRST SHOWED UP, HE LOOKED LIKE YOU, DR. SALE.
THEN I STARTED QUESTIONING HIM, AND DAMN IF HE DIDN'T TURN INTO--
THERE! YOU SEE? HE JUST DID IT AGAIN!
AND IT'S NOT JUST THE WAY H LOOKS. HE CHANG HIS BODY MASS TOO.
AND WHEN HE GOT PAST THE GUNS, HE DROPPED HIS OWN CORE TEMPERATURE DOW BELOW FIFTY FAHRENH SO AS NOT TO TRIGGER THE HEAT SEEKERS.
WHO ARE YOU?
A CUTE LITTLE CHILD, ALL ALONE IN THE GREAT BIG WORLD.
YEAH, I MEANT WHO ARE YOU UNDER THE HOLOGRAM CLOAK OR WHATEVER IT IS.
I'LL SHOW YOU.
ANY MINUTE NOW.

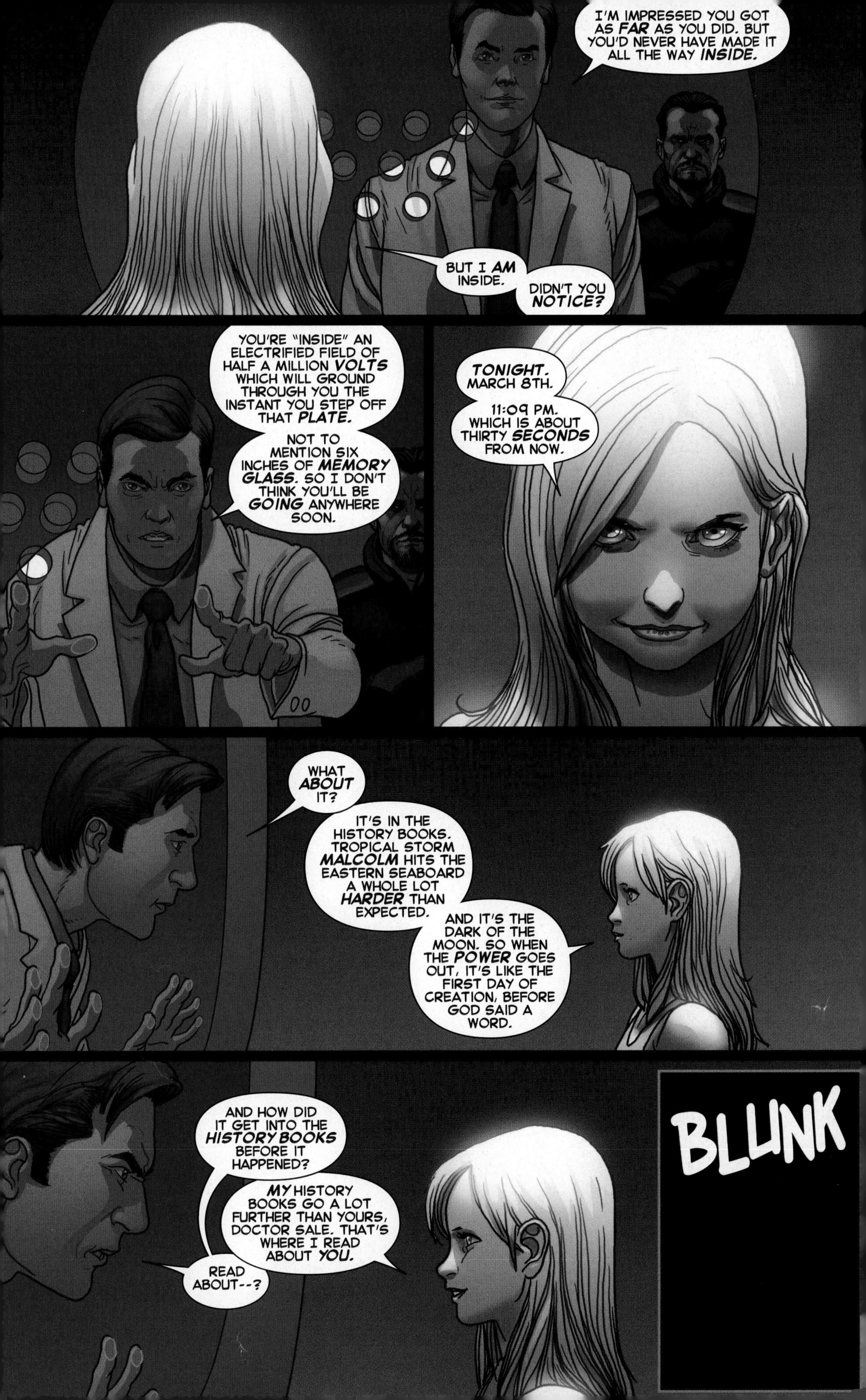
I'M IMPRESSED YOU GOT AS FAR AS YOU DID. BUT YOU'D NEVER HAVE MADE IT ALL THE WAY INSIDE.
BUT I AM INSIDE.
DIDN'T YOU NOTICE?
YOU'RE "INSIDE" AN ELECTRIFIED FIELD OF HALF A MILLION VOLTS WHICH WILL GROUND THROUGH YOU THE INSTANT YOU STEP OFF THAT PLATE.
NOT TO MENTION SIX INCHES OF MEMORY GLASS. SO I DON'T THINK YOU'LL BE GOING ANYWHERE SOON.
TONIGHT. MARCH 8TH.
11:09 PM. WHICH IS ABOUT THIRTY SECONDS FROM NOW.
WHAT ABOUT IT?
IT'S IN THE HISTORY BOOKS. TROPICAL STORM MALCOLM HITS THE EASTERN SEABOARD A WHOLE LOT HARDER THAN EXPECTED.
AND IT'S THE DARK OF THE MOON. SO WHEN THE POWER GOES OUT, IT'S LIKE THE FIRST DAY OF CREATION, BEFORE GOD SAID A WORD.
AND HOW DID IT GET INTO THE HISTORY BOOKS BEFORE IT HAPPENED?
MY HISTORY BOOKS GO A LOT FURTHER THAN YOURS, DOCTOR SALE. THAT'S WHERE I READ ABOUT YOU.
READ ABOUT--?
BLUNK

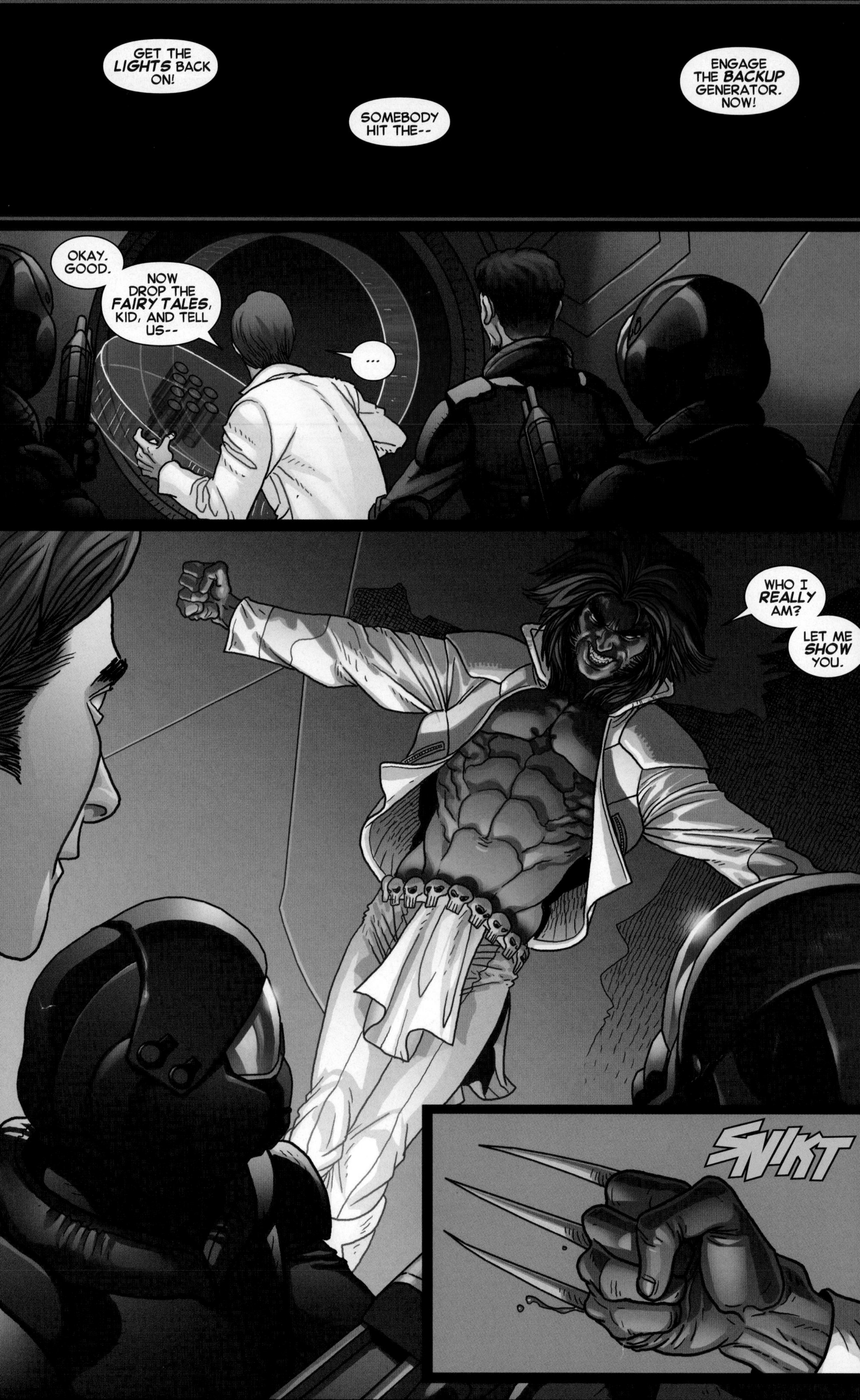
GET THE LIGHTS BACK ON!
SOMEBODY HIT THE--
ENGAGE THE BACKUP GENERATOR. NOW!
OKAY. GOOD.
NOW DROP THE FAIRY TALES, KID, AND TELL US--
...
WHO I REALLY AM?
LET ME SHOW YOU.
SNIKT

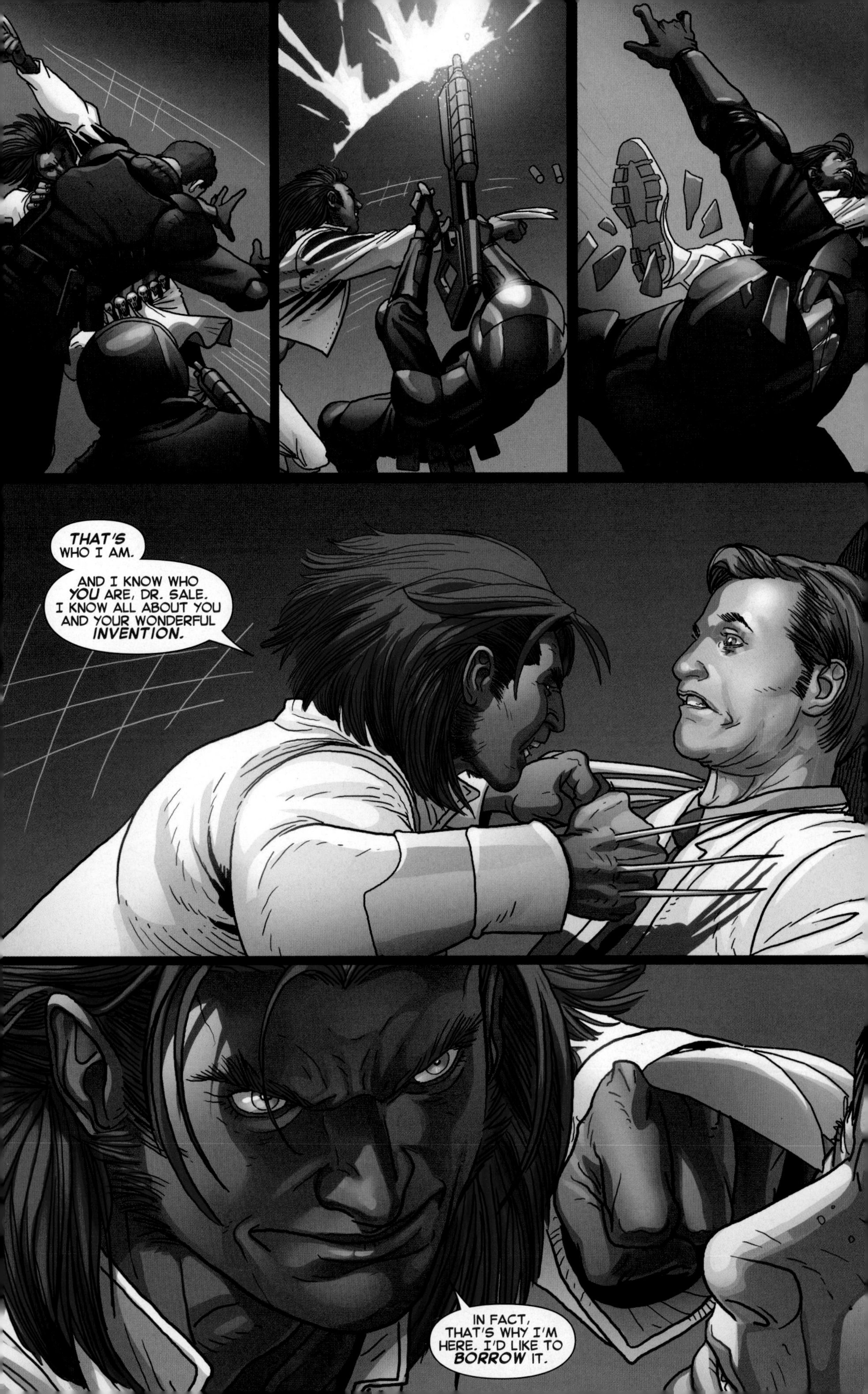
THAT'S WHO I AM.
AND I KNOW WHO YOU ARE, DR. SALE. I KNOW ALL ABOUT YOU AND YOUR WONDERFUL INVENTION.
IN FACT, THAT'S WHY I'M HERE. I'D LIKE TO BORROW IT.

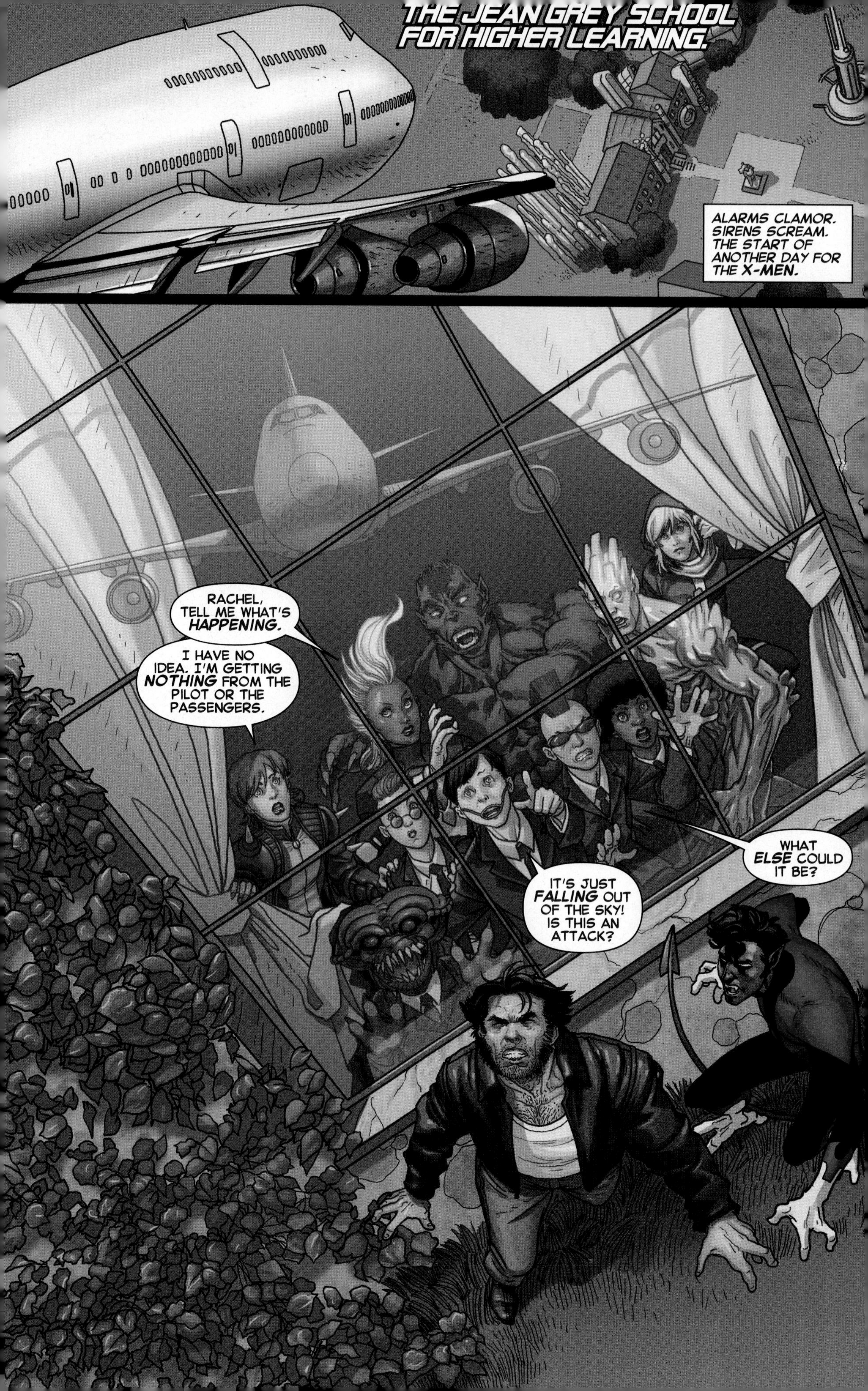
THE JEAN GREY SCHOOL FOR HIGHER LEARNING.
ALARMS CLAMOR. SIRENS SCREAM. THE START OF ANOTHER DAY FOR THE X-MEN.
RACHEL, TELL ME WHAT'S HAPPENING.
I HAVE NO IDEA. I'M GETTING NOTHING FROM THE PILOT OR THE PASSENGERS.
IT'S JUST FALLING OUT OF THE SKY! IS THIS AN ATTACK?
WHAT ELSE COULD IT BE?

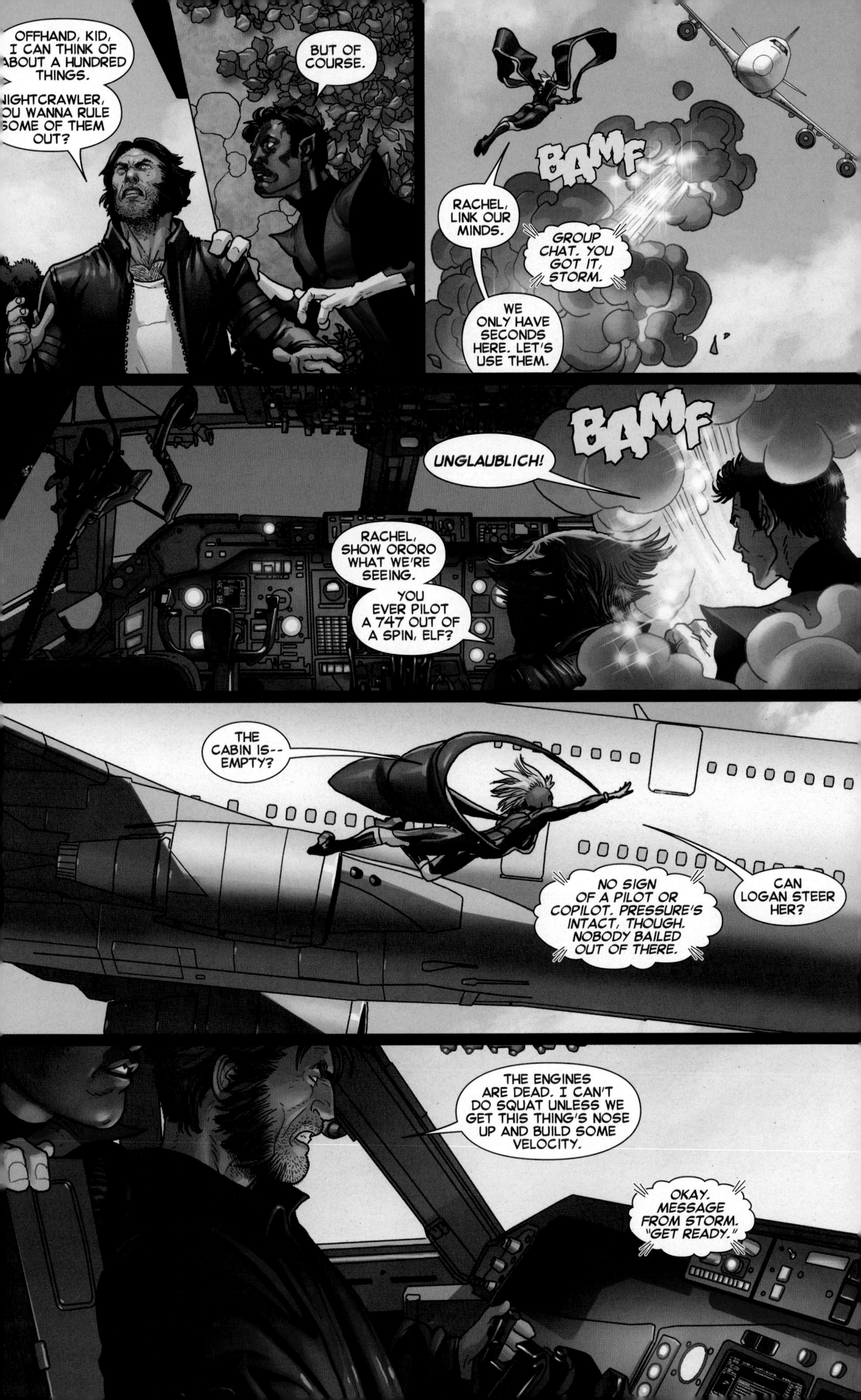
OFFHAND, KID, I CAN THINK OF ABOUT A HUNDRED THINGS.
NIGHTCRAWLER, YOU WANNA RULE SOME OF THEM OUT?
BUT OF COURSE.
BAMF
RACHEL, LINK OUR MINDS.
GROUP CHAT. YOU GOT IT, STORM.
WE ONLY HAVE SECONDS HERE. LET'S USE THEM.
BAMF
UNGLAUBLICH!
RACHEL, SHOW ORORO WHAT WE'RE SEEING.
YOU EVER PILOT A 747 OUT OF A SPIN, ELF?
THE CABIN IS--EMPTY?
NO SIGN OF A PILOT OR COPILOT. PRESSURE'S INTACT, THOUGH. NOBODY BAILED OUT OF THERE.
CAN LOGAN STEER HER?
THE ENGINES ARE DEAD. I CAN'T DO SQUAT UNLESS WE GET THIS THING'S NOSE UP AND BUILD SOME VELOCITY.
OKAY. MESSAGE FROM STORM. "GET READY."

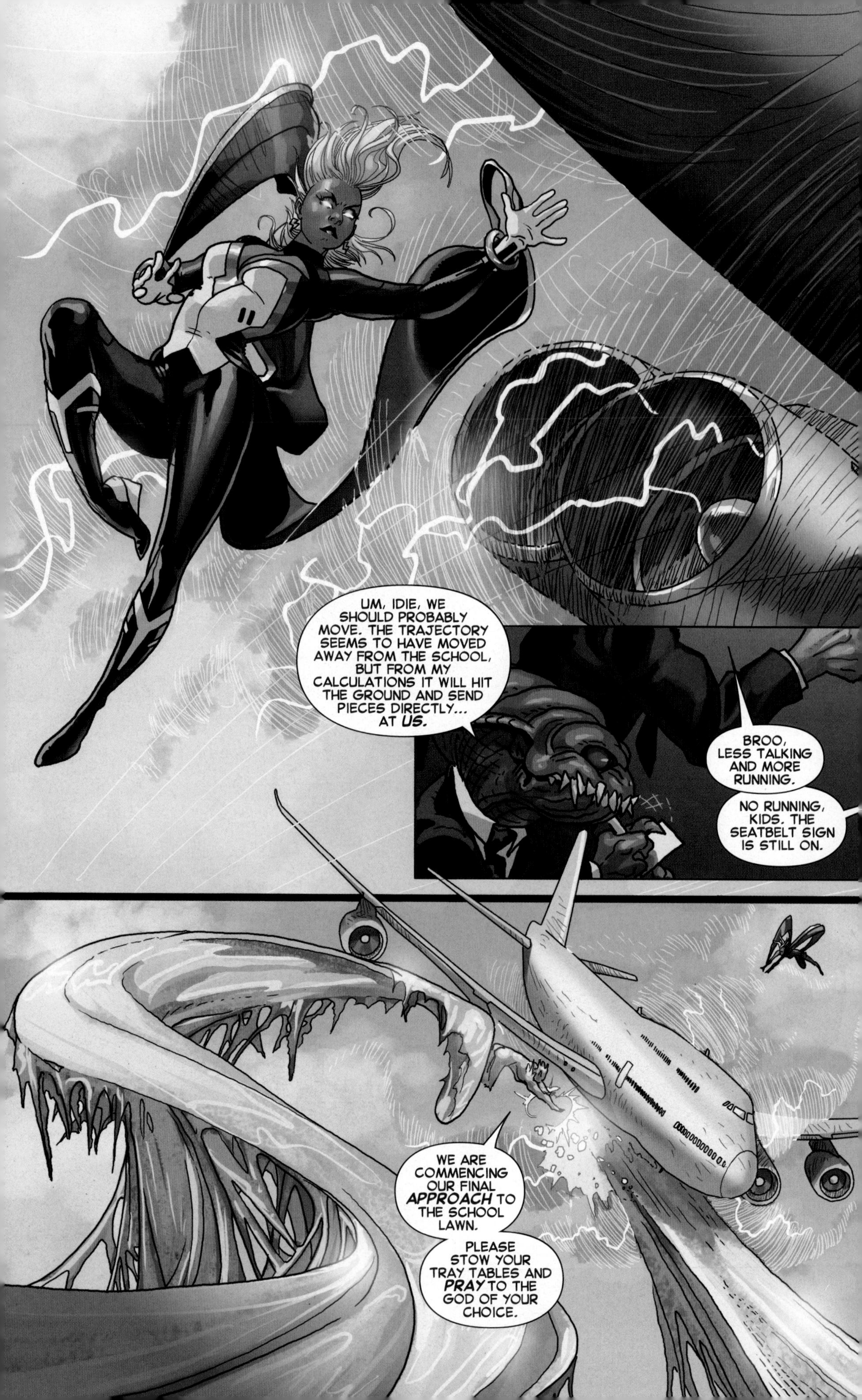
UM, IDIE, WE SHOULD PROBABLY MOVE. THE TRAJECTORY SEEMS TO HAVE MOVED AWAY FROM THE SCHOOL, BUT FROM MY CALCULATIONS IT WILL HIT THE GROUND AND SEND PIECES DIRECTLY... AT *US.*
BROO, LESS TALKING AND MORE RUNNING.
NO RUNNING, KIDS. THE SEATBELT SIGN IS STILL ON.
WE ARE COMMENCING OUR FINAL *APPROACH* TO THE SCHOOL LAWN.
PLEASE STOW YOUR TRAY TABLES AND *PRAY* TO THE GOD OF YOUR CHOICE.

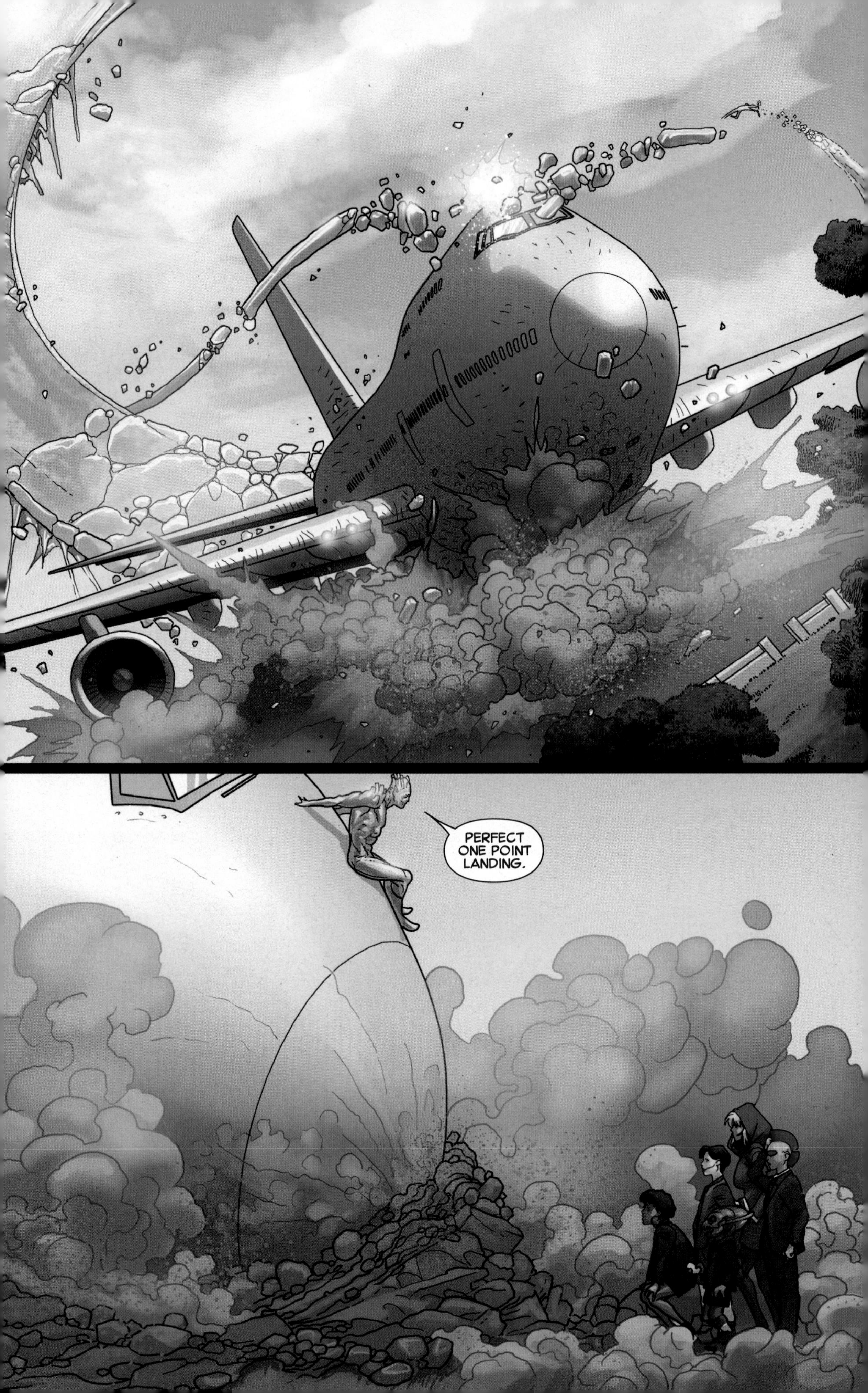
PERFECT ONE POINT LANDING.

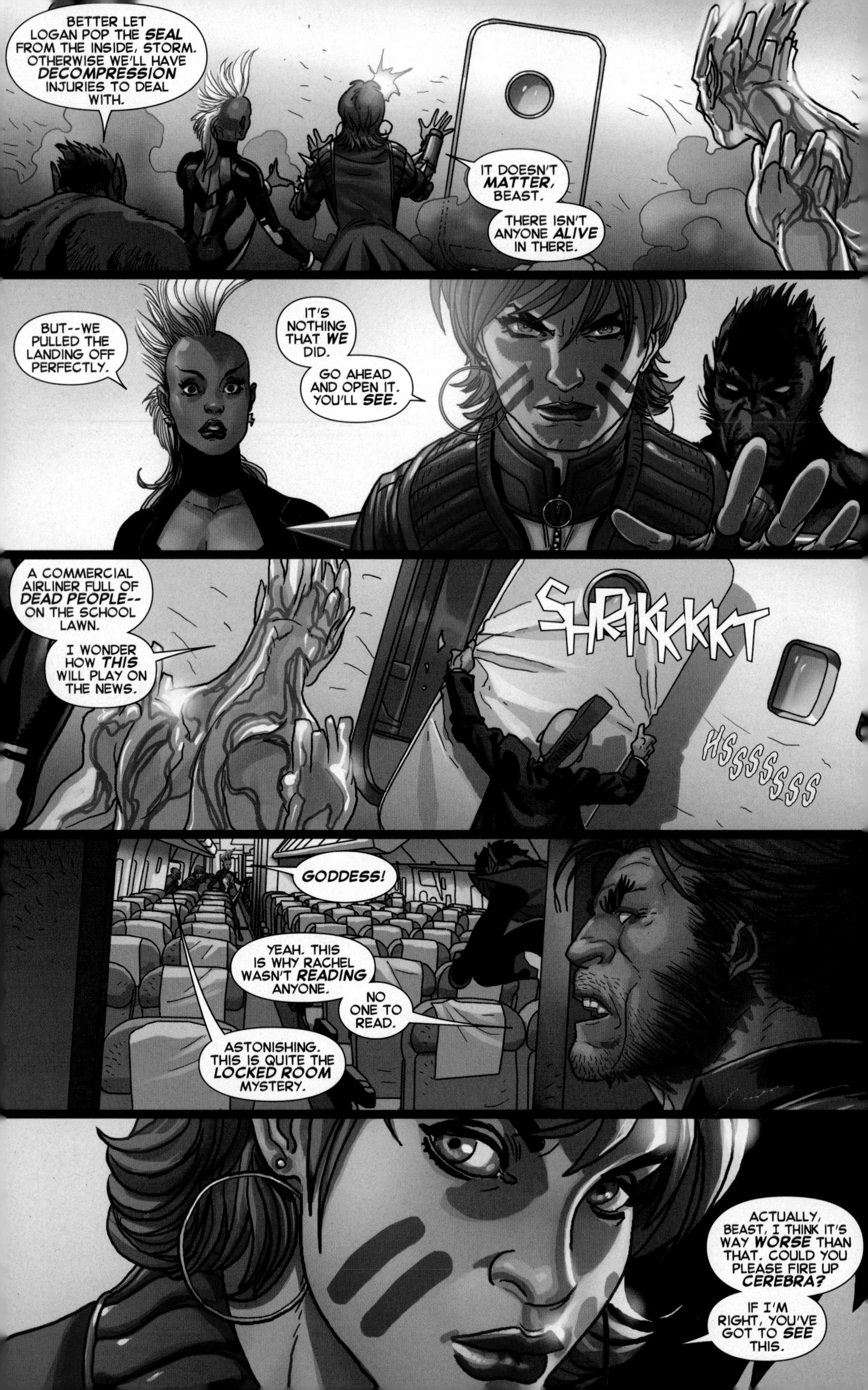
BETTER LET LOGAN POP THE SEAL FROM THE INSIDE, STORM. OTHERWISE WE'LL HAVE DECOMPRESSION INJURIES TO DEAL WITH.
IT DOESN'T MATTER, BEAST.
THERE ISN'T ANYONE ALIVE IN THERE.
BUT--WE PULLED THE LANDING OFF PERFECTLY.
IT'S NOTHING THAT WE DID.
GO AHEAD AND OPEN IT. YOU'LL SEE.
A COMMERCIAL AIRLINER FULL OF DEAD PEOPLE-- ON THE SCHOOL LAWN.
I WONDER HOW THIS WILL PLAY ON THE NEWS.
SHRIKKKKT
HSSSSSSS
GODDESS!
YEAH. THIS IS WHY RACHEL WASN'T READING ANYONE.
NO ONE TO READ.
ASTONISHING. THIS IS QUITE THE LOCKED ROOM MYSTERY.
ACTUALLY, BEAST, I THINK IT'S WAY WORSE THAN THAT. COULD YOU PLEASE FIRE UP CEREBRA?
IF I'M RIGHT, YOU'VE GOT TO SEE THIS.

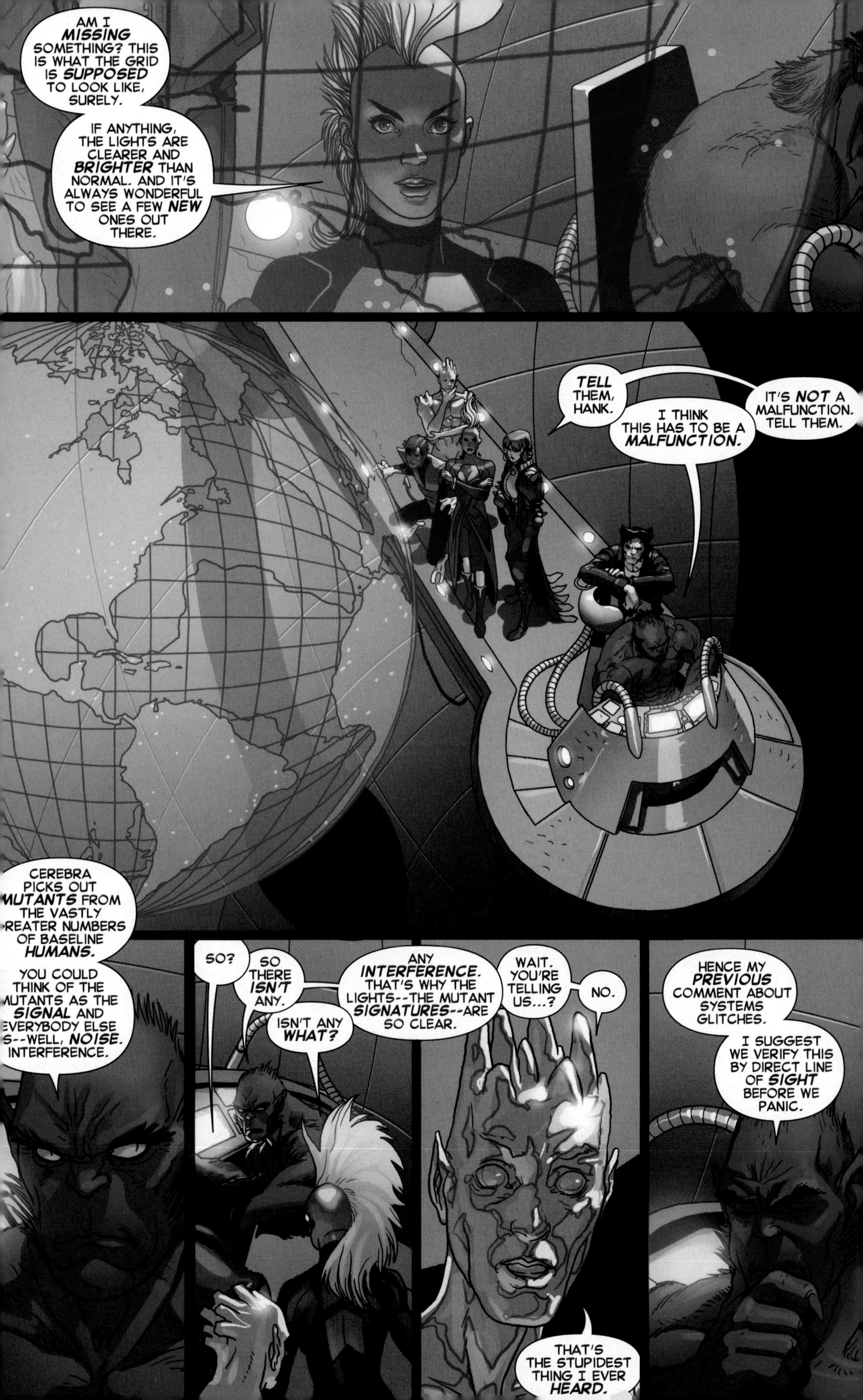
AM I MISSING SOMETHING? THIS IS WHAT THE GRID IS SUPPOSED TO LOOK LIKE, SURELY.
IF ANYTHING, THE LIGHTS ARE CLEARER AND BRIGHTER THAN NORMAL. AND IT'S ALWAYS WONDERFUL TO SEE A FEW NEW ONES OUT THERE.
TELL THEM, HANK.
IT'S NOT A MALFUNCTION. TELL THEM.
I THINK THIS HAS TO BE A MALFUNCTION.
CEREBRA PICKS OUT MUTANTS FROM THE VASTLY REATER NUMBERS OF BASELINE HUMANS.
YOU COULD THINK OF THE UTANTS AS THE SIGNAL AND VERYBODY ELSE S--WELL, NOISE. INTERFERENCE.
SO?
SO THERE ISN'T ANY.
ISN'T ANY WHAT?
ANY INTERFERENCE. THAT'S WHY THE LIGHTS--THE MUTANT SIGNATURES--ARE SO CLEAR.
WAIT. YOU'RE TELLING US...?
NO.
THAT'S THE STUPIDEST THING I EVER HEARD.
HENCE MY PREVIOUS COMMENT ABOUT SYSTEMS GLITCHES.
I SUGGEST WE VERIFY THIS BY DIRECT LINE OF SIGHT BEFORE WE PANIC.

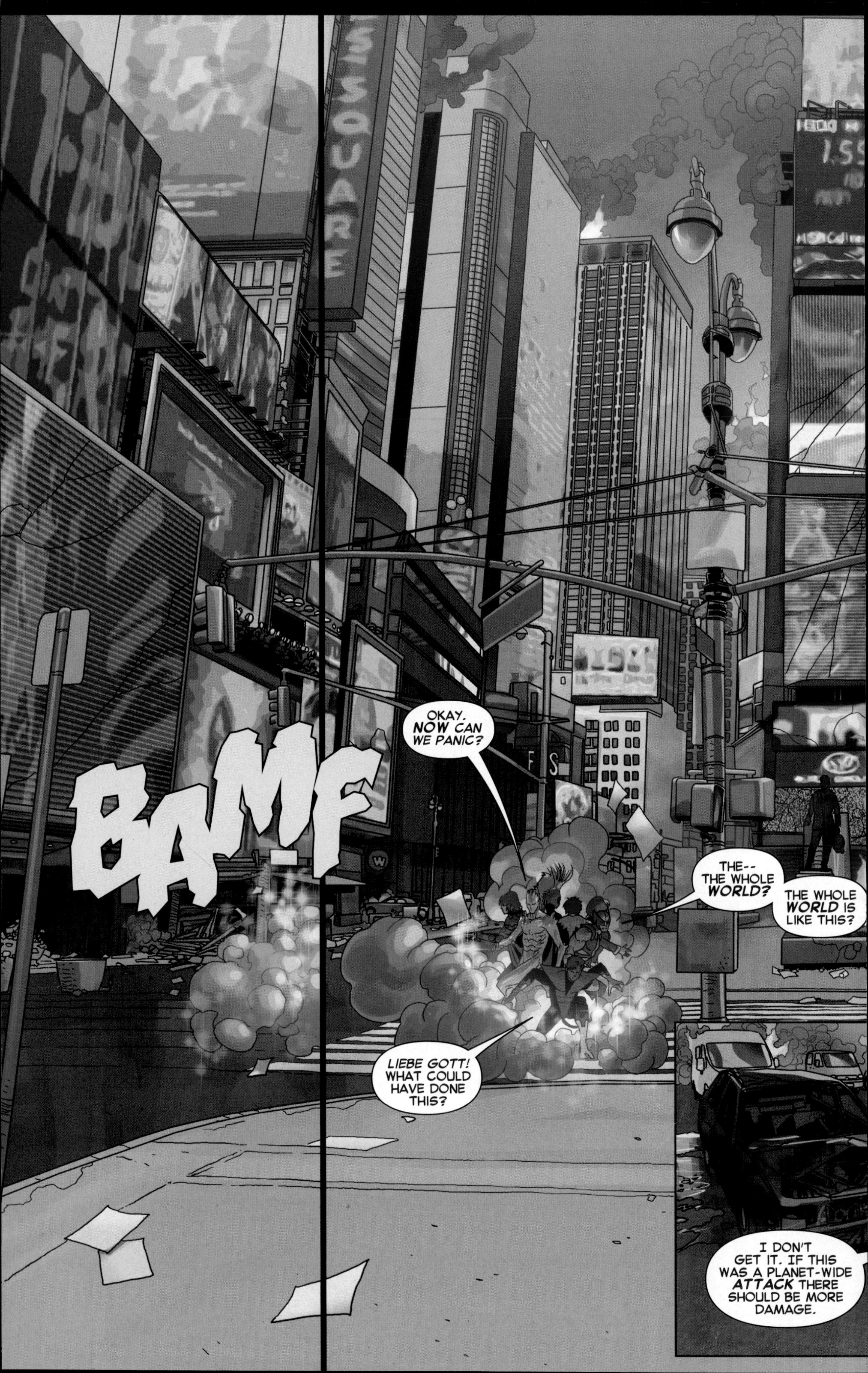
BAMF
OKAY. NOW CAN WE PANIC?
LIEBE GOTT! WHAT COULD HAVE DONE THIS?
THE-- THE WHOLE WORLD?
THE WHOLE WORLD IS LIKE THIS?
I DON'T GET IT. IF THIS WAS A PLANET-WIDE ATTACK THERE SHOULD BE MORE DAMAGE.

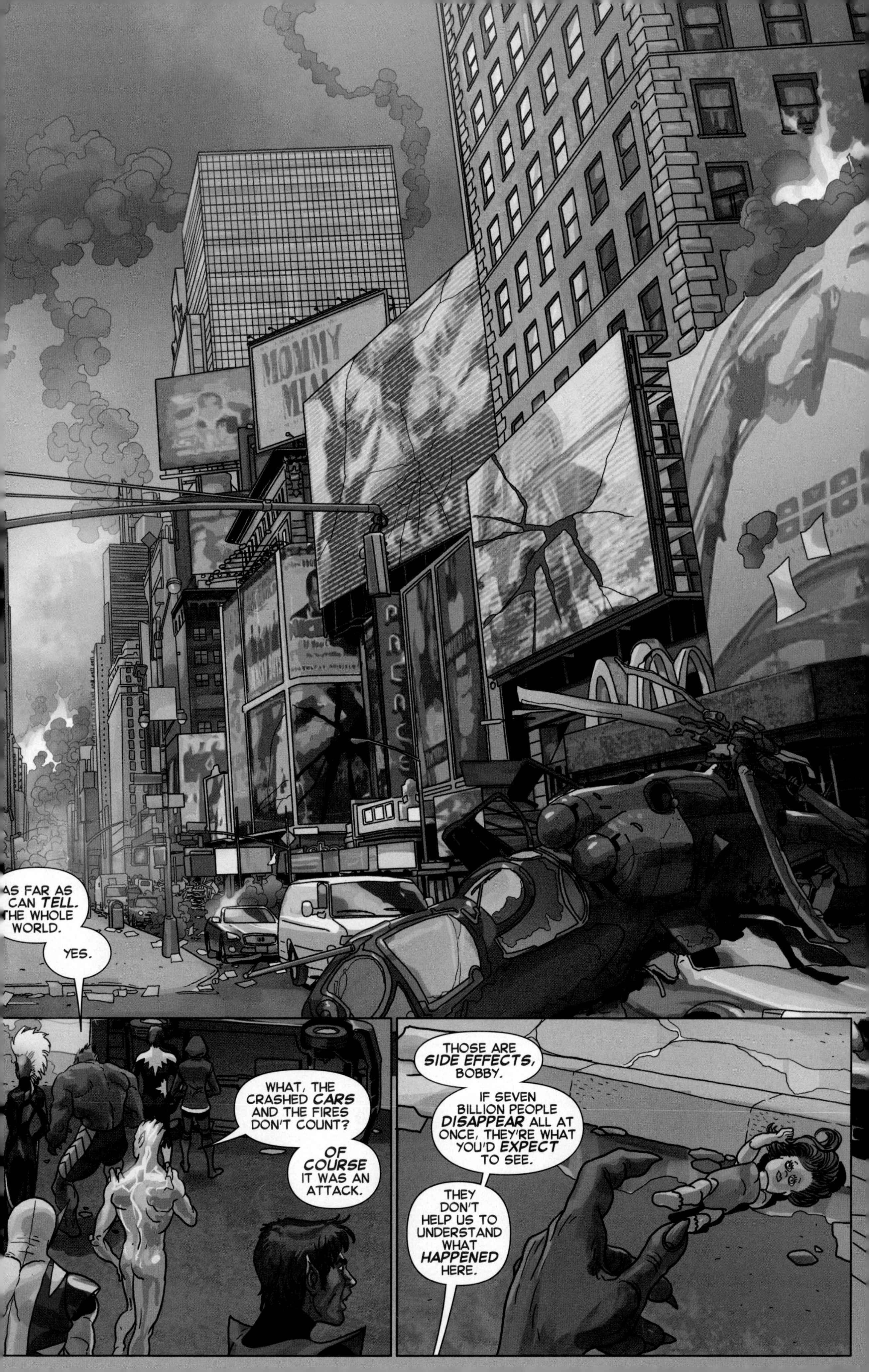
MOMMY
AS FAR AS CAN TELL. THE WHOLE WORLD.
YES.
WHAT, THE CRASHED CARS AND THE FIRES DON'T COUNT?
OF COURSE IT WAS AN ATTACK.
THOSE ARE SIDE EFFECTS, BOBBY.
IF SEVEN BILLION PEOPLE DISAPPEAR ALL AT ONCE, THEY'RE WHAT YOU'D EXPECT TO SEE.
THEY DON'T HELP US TO UNDERSTAND WHAT HAPPENED HERE.

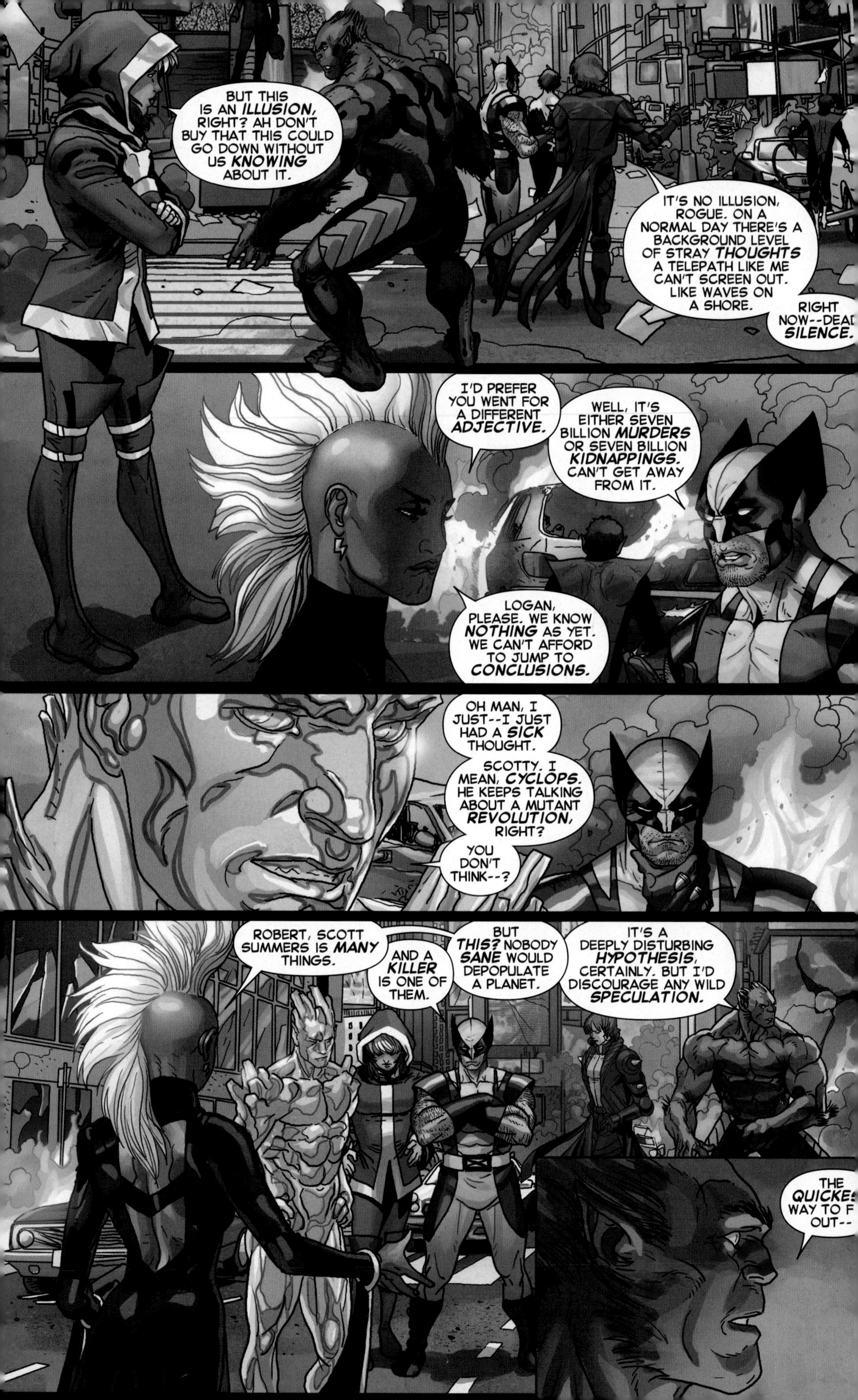
BUT THIS IS AN ILLUSION, RIGHT? AH DON'T BUY THAT THIS COULD GO DOWN WITHOUT US KNOWING ABOUT IT.
IT'S NO ILLUSION, ROGUE. ON A NORMAL DAY THERE'S A BACKGROUND LEVEL OF STRAY THOUGHTS A TELEPATH LIKE ME CAN'T SCREEN OUT. LIKE WAVES ON A SHORE.
RIGHT NOW--DEAD SILENCE.
I'D PREFER YOU WENT FOR A DIFFERENT ADJECTIVE.
WELL, IT'S EITHER SEVEN BILLION MURDERS OR SEVEN BILLION KIDNAPPINGS. CAN'T GET AWAY FROM IT.
LOGAN, PLEASE. WE KNOW NOTHING AS YET. WE CAN'T AFFORD TO JUMP TO CONCLUSIONS.
OH MAN, I JUST--I JUST HAD A SICK THOUGHT.
SCOTTY. I MEAN, CYCLOPS. HE KEEPS TALKING ABOUT A MUTANT REVOLUTION, RIGHT?
YOU DON'T THINK--?
ROBERT, SCOTT SUMMERS IS MANY THINGS.
AND A KILLER IS ONE OF THEM.
BUT THIS? NOBODY SANE WOULD DEPOPULATE A PLANET.
IT'S A DEEPLY DISTURBING HYPOTHESIS, CERTAINLY. BUT I'D DISCOURAGE ANY WILD SPECULATION.

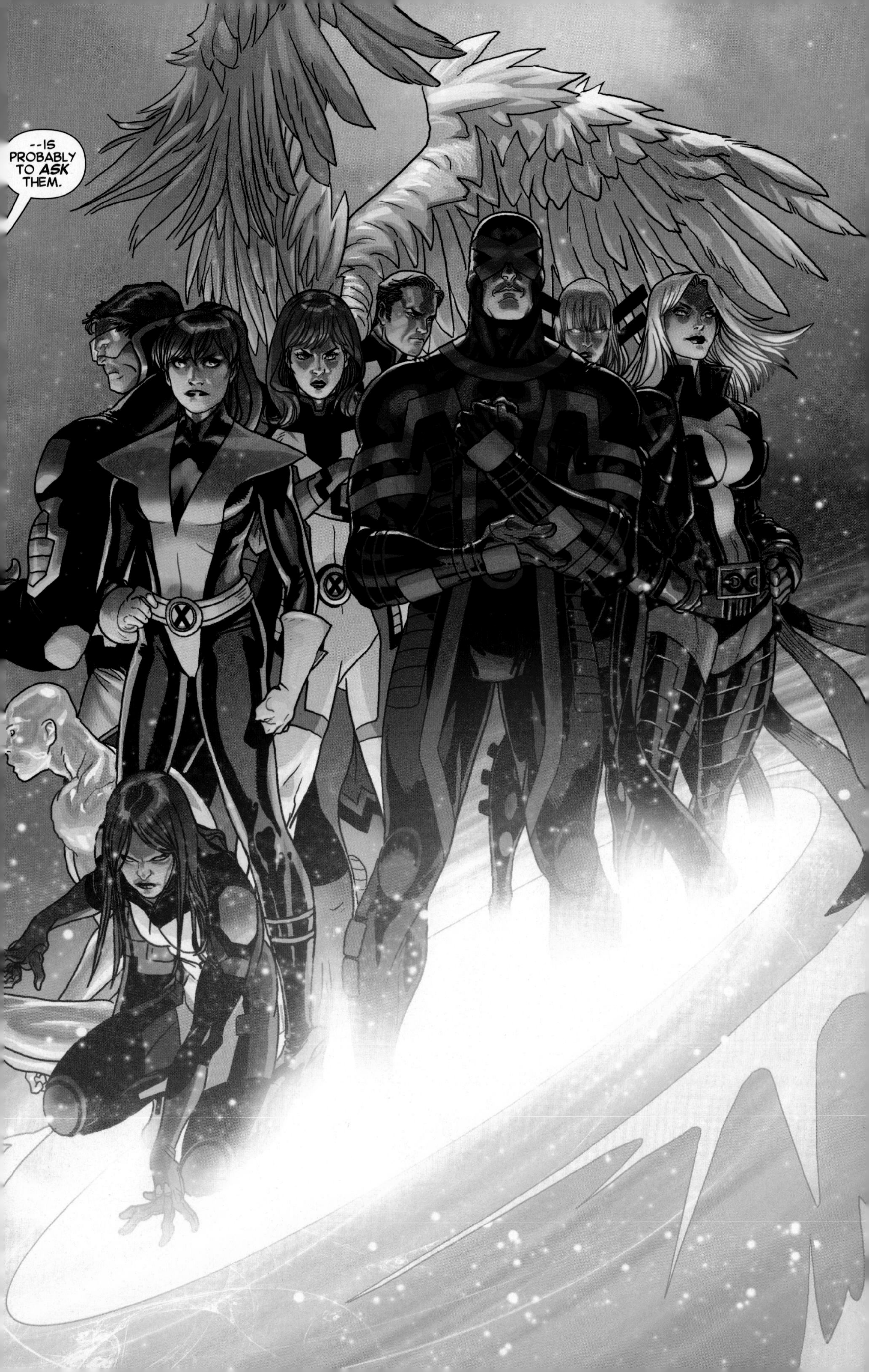
--IS PROBABLY TO ASK THEM.

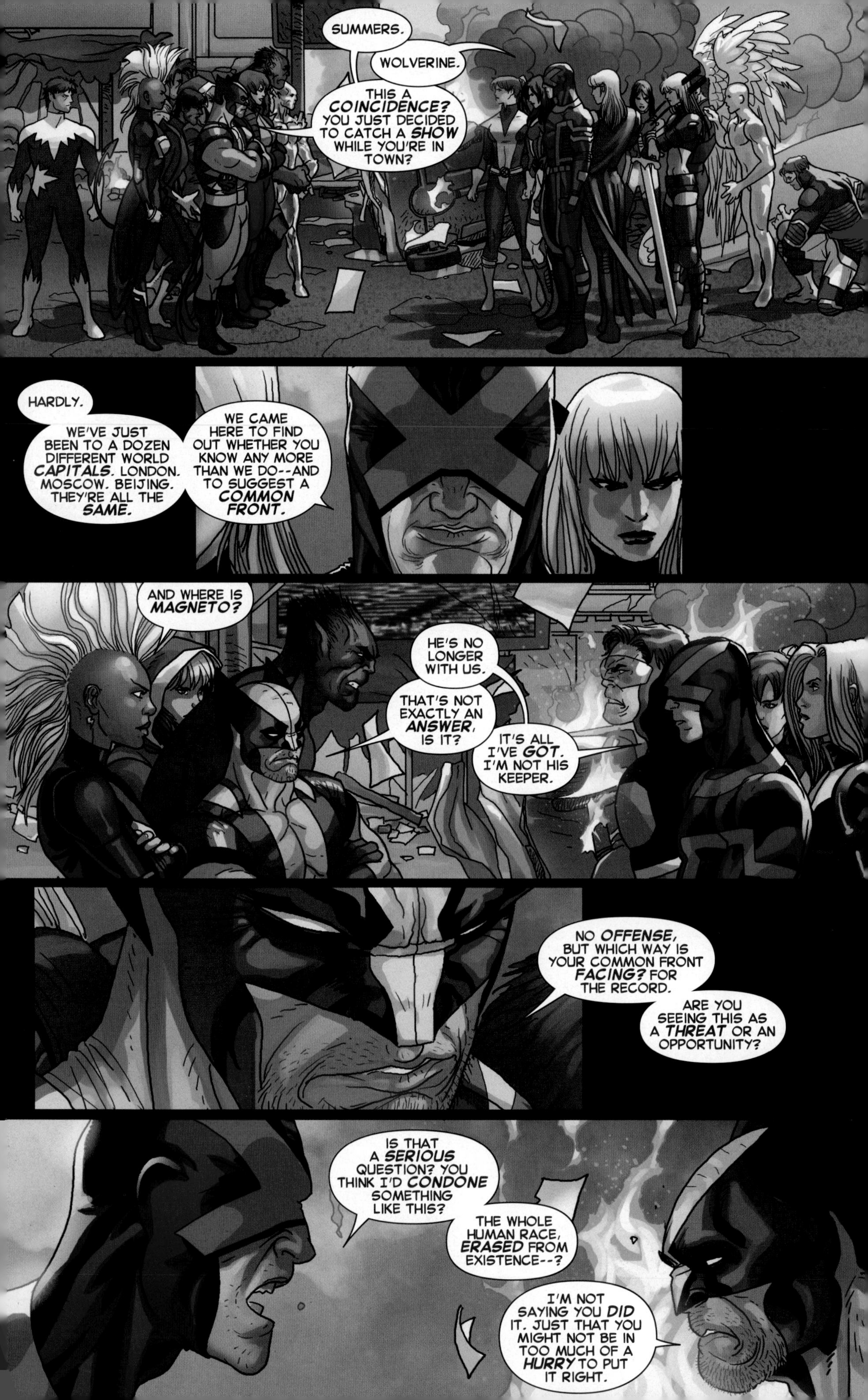
SUMMERS.
WOLVERINE.
THIS A COINCIDENCE? YOU JUST DECIDED TO CATCH A SHOW WHILE YOU'RE IN TOWN?
HARDLY.
WE'VE JUST BEEN TO A DOZEN DIFFERENT WORLD CAPITALS. LONDON. MOSCOW. BEIJING. THEY'RE ALL THE SAME.
WE CAME HERE TO FIND OUT WHETHER YOU KNOW ANY MORE THAN WE DO--AND TO SUGGEST A COMMON FRONT.
AND WHERE IS MAGNETO?
HE'S NO LONGER WITH US.
THAT'S NOT EXACTLY AN ANSWER, IS IT?
IT'S ALL I'VE GOT. I'M NOT HIS KEEPER.
NO OFFENSE, BUT WHICH WAY IS YOUR COMMON FRONT FACING? FOR THE RECORD.
ARE YOU SEEING THIS AS A THREAT OR AN OPPORTUNITY?
IS THAT A SERIOUS QUESTION? YOU THINK I'D CONDONE SOMETHING LIKE THIS?
THE WHOLE HUMAN RACE, ERASED FROM EXISTENCE--?
I'M NOT SAYING YOU DID IT. JUST THAT YOU MIGHT NOT BE IN TOO MUCH OF A HURRY TO PUT IT RIGHT.

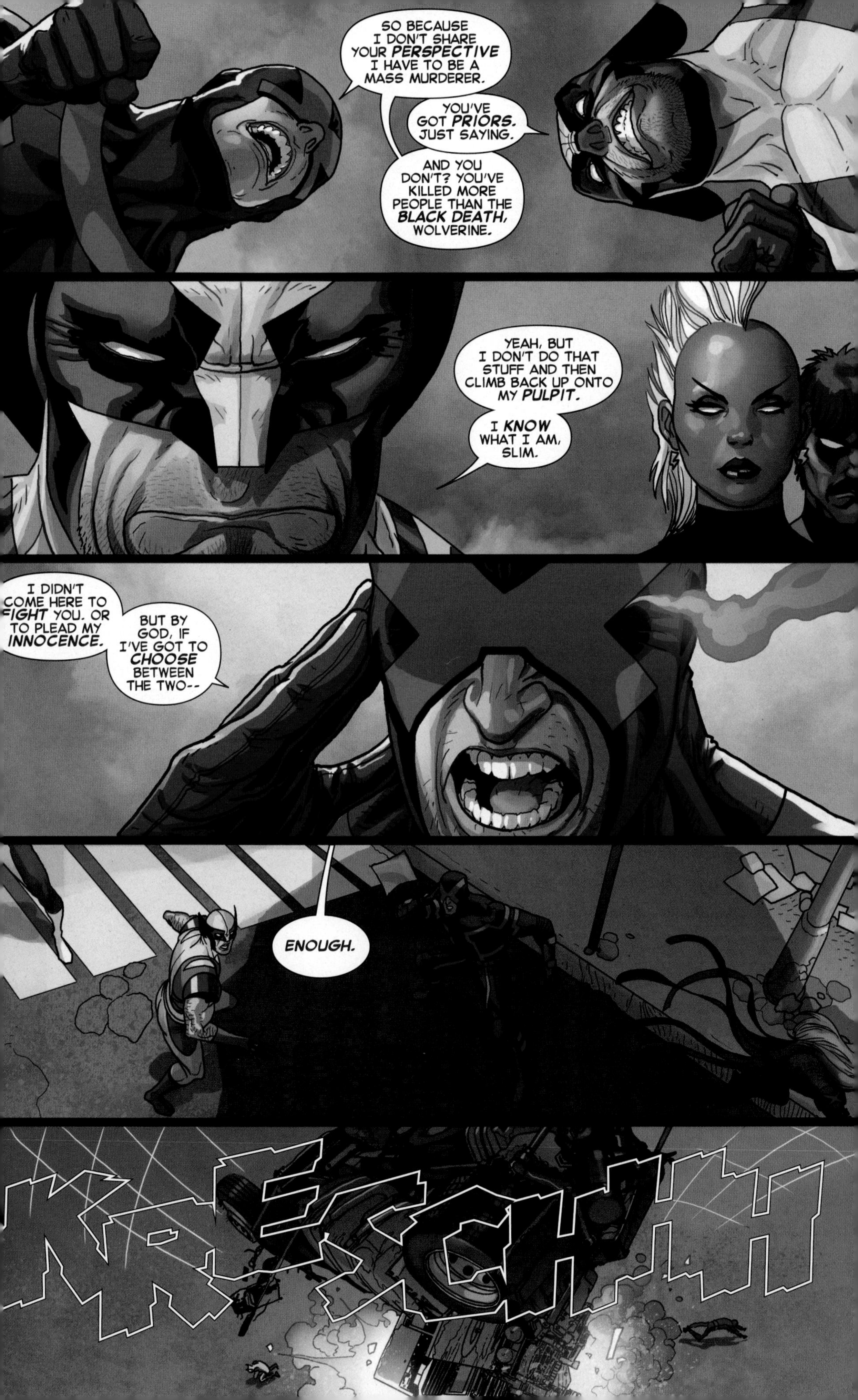
SO BECAUSE I DON'T SHARE YOUR PERSPECTIVE I HAVE TO BE A MASS MURDERER.
YOU'VE GOT PRIORS. JUST SAYING.
AND YOU DON'T? YOU'VE KILLED MORE PEOPLE THAN THE BLACK DEATH, WOLVERINE.
YEAH, BUT I DON'T DO THAT STUFF AND THEN CLIMB BACK UP ONTO MY PULPIT.
I KNOW WHAT I AM, SLIM.
I DIDN'T COME HERE TO FIGHT YOU. OR TO PLEAD MY INNOCENCE.
BUT BY GOD, IF I'VE GOT TO CHOOSE BETWEEN THE TWO--
ENOUGH.

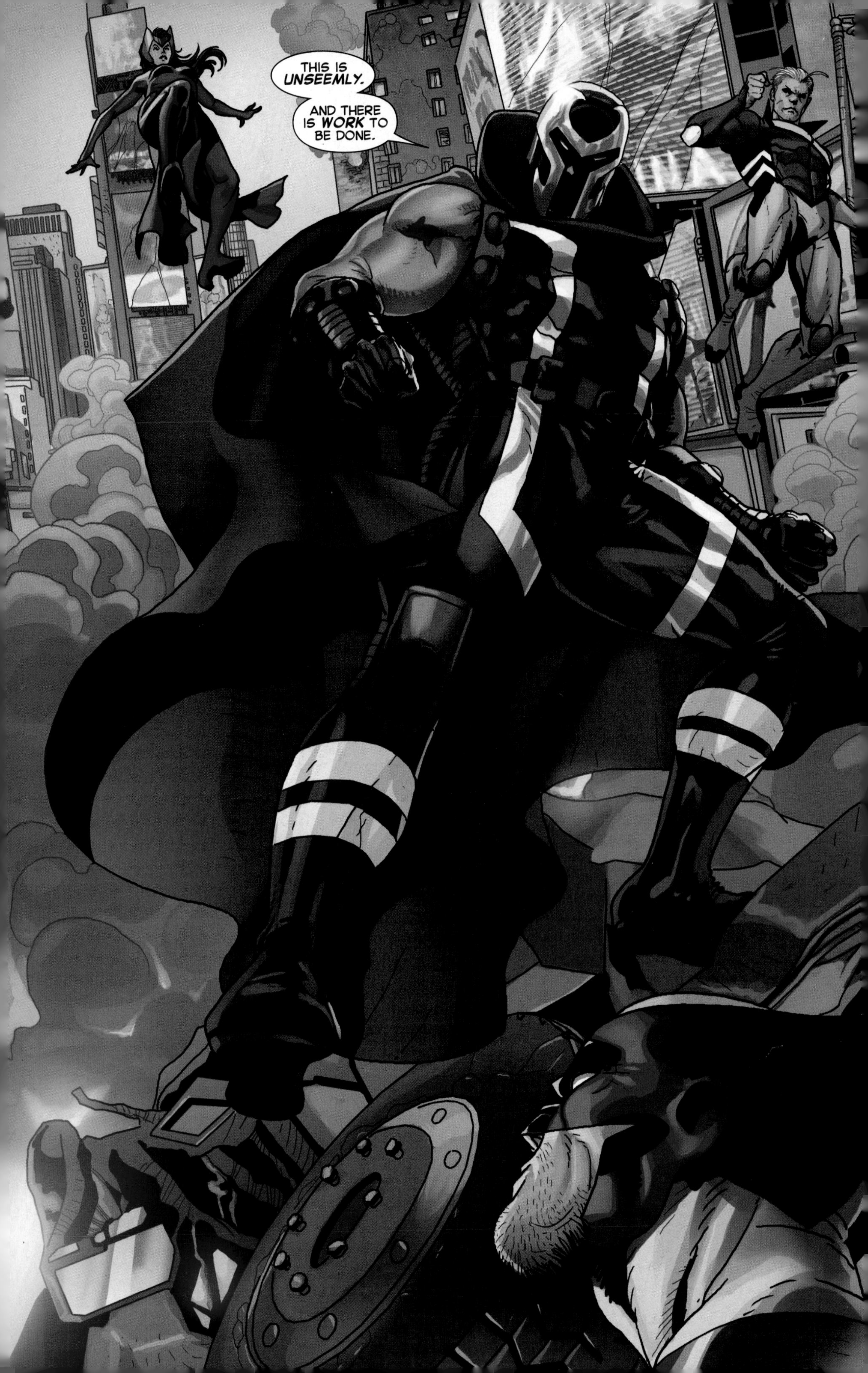
THIS IS UNSEEMLY.
AND THERE IS WORK TO BE DONE.

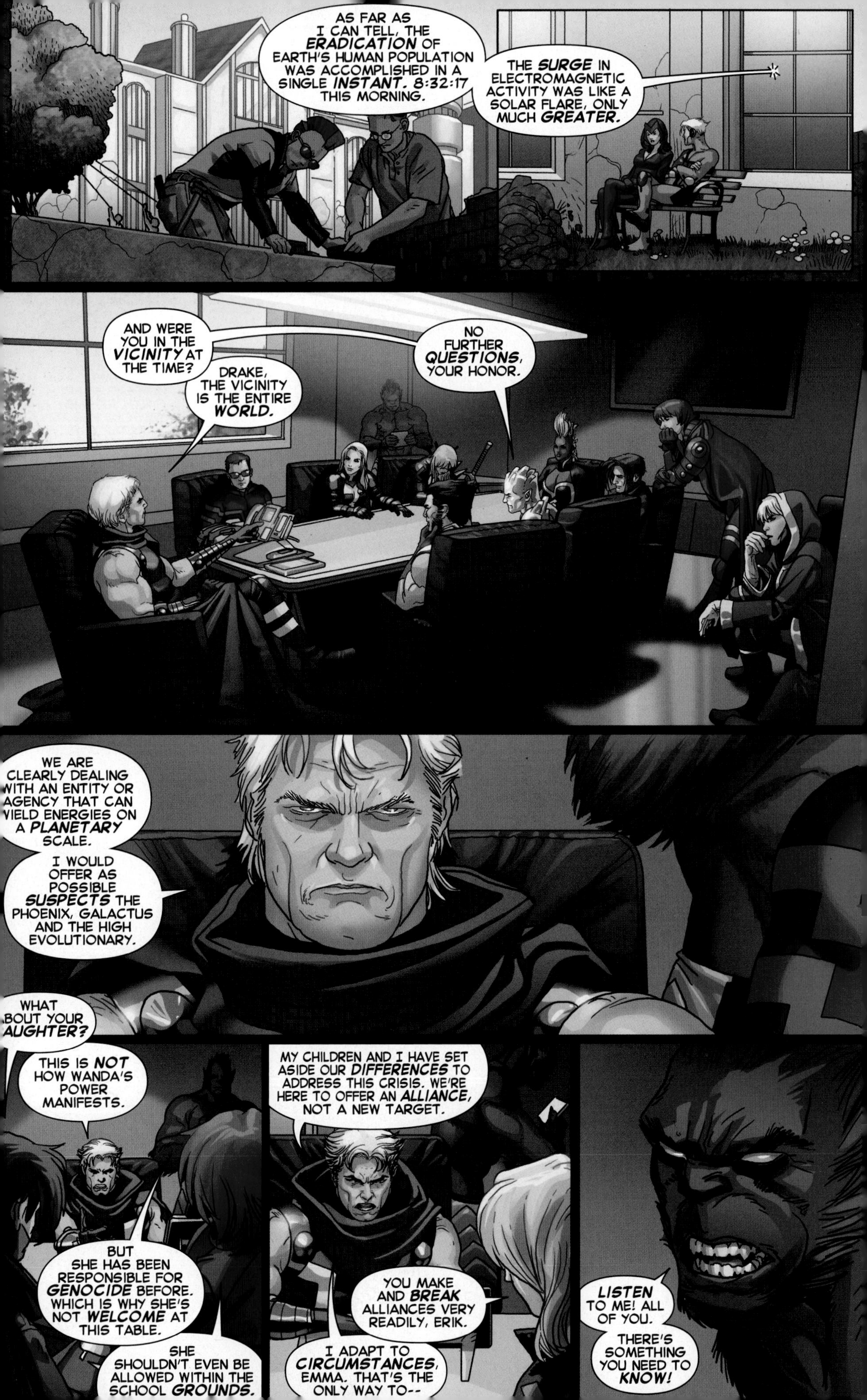
AS FAR AS I CAN TELL, THE ERADICATION OF EARTH'S HUMAN POPULATION WAS ACCOMPLISHED IN A SINGLE INSTANT. 8:32:17 THIS MORNING.
THE SURGE IN ELECTROMAGNETIC ACTIVITY WAS LIKE A SOLAR FLARE, ONLY MUCH GREATER.
AND WERE YOU IN THE VICINITY AT THE TIME?
DRAKE, THE VICINITY IS THE ENTIRE WORLD.
NO FURTHER QUESTIONS, YOUR HONOR.
WE ARE CLEARLY DEALING WITH AN ENTITY OR AGENCY THAT CAN VIELD ENERGIES ON A PLANETARY SCALE.
I WOULD OFFER AS POSSIBLE SUSPECTS THE PHOENIX, GALACTUS AND THE HIGH EVOLUTIONARY.
WHAT BOUT YOUR AUGHTER?
THIS IS NOT HOW WANDA'S POWER MANIFESTS.
BUT SHE HAS BEEN RESPONSIBLE FOR GENOCIDE BEFORE. WHICH IS WHY SHE'S NOT WELCOME AT THIS TABLE.
SHE SHOULDN'T EVEN BE ALLOWED WITHIN THE SCHOOL GROUNDS.
MY CHILDREN AND I HAVE SET ASIDE OUR DIFFERENCES TO ADDRESS THIS CRISIS. WE'RE HERE TO OFFER AN ALLIANCE, NOT A NEW TARGET.
YOU MAKE AND BREAK ALLIANCES VERY READILY, ERIK.
I ADAPT TO CIRCUMSTANCES, EMMA. THAT'S THE ONLY WAY TO--
LISTEN TO ME! ALL OF YOU.
THERE'S SOMETHING YOU NEED TO KNOW!

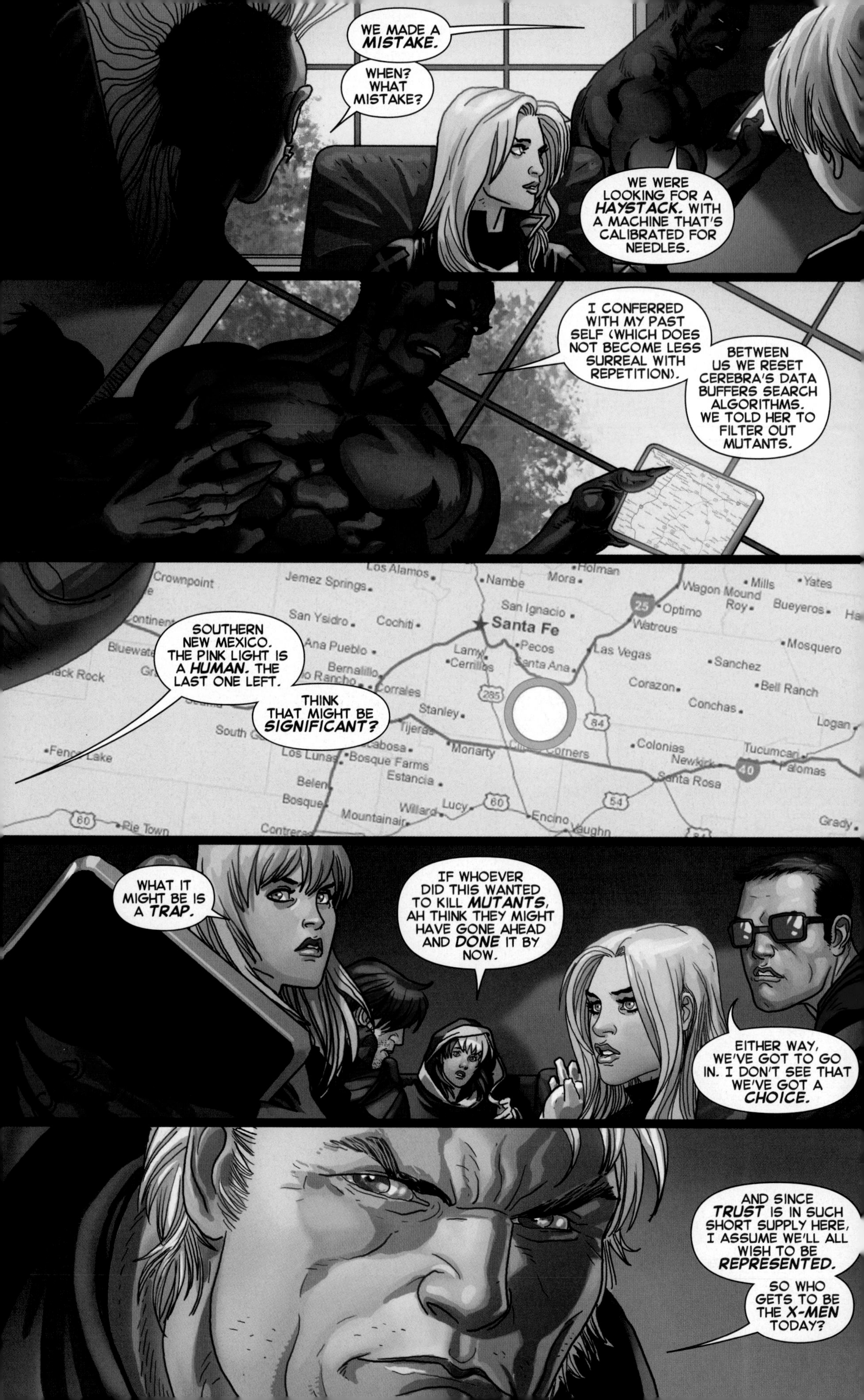

WE MADE A MISTAKE.
WHEN? WHAT MISTAKE?
WE WERE LOOKING FOR A HAYSTACK. WITH A MACHINE THAT'S CALIBRATED FOR NEEDLES.
I CONFERRED WITH MY PAST SELF (WHICH DOES NOT BECOME LESS SURREAL WITH REPETITION).
BETWEEN US WE RESET CEREBRA'S DATA BUFFERS SEARCH ALGORITHMS. WE TOLD HER TO FILTER OUT MUTANTS.
Los Alamos
Crownpoint
Jemez Springs
Nambe
Mora
Holman
Wagon Mound
Mills
Yates
San Ignacio
Roy
Bueyeros
Optimo
San Ysidro
Cochiti
Santa Fe
Watrous
Ana Pueblo
Pecos
Las Vegas
Mosquero
Lamy
Cerrillos
Santa Ana
Sanchez
Bernalillo
Corrales
Corazon
Bell Ranch
Stanley
Conchas
Logan
Tijeras
South
Colonias
Moriarty
Tucumcari
Los Lunas
Bosque Farms
Newkirk
Palomas
Estancia
Santa Rosa
Belen
Bosque
Lucy
Willard
Mountainair
Encino
Vaughn
Pie Town
Grady
25
285
84
40
60
54
SOUTHERN NEW MEXICO. THE PINK LIGHT IS A HUMAN. THE LAST ONE LEFT.
THINK THAT MIGHT BE SIGNIFICANT?
WHAT IT MIGHT BE IS A TRAP.
IF WHOEVER DID THIS WANTED TO KILL MUTANTS, AH THINK THEY MIGHT HAVE GONE AHEAD AND DONE IT BY NOW.
EITHER WAY, WE'VE GOT TO GO IN. I DON'T SEE THAT WE'VE GOT A CHOICE.
AND SINCE TRUST IS IN SUCH SHORT SUPPLY HERE, I ASSUME WE'LL ALL WISH TO BE REPRESENTED.
SO WHO GETS TO BE THE X-MEN TODAY?

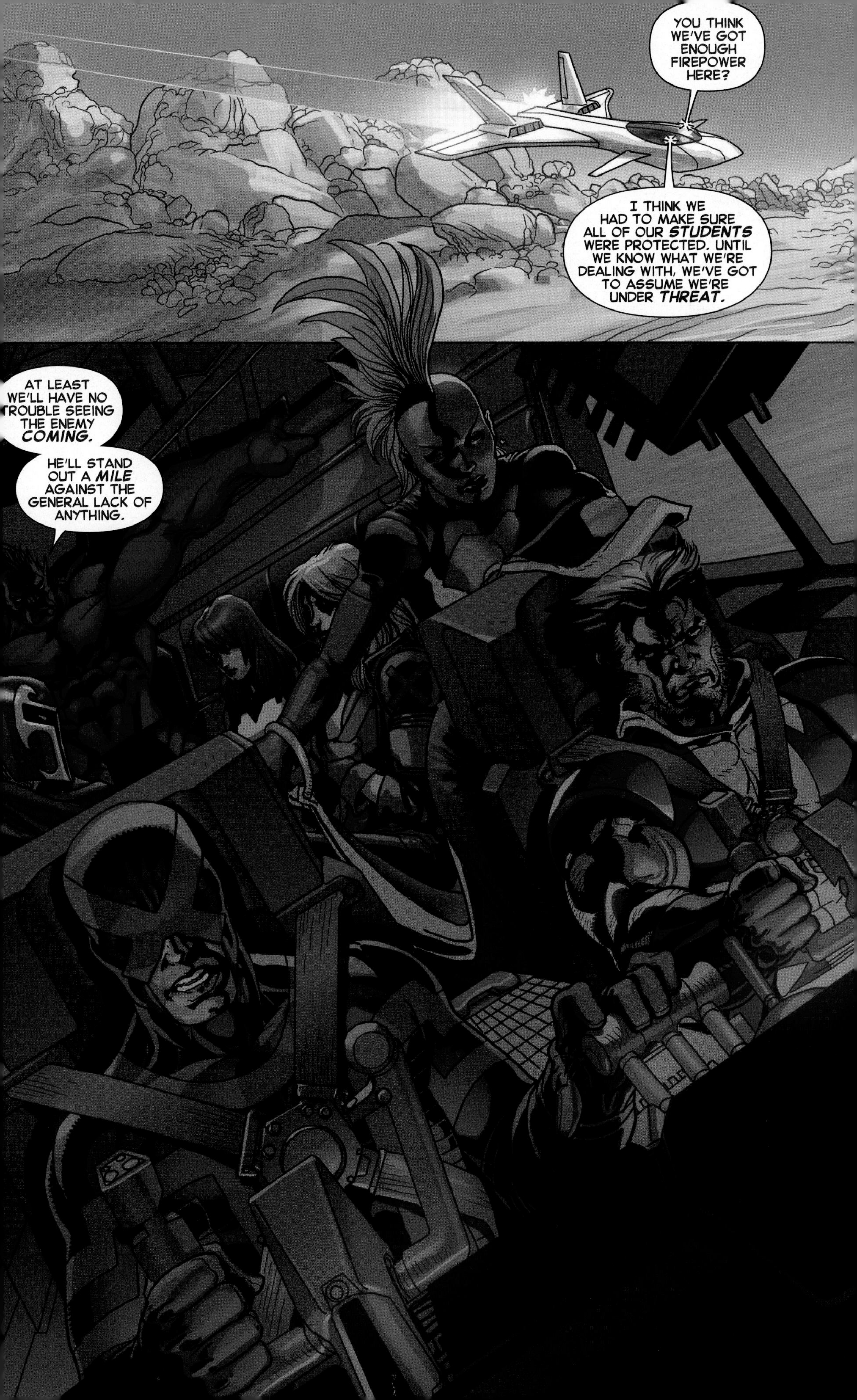
YOU THINK WE'VE GOT ENOUGH FIREPOWER HERE?
I THINK WE HAD TO MAKE SURE ALL OF OUR STUDENTS WERE PROTECTED. UNTIL WE KNOW WHAT WE'RE DEALING WITH, WE'VE GOT TO ASSUME WE'RE UNDER THREAT.
AT LEAST WE'LL HAVE NO TROUBLE SEEING THE ENEMY COMING.
HE'LL STAND OUT A MILE AGAINST THE GENERAL LACK OF ANYTHING.

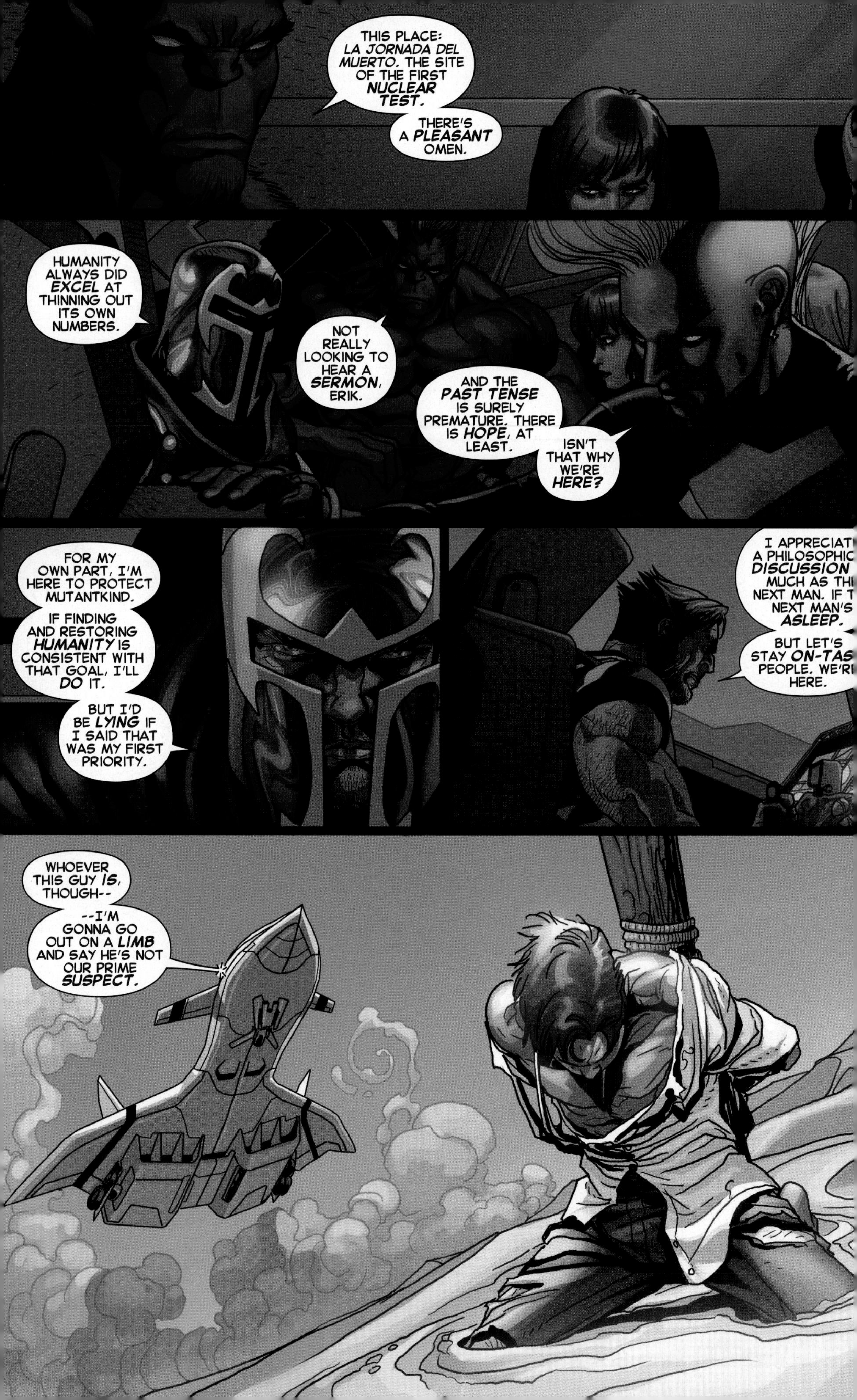
THIS PLACE: LA JORNADA DEL MUERTO. THE SITE OF THE FIRST NUCLEAR TEST.
THERE'S A PLEASANT OMEN.
HUMANITY ALWAYS DID EXCEL AT THINNING OUT ITS OWN NUMBERS.
NOT REALLY LOOKING TO HEAR A SERMON, ERIK.
AND THE PAST TENSE IS SURELY PREMATURE. THERE IS HOPE, AT LEAST.
ISN'T THAT WHY WE'RE HERE?
FOR MY OWN PART, I'M HERE TO PROTECT MUTANTKIND.
IF FINDING AND RESTORING HUMANITY IS CONSISTENT WITH THAT GOAL, I'LL DO IT.
BUT I'D BE LYING IF I SAID THAT WAS MY FIRST PRIORITY.
I APPRECIAT A PHILOSOPHIC DISCUSSION MUCH AS TH NEXT MAN. IF T NEXT MAN'S ASLEEP.
BUT LET'S STAY ON-TAS PEOPLE. WE'R HERE.
WHOEVER THIS GUY IS, THOUGH--
--I'M GONNA GO OUT ON A LIMB AND SAY HE'S NOT OUR PRIME SUSPECT.

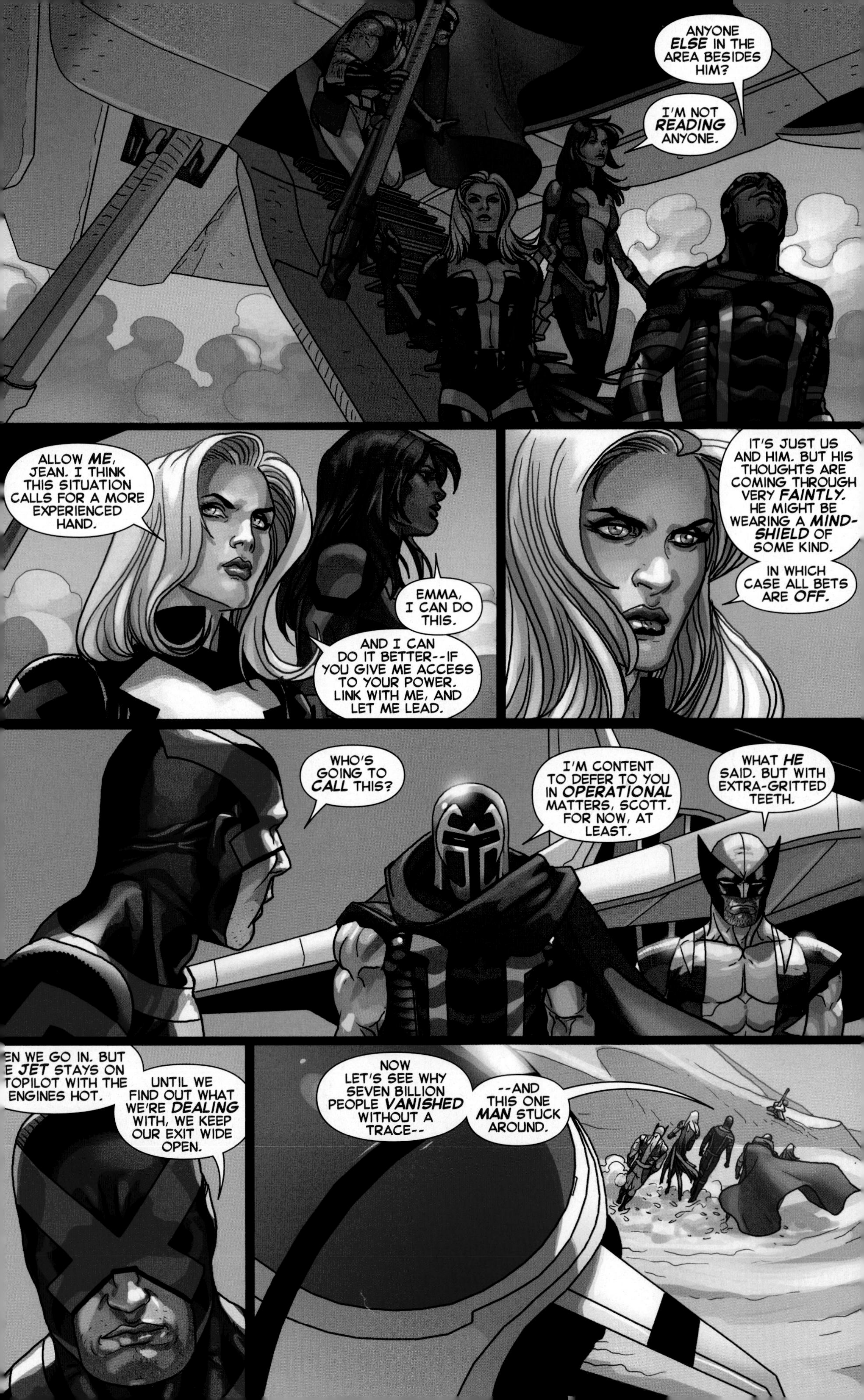
ANYONE ELSE IN THE AREA BESIDES HIM?
I'M NOT READING ANYONE.
ALLOW ME, JEAN. I THINK THIS SITUATION CALLS FOR A MORE EXPERIENCED HAND.
EMMA, I CAN DO THIS.
AND I CAN DO IT BETTER--IF YOU GIVE ME ACCESS TO YOUR POWER. LINK WITH ME, AND LET ME LEAD.
IT'S JUST US AND HIM. BUT HIS THOUGHTS ARE COMING THROUGH VERY FAINTLY. HE MIGHT BE WEARING A MIND-SHIELD OF SOME KIND.
IN WHICH CASE ALL BETS ARE OFF.
WHO'S GOING TO CALL THIS?
I'M CONTENT TO DEFER TO YOU IN OPERATIONAL MATTERS, SCOTT. FOR NOW, AT LEAST.
WHAT HE SAID. BUT WITH EXTRA-GRITTED TEETH.
EN WE GO IN. BUT E JET STAYS ON TOPILOT WITH THE ENGINES HOT.
UNTIL WE FIND OUT WHAT WE'RE DEALING WITH, WE KEEP OUR EXIT WIDE OPEN.
NOW LET'S SEE WHY SEVEN BILLION PEOPLE VANISHED WITHOUT A TRACE--
--AND THIS ONE MAN STUCK AROUND.

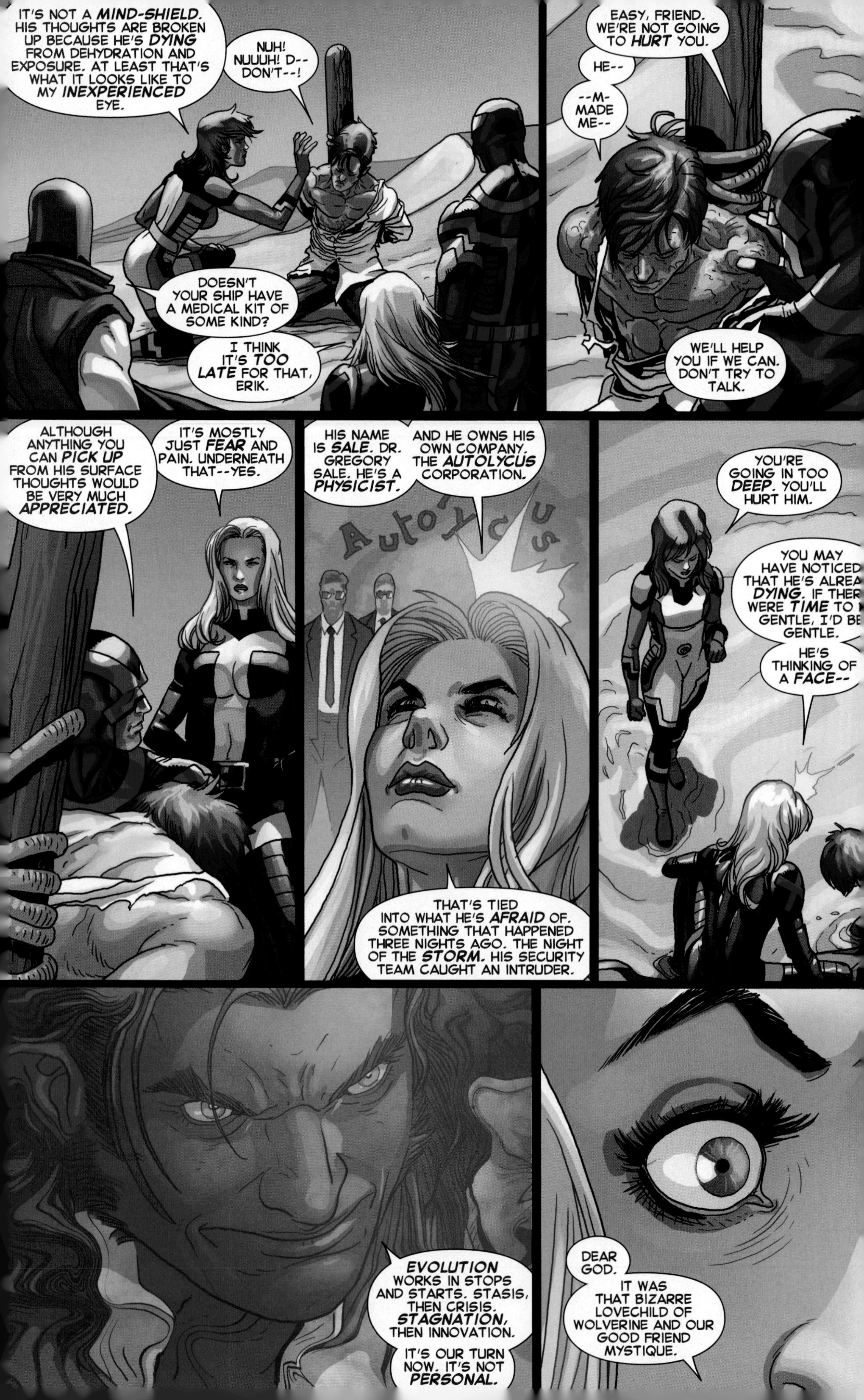

IT'S NOT A MIND-SHIELD. HIS THOUGHTS ARE BROKEN UP BECAUSE HE'S DYING FROM DEHYDRATION AND EXPOSURE. AT LEAST THAT'S WHAT IT LOOKS LIKE TO MY INEXPERIENCED EYE.
NUH! NUUUH! D-- DON'T--!
DOESN'T YOUR SHIP HAVE A MEDICAL KIT OF SOME KIND?
I THINK IT'S TOO LATE FOR THAT, ERIK.
EASY, FRIEND. WE'RE NOT GOING TO HURT YOU.
HE--
--M- MADE ME--
WE'LL HELP YOU IF WE CAN. DON'T TRY TO TALK.
ALTHOUGH ANYTHING YOU CAN PICK UP FROM HIS SURFACE THOUGHTS WOULD BE VERY MUCH APPRECIATED.
IT'S MOSTLY JUST FEAR AND PAIN. UNDERNEATH THAT--YES.
HIS NAME IS SALE. DR. GREGORY SALE. HE'S A PHYSICIST.
AND HE OWNS HIS OWN COMPANY. THE AUTOLYCUS CORPORATION.
Autolycus
THAT'S TIED INTO WHAT HE'S AFRAID OF. SOMETHING THAT HAPPENED THREE NIGHTS AGO. THE NIGHT OF THE STORM. HIS SECURITY TEAM CAUGHT AN INTRUDER.
YOU'RE GOING IN TOO DEEP. YOU'LL HURT HIM.
YOU MAY HAVE NOTICED THAT HE'S ALREA DYING. IF THER WERE TIME TO GENTLE, I'D BE GENTLE.
HE'S THINKING OF A FACE--
EVOLUTION WORKS IN STOPS AND STARTS. STASIS, THEN CRISIS. STAGNATION, THEN INNOVATION.
IT'S OUR TURN NOW. IT'S NOT PERSONAL.
DEAR GOD.
IT WAS THAT BIZARRE LOVECHILD OF WOLVERINE AND OUR GOOD FRIEND MYSTIQUE.

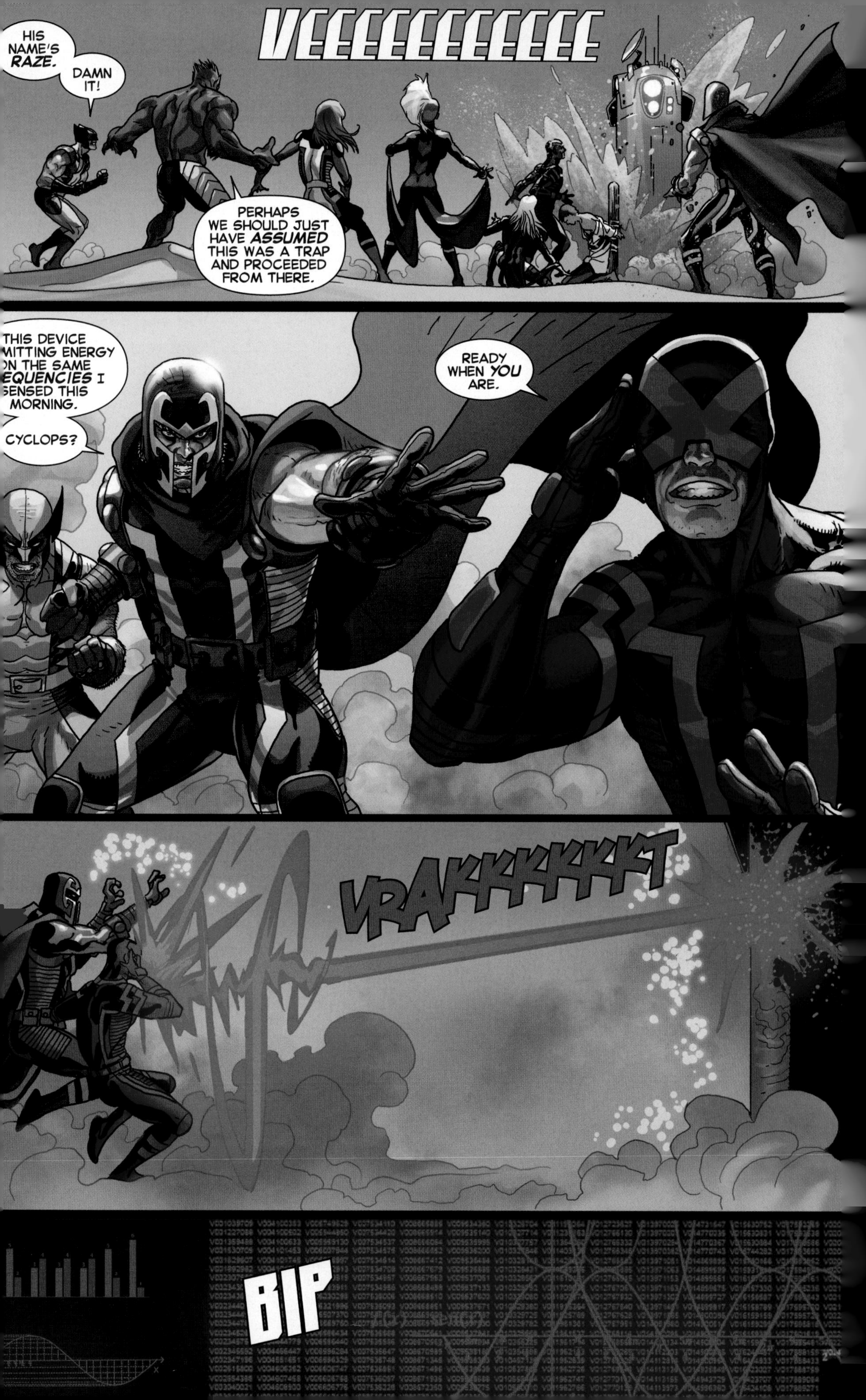
VEEEEEEEEEEEE
HIS NAME'S RAZE.
DAMN IT!
PERHAPS WE SHOULD JUST HAVE ASSUMED THIS WAS A TRAP AND PROCEEDED FROM THERE.
THIS DEVICE MITTING ENERGY ON THE SAME EQUENCIES I SENSED THIS MORNING.
CYCLOPS?
READY WHEN YOU ARE.
VRAKKKKKKT
BIP

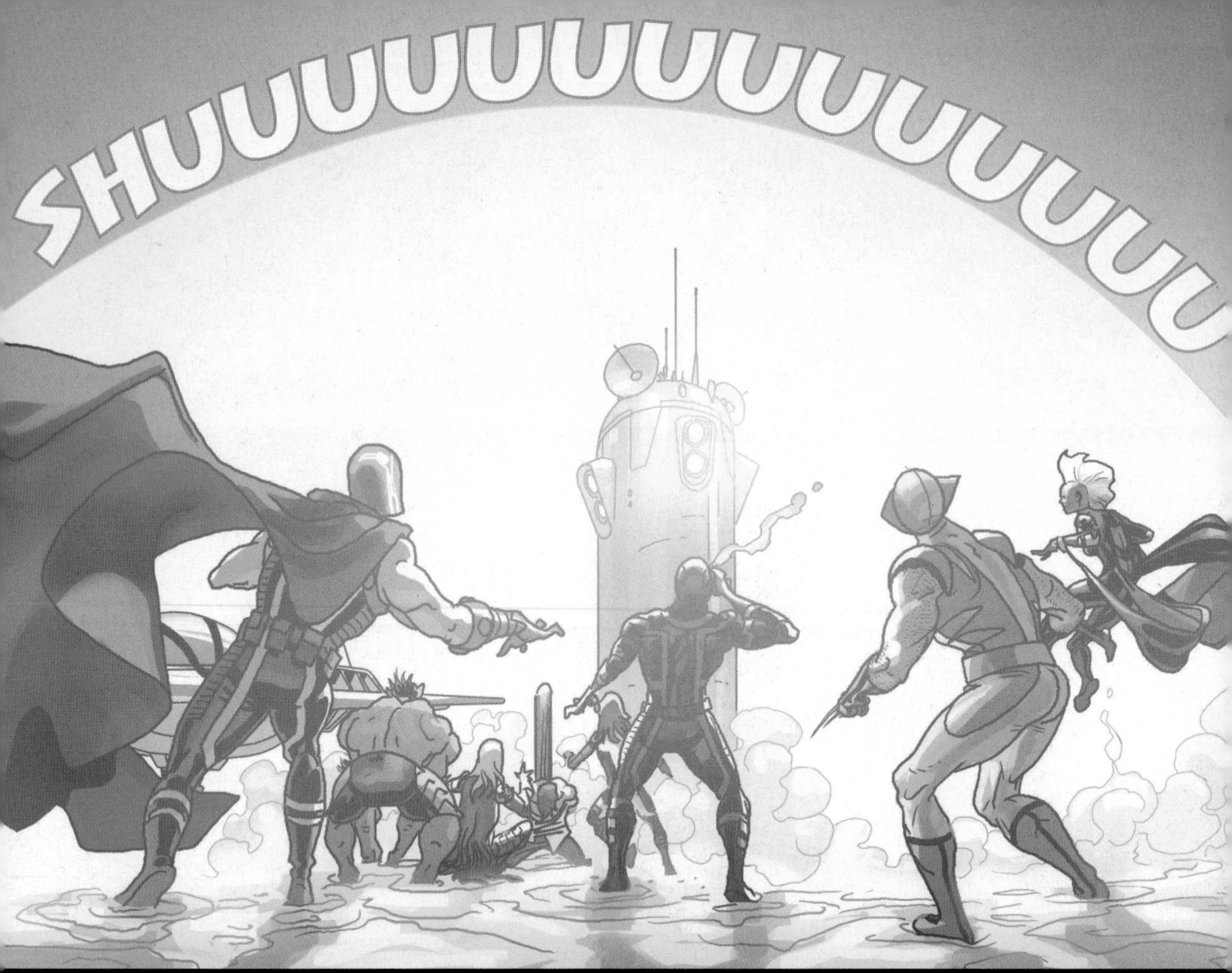
SHUUUUUUUUUUUUUU

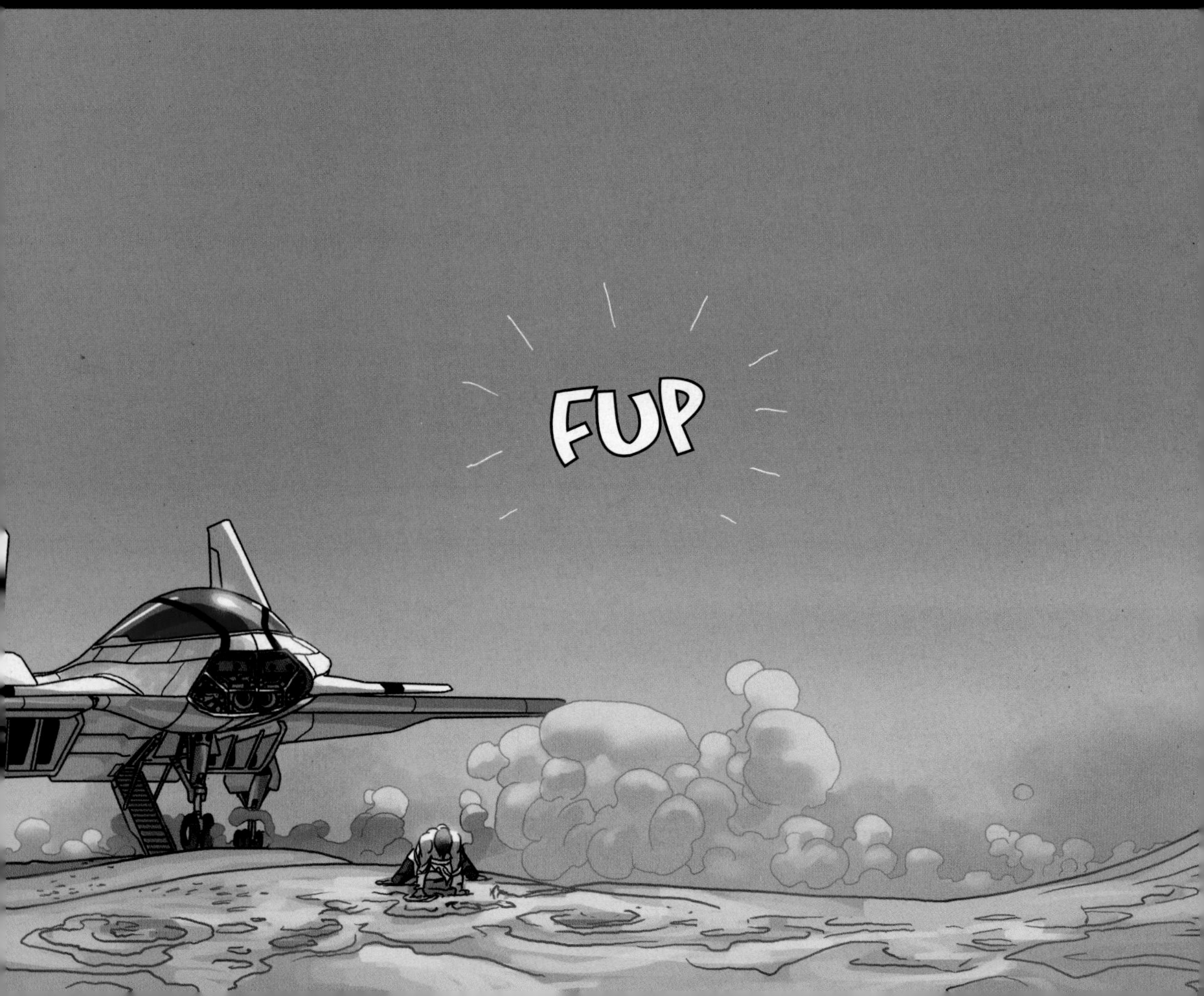
FUP

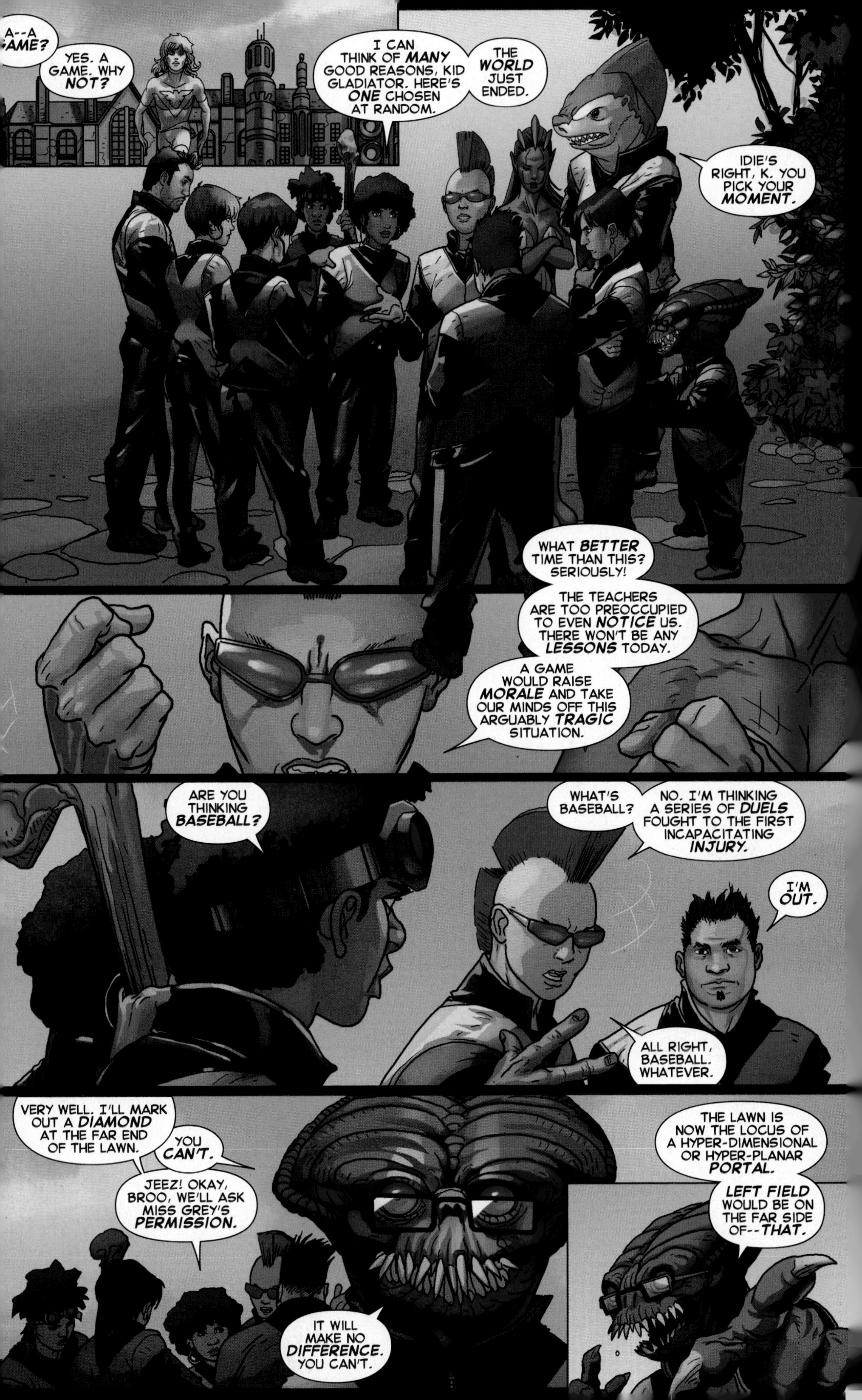
A--A GAME?
YES. A GAME. WHY NOT?
I CAN THINK OF MANY GOOD REASONS, KID GLADIATOR. HERE'S ONE CHOSEN AT RANDOM.
THE WORLD JUST ENDED.
IDIE'S RIGHT, K. YOU PICK YOUR MOMENT.
WHAT BETTER TIME THAN THIS? SERIOUSLY!
THE TEACHERS ARE TOO PREOCCUPIED TO EVEN NOTICE US. THERE WON'T BE ANY LESSONS TODAY.
A GAME WOULD RAISE MORALE AND TAKE OUR MINDS OFF THIS ARGUABLY TRAGIC SITUATION.
ARE YOU THINKING BASEBALL?
WHAT'S BASEBALL?
NO. I'M THINKING A SERIES OF DUELS FOUGHT TO THE FIRST INCAPACITATING INJURY.
I'M OUT.
ALL RIGHT, BASEBALL. WHATEVER.
VERY WELL. I'LL MARK OUT A DIAMOND AT THE FAR END OF THE LAWN.
YOU CAN'T.
JEEZ! OKAY, BROO, WE'LL ASK MISS GREY'S PERMISSION.
IT WILL MAKE NO DIFFERENCE. YOU CAN'T.
THE LAWN IS NOW THE LOCUS OF A HYPER-DIMENSIONAL OR HYPER-PLANAR PORTAL.
LEFT FIELD WOULD BE ON THE FAR SIDE OF--THAT.

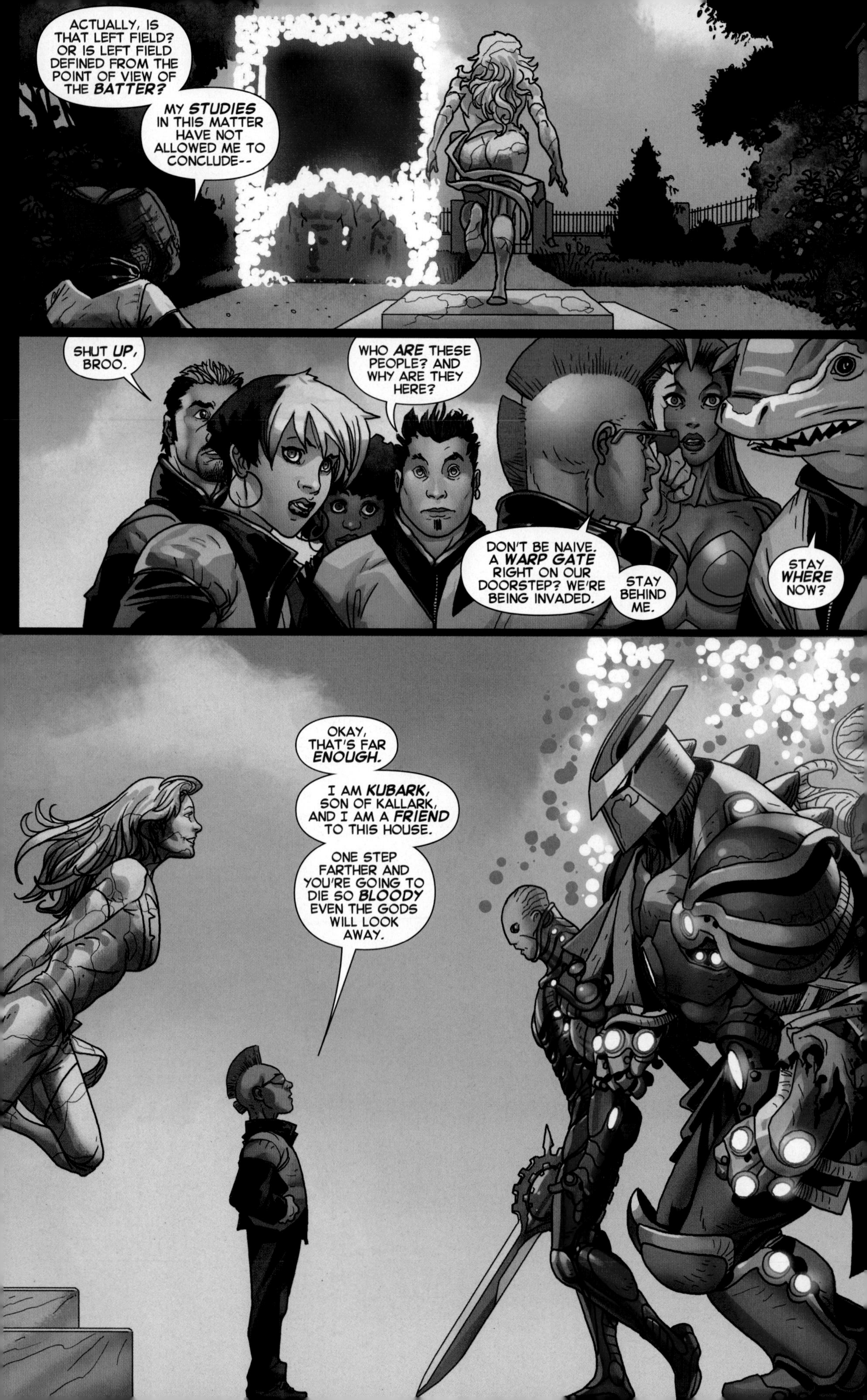
ACTUALLY, IS THAT LEFT FIELD? OR IS LEFT FIELD DEFINED FROM THE POINT OF VIEW OF THE BATTER?
MY STUDIES IN THIS MATTER HAVE NOT ALLOWED ME TO CONCLUDE--
SHUT UP, BROO.
WHO ARE THESE PEOPLE? AND WHY ARE THEY HERE?
DON'T BE NAIVE. A WARP GATE RIGHT ON OUR DOORSTEP? WE'RE BEING INVADED.
STAY BEHIND ME.
STAY WHERE NOW?
OKAY, THAT'S FAR ENOUGH.
I AM KUBARK, SON OF KALLARK, AND I AM A FRIEND TO THIS HOUSE.
ONE STEP FARTHER AND YOU'RE GOING TO DIE SO BLOODY EVEN THE GODS WILL LOOK AWAY.

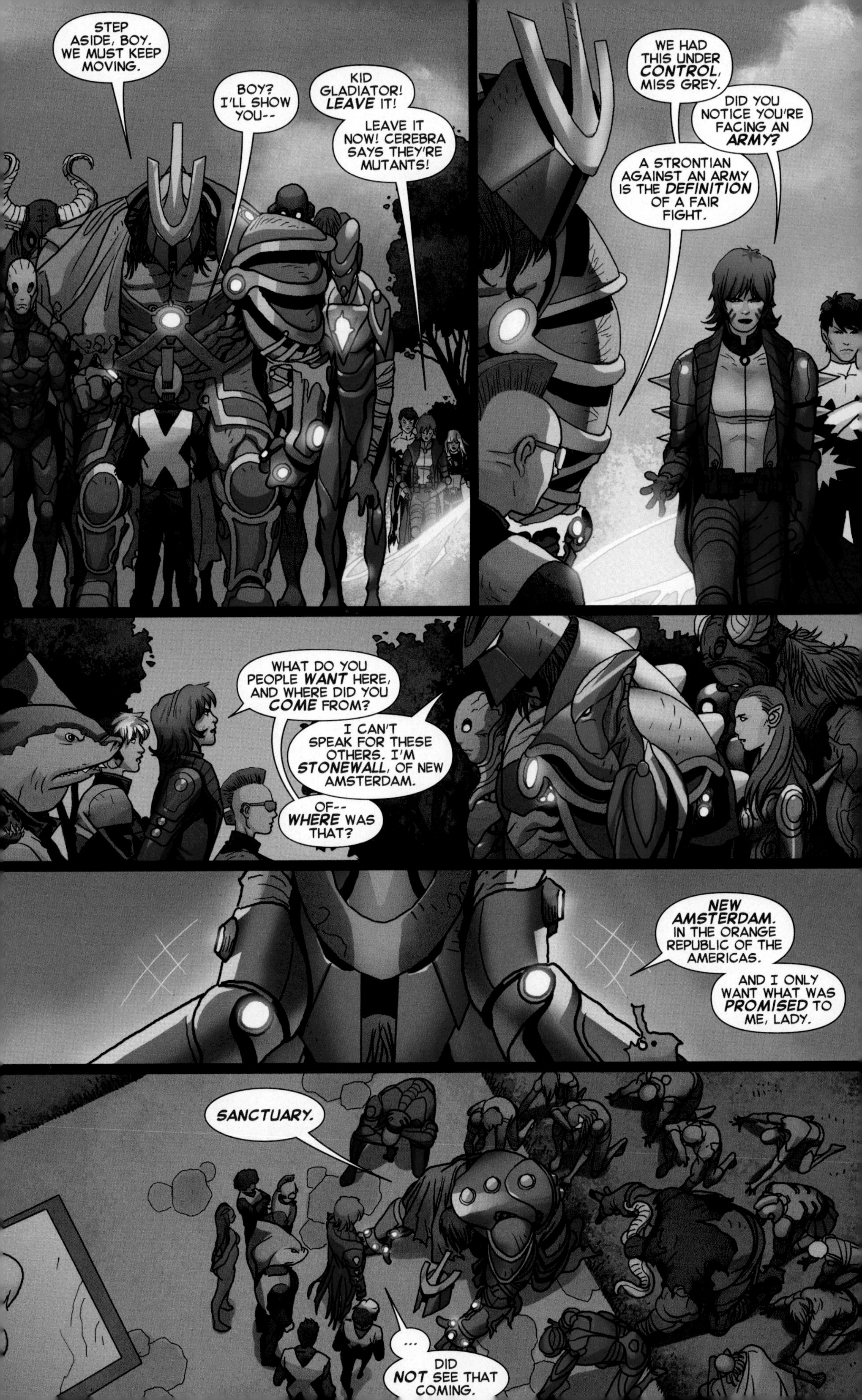
STEP ASIDE, BOY. WE MUST KEEP MOVING.
BOY? I'LL SHOW YOU--
KID GLADIATOR! LEAVE IT!
LEAVE IT NOW! CEREBRA SAYS THEY'RE MUTANTS!
WE HAD THIS UNDER CONTROL, MISS GREY.
DID YOU NOTICE YOU'RE FACING AN ARMY?
A STRONTIAN AGAINST AN ARMY IS THE DEFINITION OF A FAIR FIGHT.
WHAT DO YOU PEOPLE WANT HERE, AND WHERE DID YOU COME FROM?
I CAN'T SPEAK FOR THESE OTHERS. I'M STONEWALL, OF NEW AMSTERDAM.
OF-- WHERE WAS THAT?
NEW AMSTERDAM. IN THE ORANGE REPUBLIC OF THE AMERICAS.
AND I ONLY WANT WHAT WAS PROMISED TO ME, LADY.
SANCTUARY.
... DID NOT SEE THAT COMING.

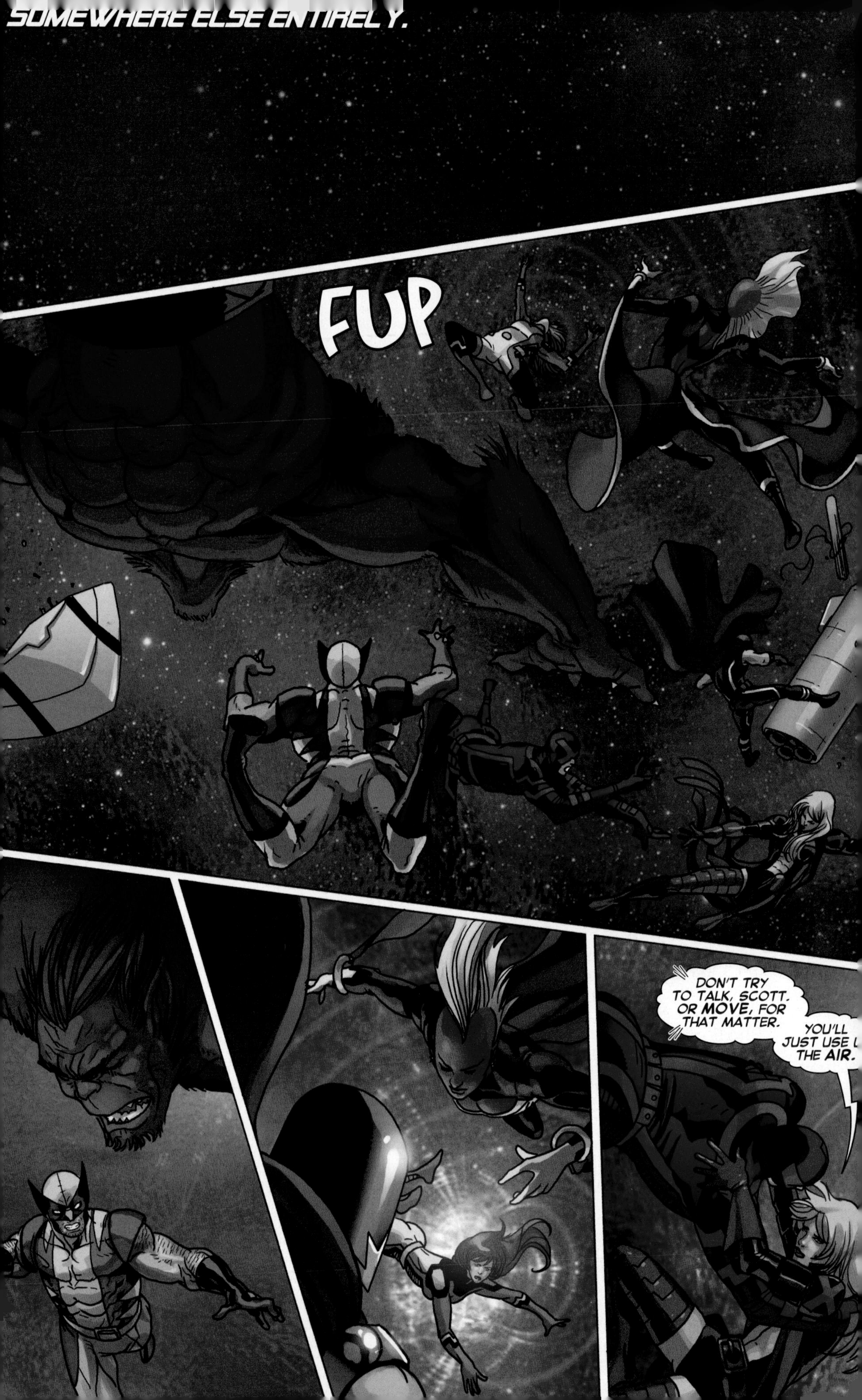
SOMEWHERE ELSE ENTIRELY.
FUP
DON'T TRY TO TALK, SCOTT. OR MOVE, FOR THAT MATTER.
YOU'LL JUST USE U THE AIR.

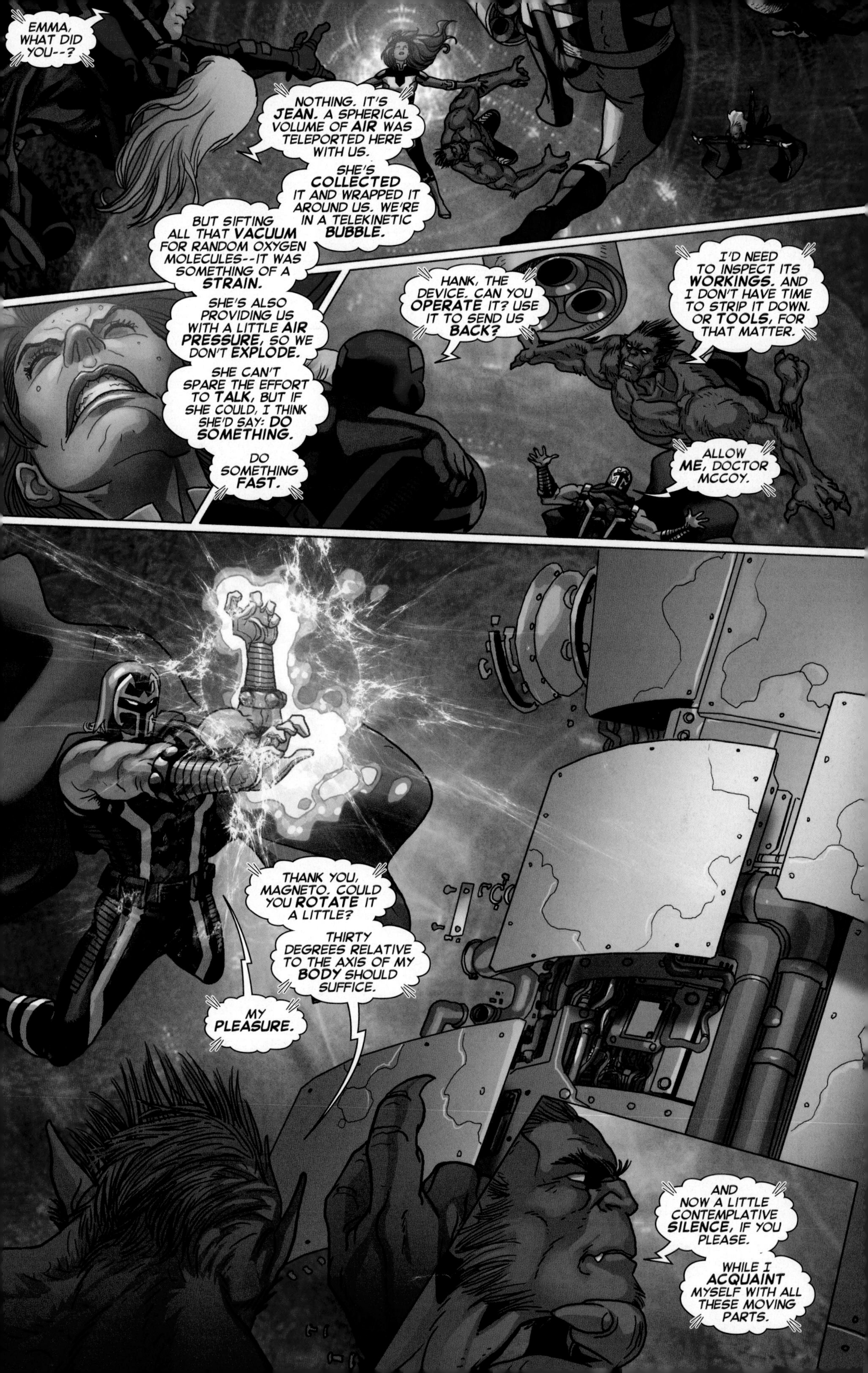
EMMA, WHAT DID YOU--?
NOTHING. IT'S JEAN. A SPHERICAL VOLUME OF AIR WAS TELEPORTED HERE WITH US.
SHE'S COLLECTED IT AND WRAPPED IT AROUND US. WE'RE IN A TELEKINETIC BUBBLE.
BUT SIFTING ALL THAT VACUUM FOR RANDOM OXYGEN MOLECULES--IT WAS SOMETHING OF A STRAIN.
SHE'S ALSO PROVIDING US WITH A LITTLE AIR PRESSURE, SO WE DON'T EXPLODE.
SHE CAN'T SPARE THE EFFORT TO TALK, BUT IF SHE COULD, I THINK SHE'D SAY: DO SOMETHING.
DO SOMETHING FAST.
HANK, THE DEVICE. CAN YOU OPERATE IT? USE IT TO SEND US BACK?
I'D NEED TO INSPECT ITS WORKINGS. AND I DON'T HAVE TIME TO STRIP IT DOWN. OR TOOLS, FOR THAT MATTER.
ALLOW ME, DOCTOR MCCOY.
THANK YOU, MAGNETO. COULD YOU ROTATE IT A LITTLE?
THIRTY DEGREES RELATIVE TO THE AXIS OF MY BODY SHOULD SUFFICE.
MY PLEASURE.
AND NOW A LITTLE CONTEMPLATIVE SILENCE, IF YOU PLEASE.
WHILE I ACQUAINT MYSELF WITH ALL THESE MOVING PARTS.

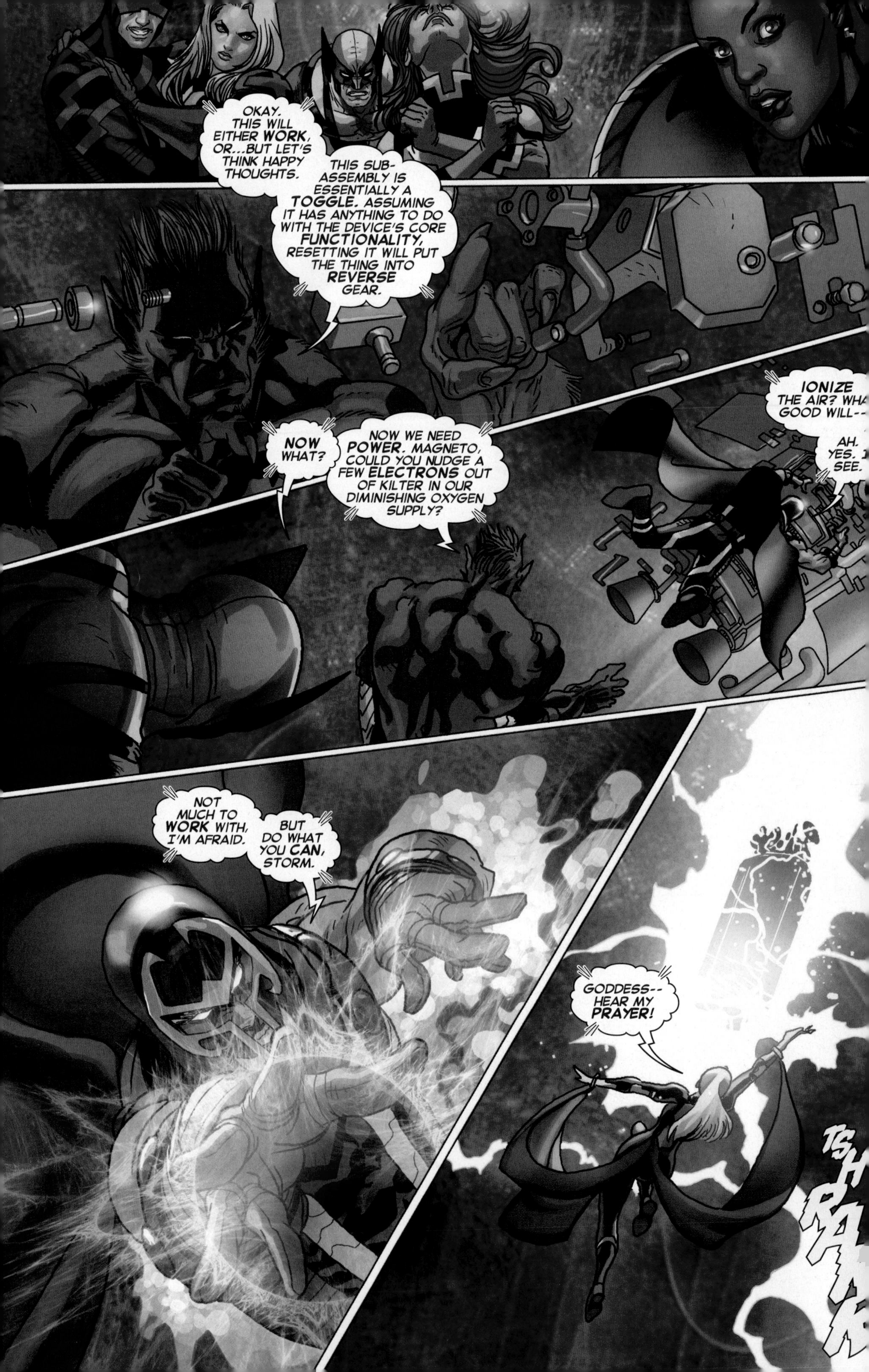
OKAY. THIS WILL EITHER WORK, OR...BUT LET'S THINK HAPPY THOUGHTS.
THIS SUB-ASSEMBLY IS ESSENTIALLY A TOGGLE. ASSUMING IT HAS ANYTHING TO DO WITH THE DEVICE'S CORE FUNCTIONALITY, RESETTING IT WILL PUT THE THING INTO REVERSE GEAR.
NOW WHAT?
NOW WE NEED POWER. MAGNETO, COULD YOU NUDGE A FEW ELECTRONS OUT OF KILTER IN OUR DIMINISHING OXYGEN SUPPLY?
IONIZE THE AIR? WHA GOOD WILL--
AH. YES. SEE.
NOT MUCH TO WORK WITH, I'M AFRAID.
BUT DO WHAT YOU CAN, STORM.
GODDESS--HEAR MY PRAYER!
TSHRAK

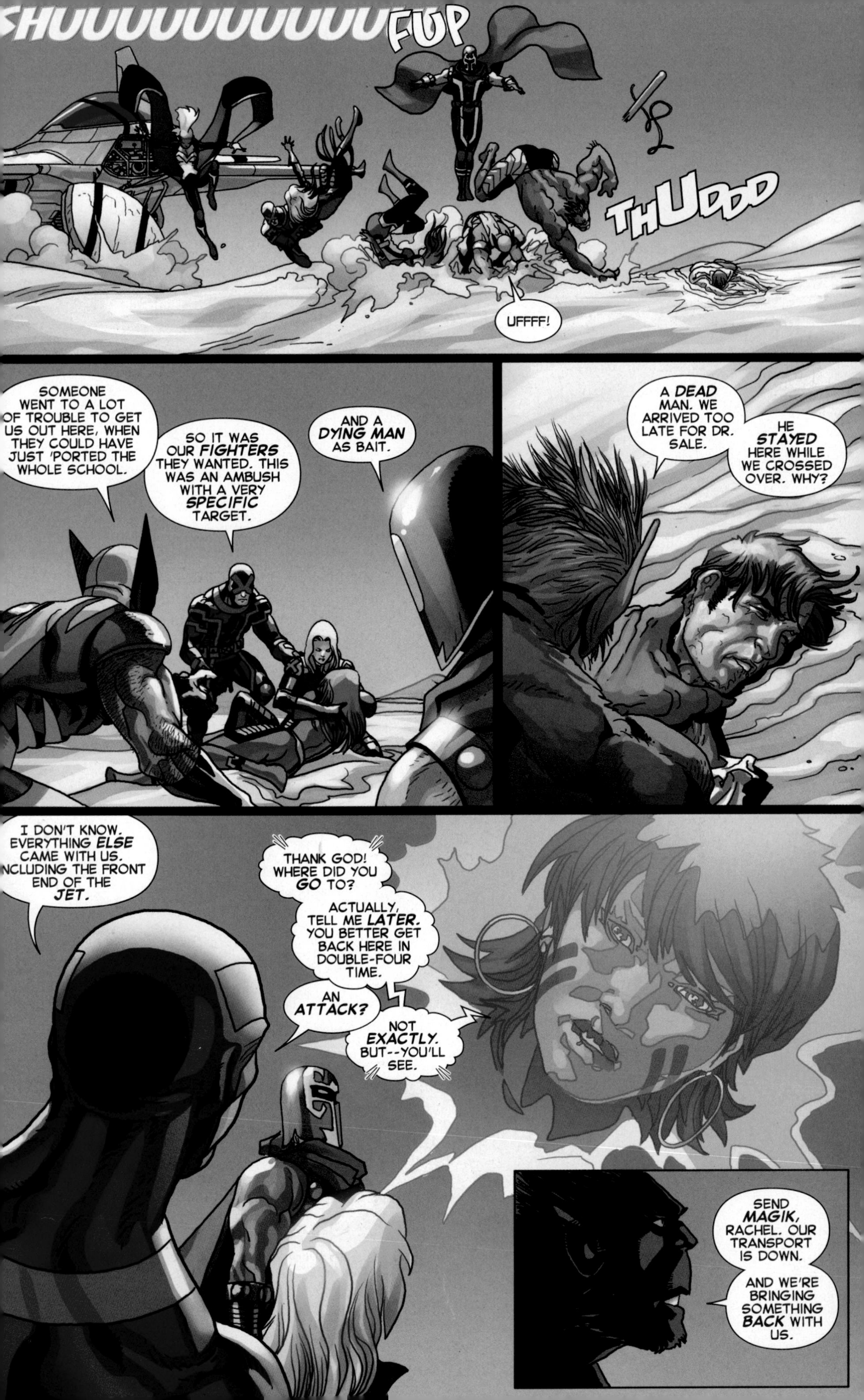
SHUUUUUUUUUUUFUP
THUDDD
UFFFF!
SOMEONE WENT TO A LOT OF TROUBLE TO GET US OUT HERE, WHEN THEY COULD HAVE JUST 'PORTED THE WHOLE SCHOOL.
SO IT WAS OUR FIGHTERS THEY WANTED. THIS WAS AN AMBUSH WITH A VERY SPECIFIC TARGET.
AND A DYING MAN AS BAIT.
A DEAD MAN. WE ARRIVED TOO LATE FOR DR. SALE.
HE STAYED HERE WHILE WE CROSSED OVER. WHY?
I DON'T KNOW. EVERYTHING ELSE CAME WITH US. NCLUDING THE FRONT END OF THE JET.
THANK GOD! WHERE DID YOU GO TO?
ACTUALLY, TELL ME LATER. YOU BETTER GET BACK HERE IN DOUBLE-FOUR TIME.
AN ATTACK?
NOT EXACTLY. BUT--YOU'LL SEE.
SEND MAGIK, RACHEL. OUR TRANSPORT IS DOWN.
AND WE'RE BRINGING SOMETHING BACK WITH US.

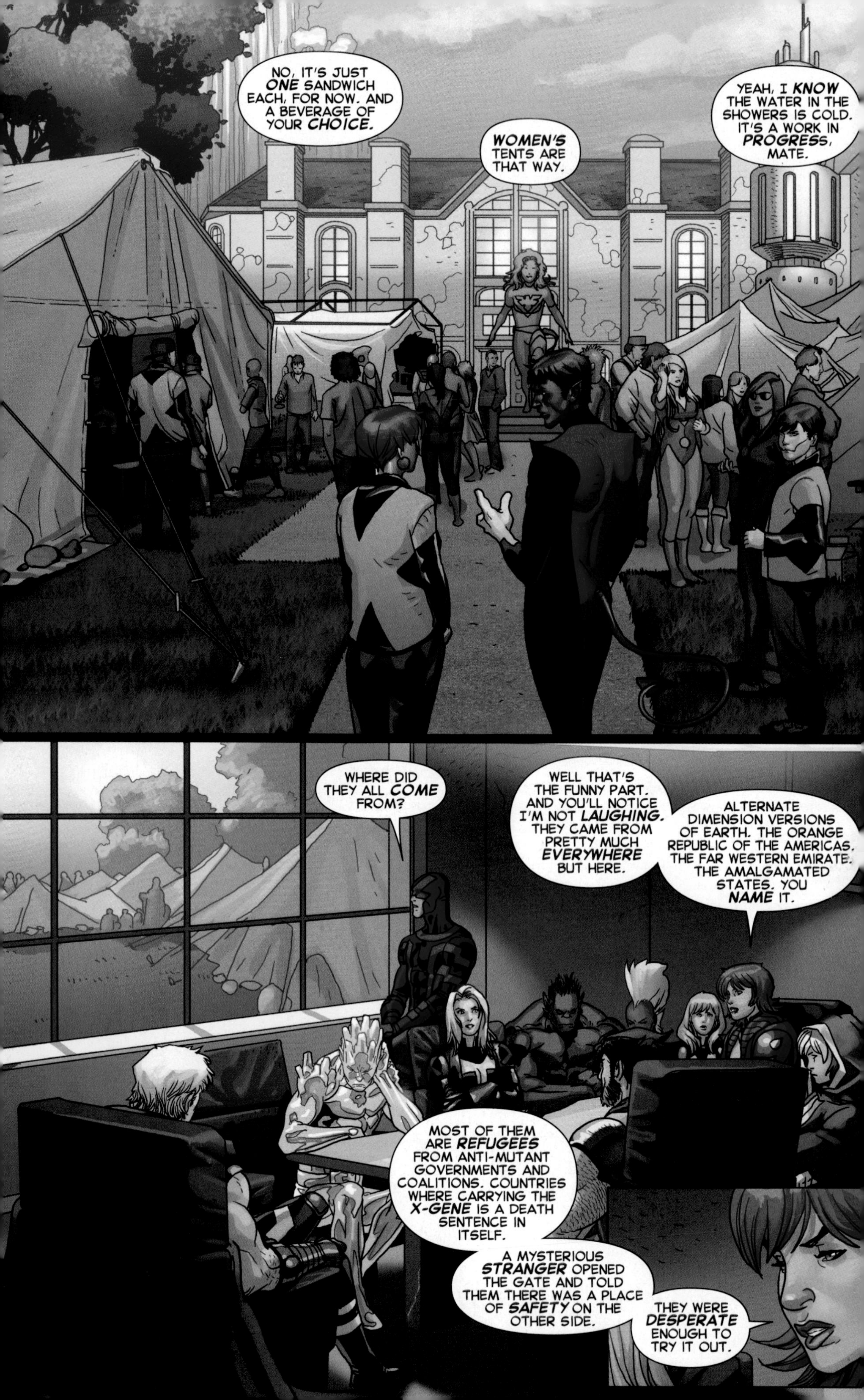
NO, IT'S JUST ONE SANDWICH EACH, FOR NOW. AND A BEVERAGE OF YOUR CHOICE.
WOMEN'S TENTS ARE THAT WAY.
YEAH, I KNOW THE WATER IN THE SHOWERS IS COLD. IT'S A WORK IN PROGRESS, MATE.
WHERE DID THEY ALL COME FROM?
WELL THAT'S THE FUNNY PART. AND YOU'LL NOTICE I'M NOT LAUGHING. THEY CAME FROM PRETTY MUCH EVERYWHERE BUT HERE.
ALTERNATE DIMENSION VERSIONS OF EARTH. THE ORANGE REPUBLIC OF THE AMERICAS. THE FAR WESTERN EMIRATE. THE AMALGAMATED STATES. YOU NAME IT.
MOST OF THEM ARE REFUGEES FROM ANTI-MUTANT GOVERNMENTS AND COALITIONS. COUNTRIES WHERE CARRYING THE X-GENE IS A DEATH SENTENCE IN ITSELF.
A MYSTERIOUS STRANGER OPENED THE GATE AND TOLD THEM THERE WAS A PLACE OF SAFETY ON THE OTHER SIDE.
THEY WERE DESPERATE ENOUGH TO TRY IT OUT.

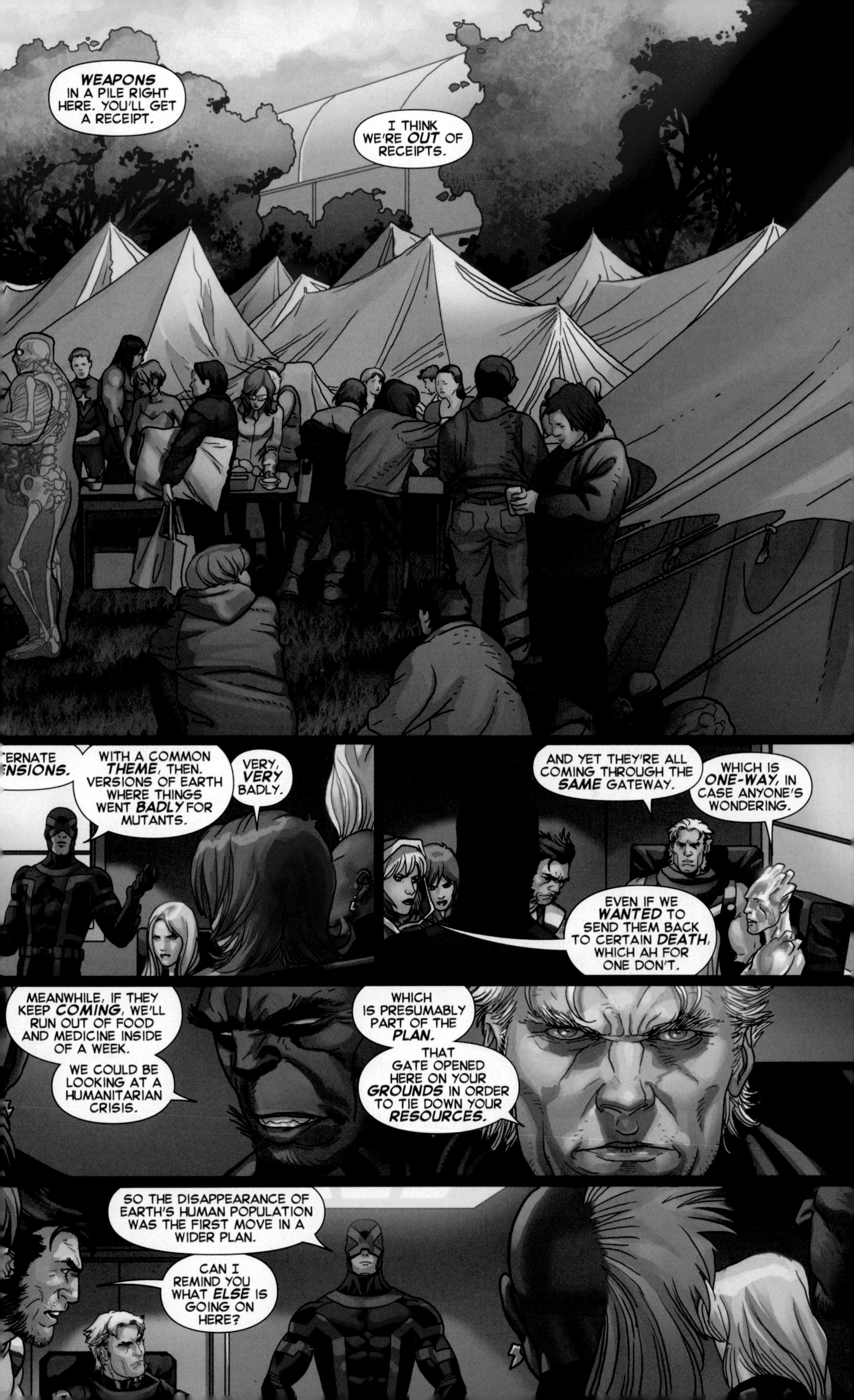
WEAPONS IN A PILE RIGHT HERE. YOU'LL GET A RECEIPT.
I THINK WE'RE OUT OF RECEIPTS.
ERNATE ENSIONS.
WITH A COMMON THEME, THEN. VERSIONS OF EARTH WHERE THINGS WENT BADLY FOR MUTANTS.
VERY, VERY BADLY.
AND YET THEY'RE ALL COMING THROUGH THE SAME GATEWAY.
WHICH IS ONE-WAY, IN CASE ANYONE'S WONDERING.
EVEN IF WE WANTED TO SEND THEM BACK TO CERTAIN DEATH, WHICH AH FOR ONE DON'T.
MEANWHILE, IF THEY KEEP COMING, WE'LL RUN OUT OF FOOD AND MEDICINE INSIDE OF A WEEK.
WE COULD BE LOOKING AT A HUMANITARIAN CRISIS.
WHICH IS PRESUMABLY PART OF THE PLAN.
THAT GATE OPENED HERE ON YOUR GROUNDS IN ORDER TO TIE DOWN YOUR RESOURCES.
SO THE DISAPPEARANCE OF EARTH'S HUMAN POPULATION WAS THE FIRST MOVE IN A WIDER PLAN.
CAN I REMIND YOU WHAT ELSE IS GOING ON HERE?

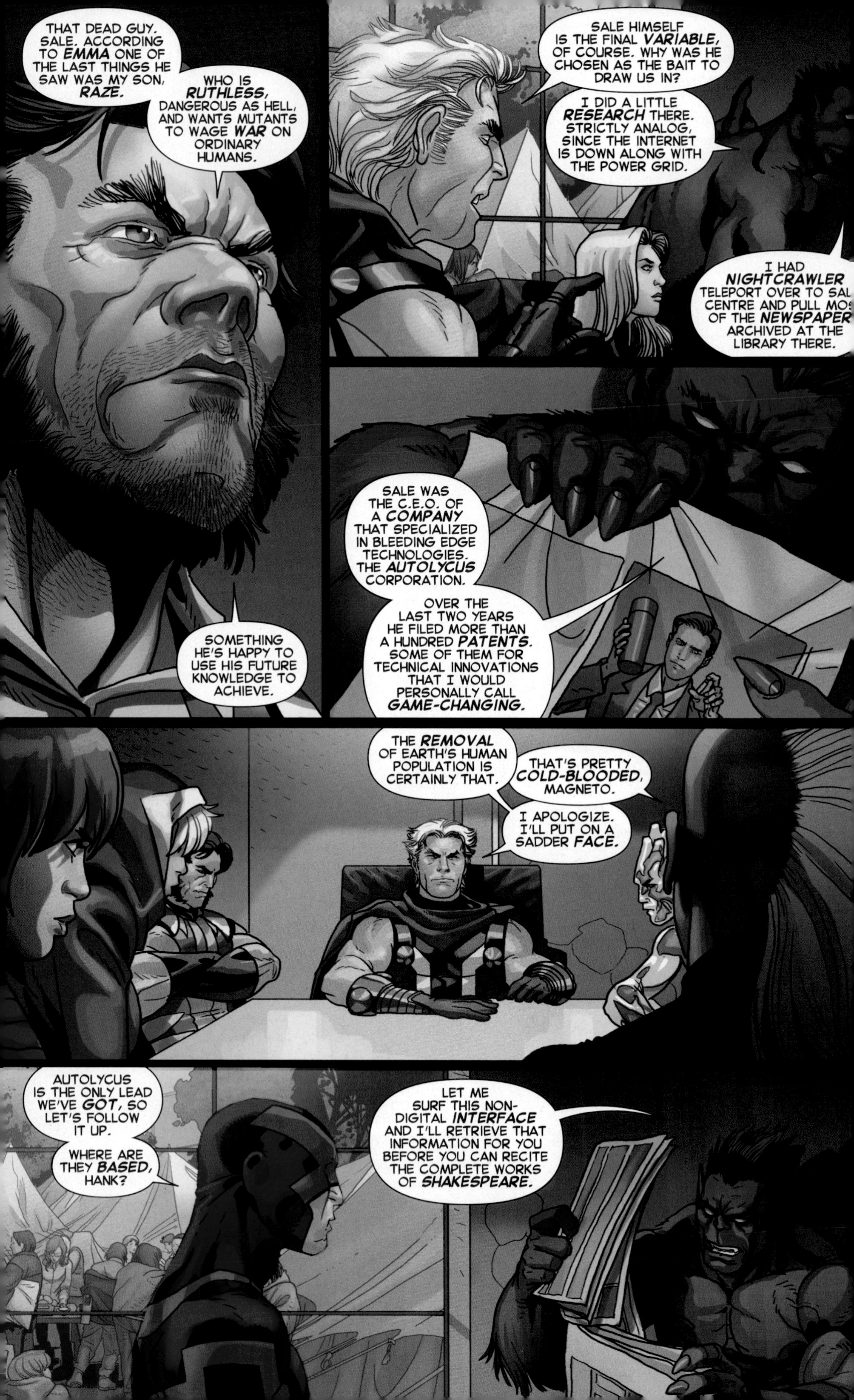
THAT DEAD GUY. SALE. ACCORDING TO EMMA ONE OF THE LAST THINGS HE SAW WAS MY SON, RAZE.
WHO IS RUTHLESS, DANGEROUS AS HELL, AND WANTS MUTANTS TO WAGE WAR ON ORDINARY HUMANS.
SOMETHING HE'S HAPPY TO USE HIS FUTURE KNOWLEDGE TO ACHIEVE.
SALE HIMSELF IS THE FINAL VARIABLE, OF COURSE. WHY WAS HE CHOSEN AS THE BAIT TO DRAW US IN?
I DID A LITTLE RESEARCH THERE. STRICTLY ANALOG, SINCE THE INTERNET IS DOWN ALONG WITH THE POWER GRID.
I HAD NIGHTCRAWLER TELEPORT OVER TO SAL CENTRE AND PULL MOS OF THE NEWSPAPER ARCHIVED AT THE LIBRARY THERE.
SALE WAS THE C.E.O. OF A COMPANY THAT SPECIALIZED IN BLEEDING EDGE TECHNOLOGIES. THE AUTOLYCUS CORPORATION.
OVER THE LAST TWO YEARS HE FILED MORE THAN A HUNDRED PATENTS. SOME OF THEM FOR TECHNICAL INNOVATIONS THAT I WOULD PERSONALLY CALL GAME-CHANGING.
THE REMOVAL OF EARTH'S HUMAN POPULATION IS CERTAINLY THAT.
THAT'S PRETTY COLD-BLOODED, MAGNETO.
I APOLOGIZE. I'LL PUT ON A SADDER FACE.
AUTOLYCUS IS THE ONLY LEAD WE'VE GOT, SO LET'S FOLLOW IT UP.
WHERE ARE THEY BASED, HANK?
LET ME SURF THIS NON-DIGITAL INTERFACE AND I'LL RETRIEVE THAT INFORMATION FOR YOU BEFORE YOU CAN RECITE THE COMPLETE WORKS OF SHAKESPEARE.

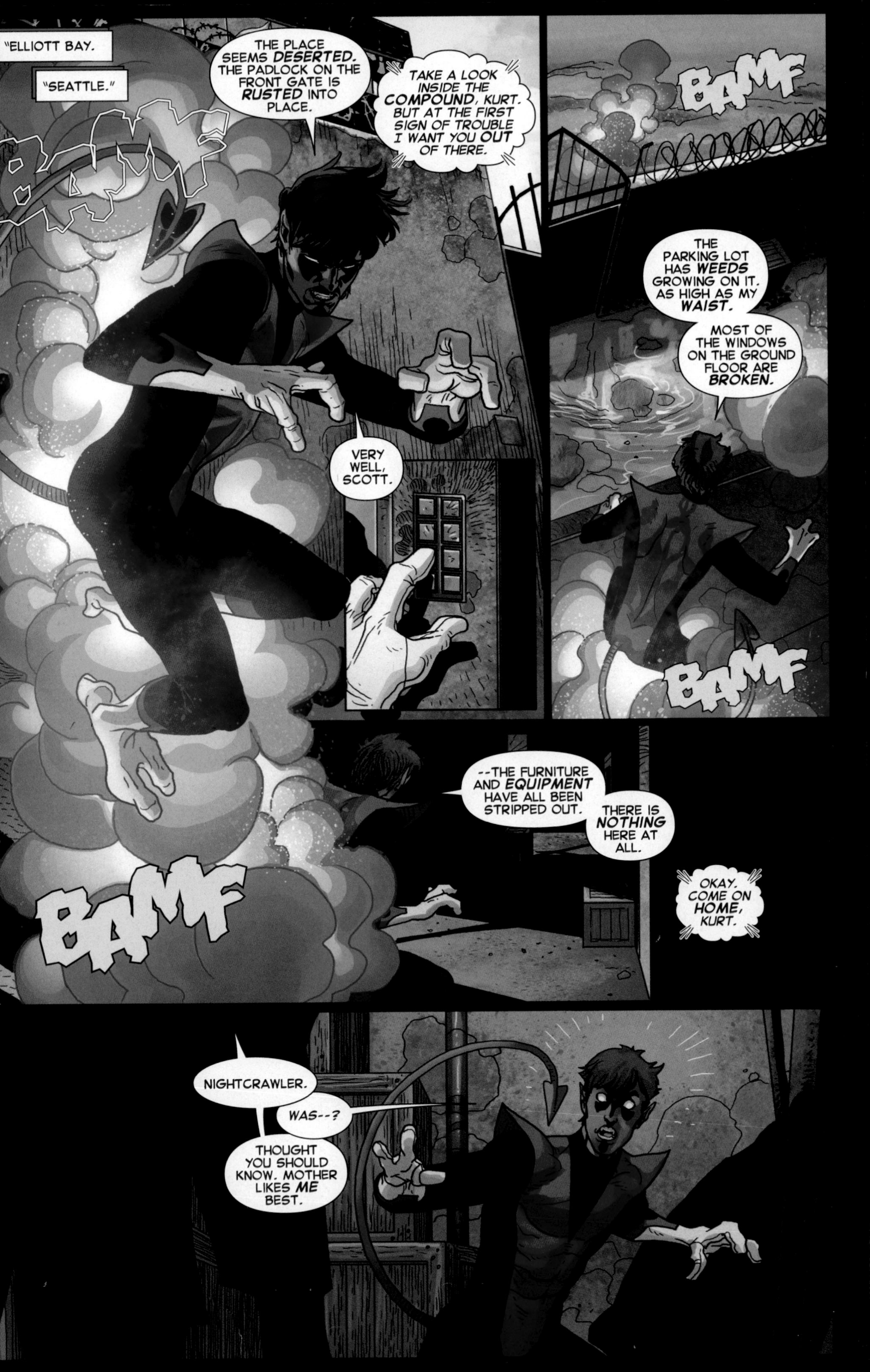
"ELLIOTT BAY.
"SEATTLE."
THE PLACE SEEMS DESERTED. THE PADLOCK ON THE FRONT GATE IS RUSTED INTO PLACE.
TAKE A LOOK INSIDE THE COMPOUND, KURT. BUT AT THE FIRST SIGN OF TROUBLE I WANT YOU OUT OF THERE.
BAMF
VERY WELL, SCOTT.
BAMF
THE PARKING LOT HAS WEEDS GROWING ON IT. AS HIGH AS MY WAIST.
MOST OF THE WINDOWS ON THE GROUND FLOOR ARE BROKEN.
BAMF
BAMF
--THE FURNITURE AND EQUIPMENT HAVE ALL BEEN STRIPPED OUT.
THERE IS NOTHING HERE AT ALL.
OKAY. COME ON HOME, KURT.
NIGHTCRAWLER.
WAS--?
THOUGHT YOU SHOULD KNOW. MOTHER LIKES ME BEST.

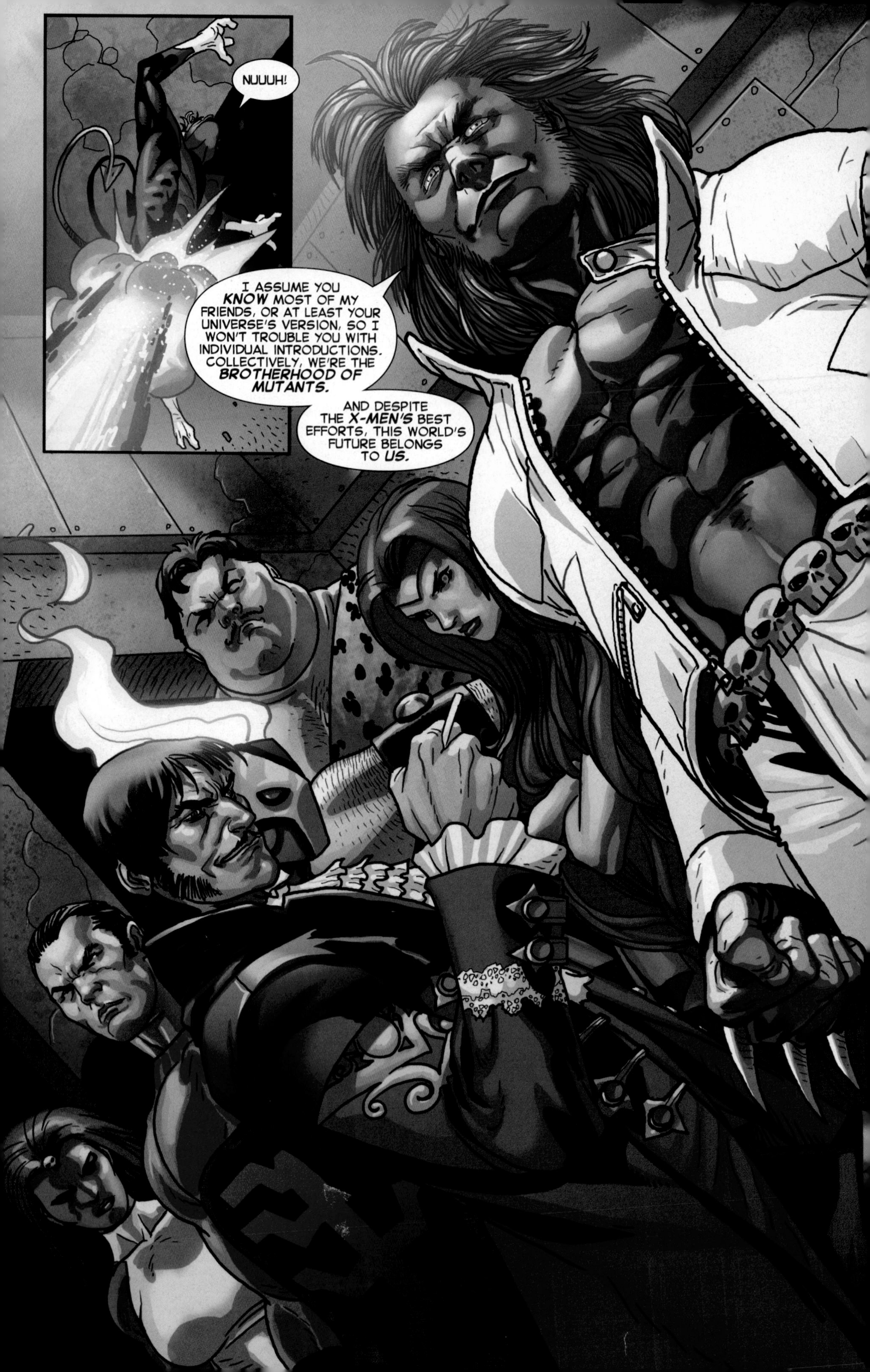
NUUUH!
I ASSUME YOU KNOW MOST OF MY FRIENDS, OR AT LEAST YOUR UNIVERSE'S VERSION, SO I WON'T TROUBLE YOU WITH INDIVIDUAL INTRODUCTIONS. COLLECTIVELY, WE'RE THE BROTHERHOOD OF MUTANTS.
AND DESPITE THE X-MEN'S BEST EFFORTS, THIS WORLD'S FUTURE BELONGS TO US.

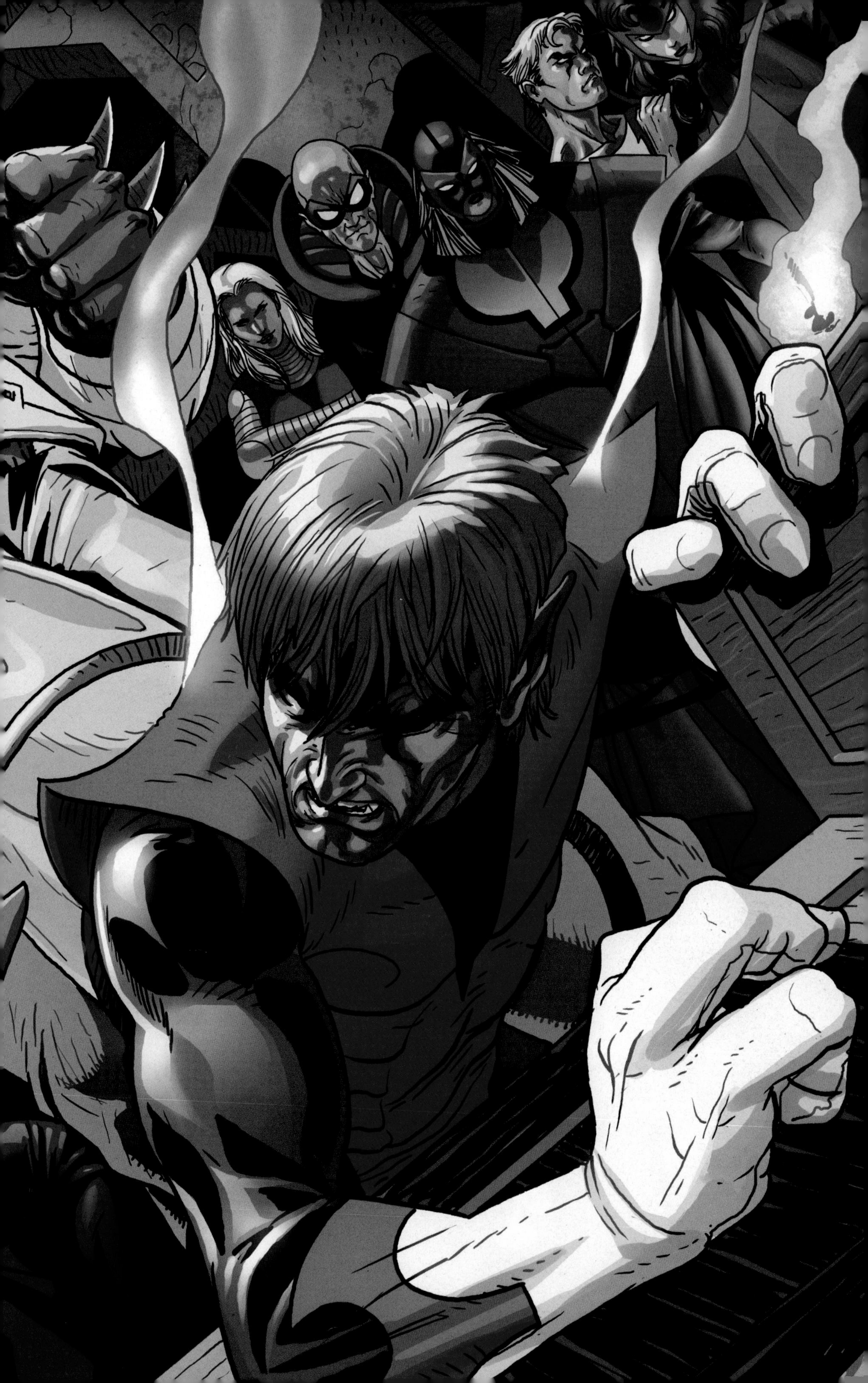

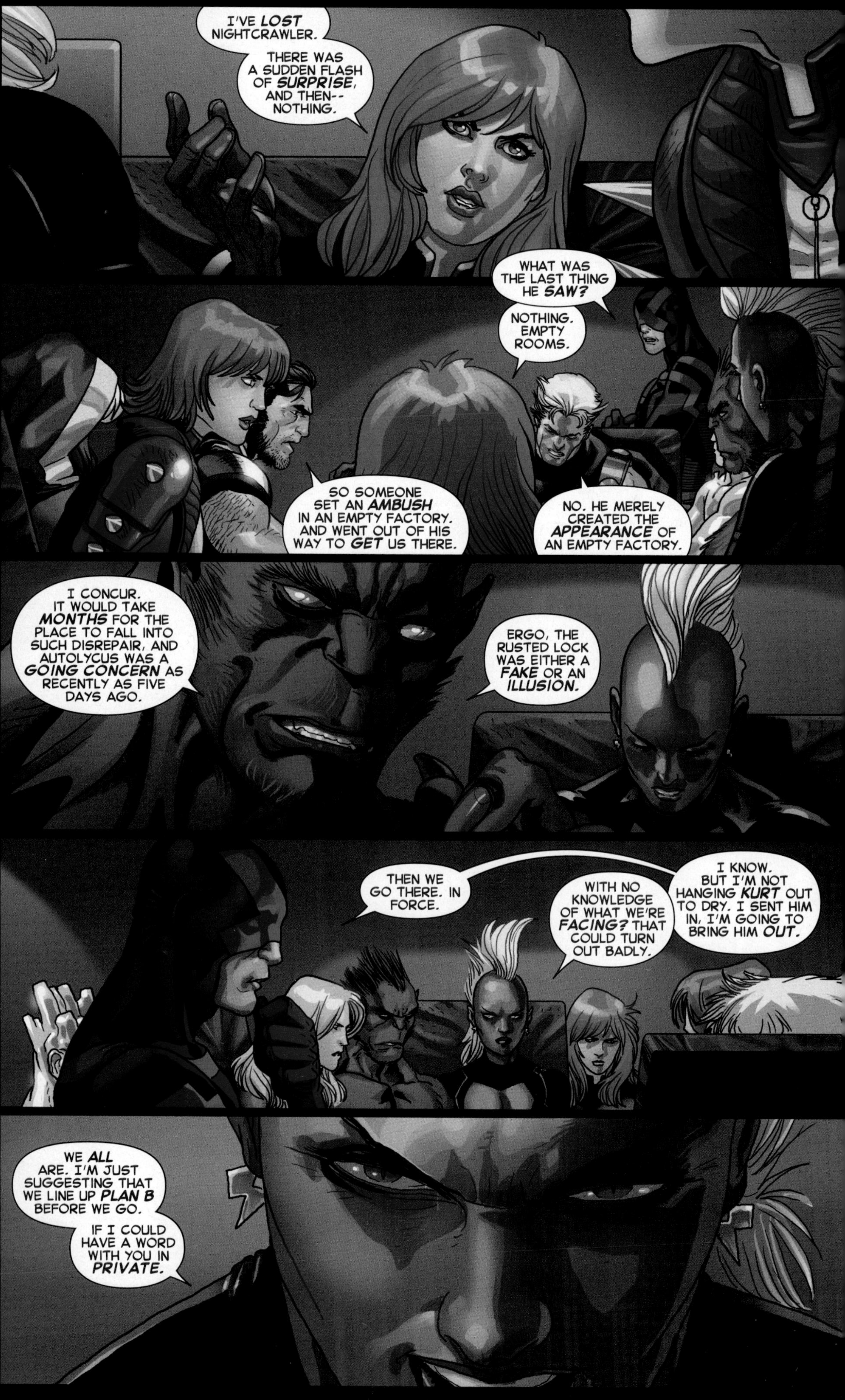
I'VE LOST NIGHTCRAWLER.
THERE WAS A SUDDEN FLASH OF SURPRISE, AND THEN-- NOTHING.
WHAT WAS THE LAST THING HE SAW?
NOTHING. EMPTY ROOMS.
SO SOMEONE SET AN AMBUSH IN AN EMPTY FACTORY. AND WENT OUT OF HIS WAY TO GET US THERE.
NO. HE MERELY CREATED THE APPEARANCE OF AN EMPTY FACTORY.
I CONCUR. IT WOULD TAKE MONTHS FOR THE PLACE TO FALL INTO SUCH DISREPAIR, AND AUTOLYCUS WAS A GOING CONCERN AS RECENTLY AS FIVE DAYS AGO.
ERGO, THE RUSTED LOCK WAS EITHER A FAKE OR AN ILLUSION.
THEN WE GO THERE. IN FORCE.
WITH NO KNOWLEDGE OF WHAT WE'RE FACING? THAT COULD TURN OUT BADLY.
I KNOW. BUT I'M NOT HANGING KURT OUT TO DRY. I SENT HIM IN, I'M GOING TO BRING HIM OUT.
WE ALL ARE. I'M JUST SUGGESTING THAT WE LINE UP PLAN B BEFORE WE GO.
IF I COULD HAVE A WORD WITH YOU IN PRIVATE.

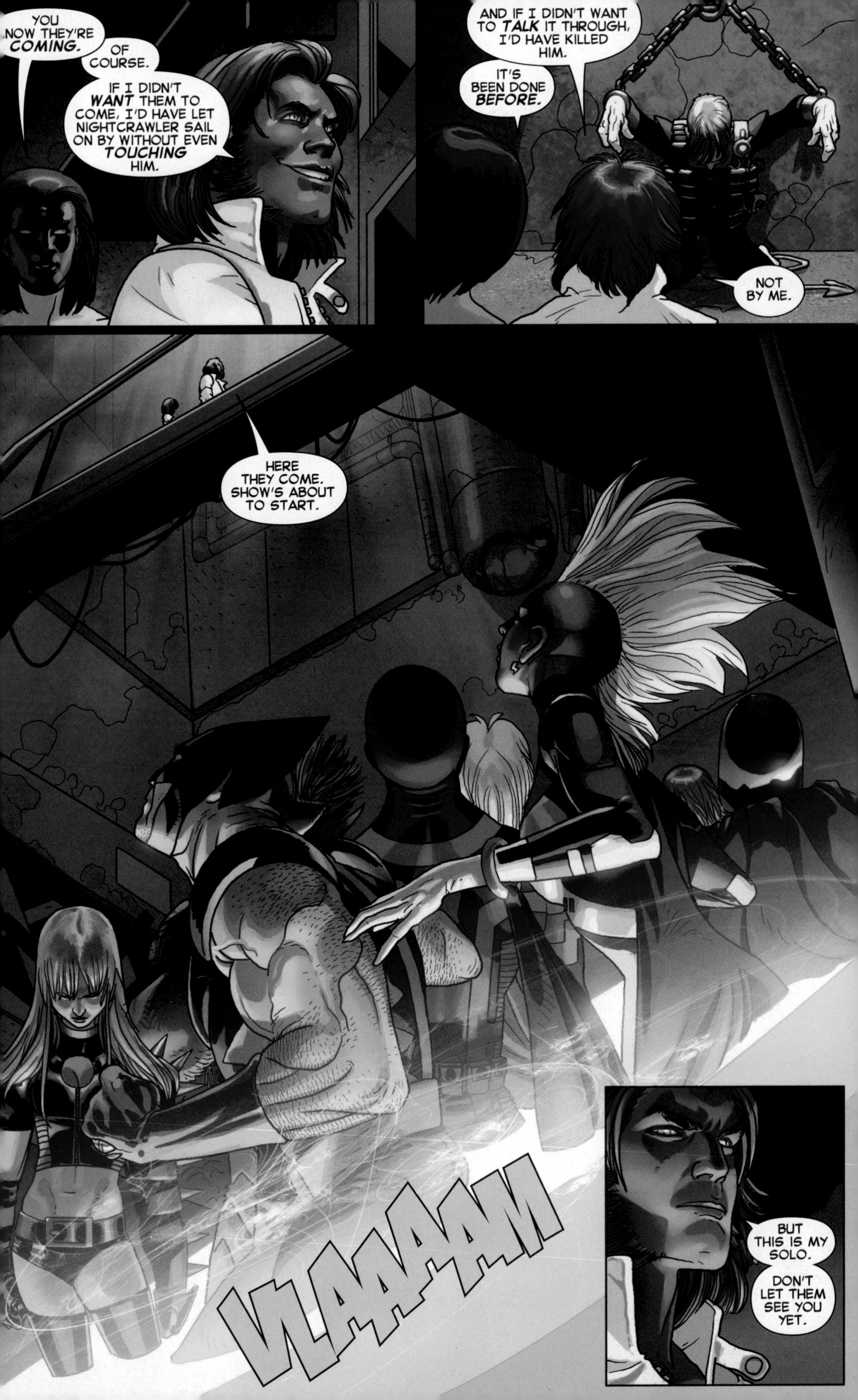
YOU KNOW THEY'RE COMING.
OF COURSE.
IF I DIDN'T WANT THEM TO COME, I'D HAVE LET NIGHTCRAWLER SAIL ON BY WITHOUT EVEN TOUCHING HIM.
AND IF I DIDN'T WANT TO TALK IT THROUGH, I'D HAVE KILLED HIM.
IT'S BEEN DONE BEFORE.
NOT BY ME.
HERE THEY COME. SHOW'S ABOUT TO START.
VLAAAAM
BUT THIS IS MY SOLO.
DON'T LET THEM SEE YOU YET.

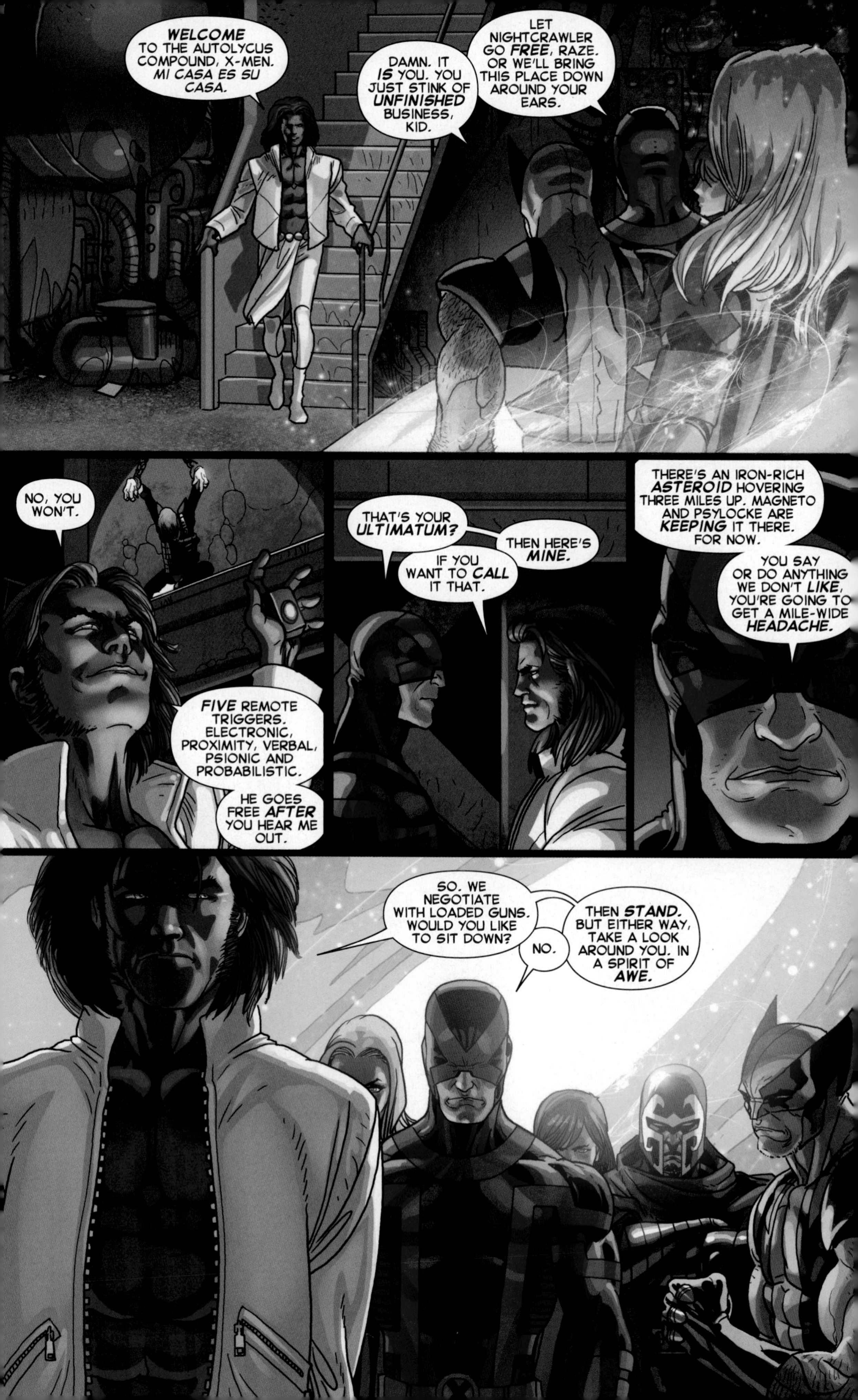
WELCOME TO THE AUTOLYCUS COMPOUND, X-MEN. MI CASA ES SU CASA.
DAMN. IT IS YOU. YOU JUST STINK OF UNFINISHED BUSINESS, KID.
LET NIGHTCRAWLER GO FREE, RAZE. OR WE'LL BRING THIS PLACE DOWN AROUND YOUR EARS.
NO, YOU WON'T.
FIVE REMOTE TRIGGERS. ELECTRONIC, PROXIMITY, VERBAL, PSIONIC AND PROBABILISTIC.
HE GOES FREE AFTER YOU HEAR ME OUT.
THAT'S YOUR ULTIMATUM?
THEN HERE'S MINE.
IF YOU WANT TO CALL IT THAT.
THERE'S AN IRON-RICH ASTEROID HOVERING THREE MILES UP. MAGNETO AND PSYLOCKE ARE KEEPING IT THERE. FOR NOW.
YOU SAY OR DO ANYTHING WE DON'T LIKE, YOU'RE GOING TO GET A MILE-WIDE HEADACHE.
SO. WE NEGOTIATE WITH LOADED GUNS. WOULD YOU LIKE TO SIT DOWN?
NO.
THEN STAND. BUT EITHER WAY, TAKE A LOOK AROUND YOU. IN A SPIRIT OF AWE.

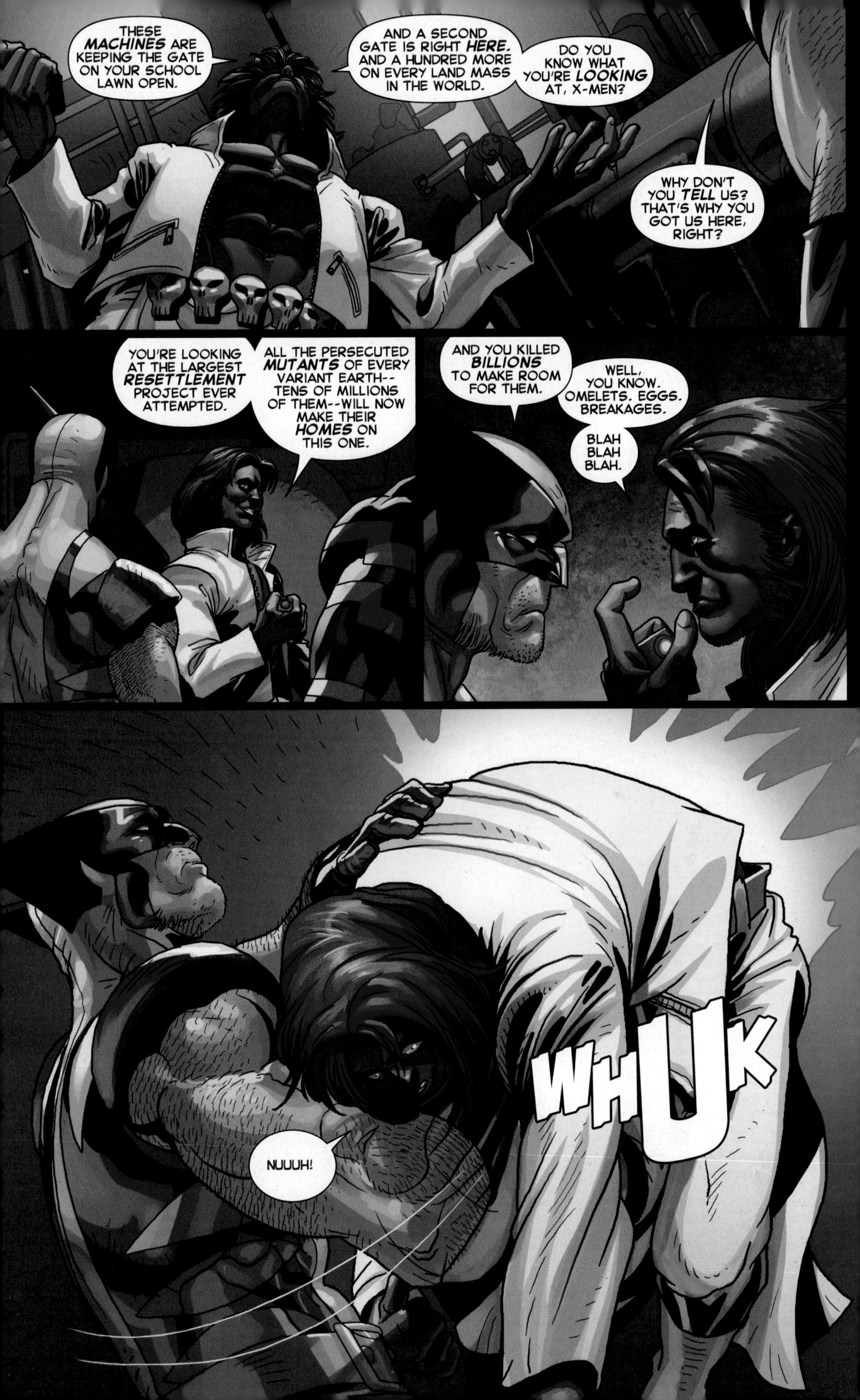

THESE MACHINES ARE KEEPING THE GATE ON YOUR SCHOOL LAWN OPEN.
AND A SECOND GATE IS RIGHT HERE. AND A HUNDRED MORE ON EVERY LAND MASS IN THE WORLD.
DO YOU KNOW WHAT YOU'RE LOOKING AT, X-MEN?
WHY DON'T YOU TELL US? THAT'S WHY YOU GOT US HERE, RIGHT?
YOU'RE LOOKING AT THE LARGEST RESETTLEMENT PROJECT EVER ATTEMPTED.
ALL THE PERSECUTED MUTANTS OF EVERY VARIANT EARTH--TENS OF MILLIONS OF THEM--WILL NOW MAKE THEIR HOMES ON THIS ONE.
AND YOU KILLED BILLIONS TO MAKE ROOM FOR THEM.
WELL, YOU KNOW. OMELETS. EGGS. BREAKAGES.
BLAH BLAH BLAH.
WHUK
NUUUH!

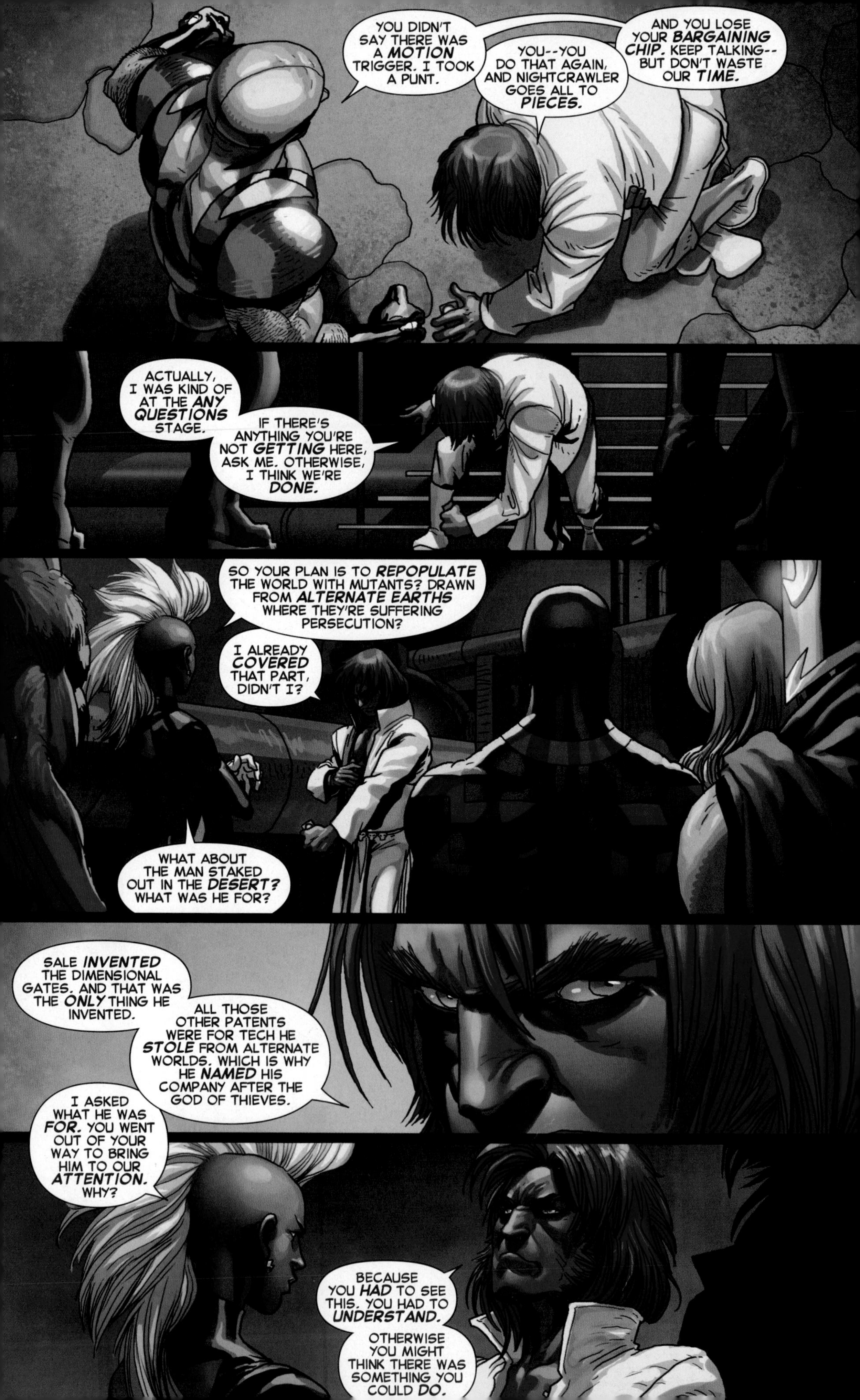
YOU DIDN'T SAY THERE WAS A MOTION TRIGGER. I TOOK A PUNT.
AND YOU LOSE YOUR BARGAINING CHIP. KEEP TALKING-- BUT DON'T WASTE OUR TIME.
YOU--YOU DO THAT AGAIN, AND NIGHTCRAWLER GOES ALL TO PIECES.
ACTUALLY, I WAS KIND OF AT THE ANY QUESTIONS STAGE.
IF THERE'S ANYTHING YOU'RE NOT GETTING HERE, ASK ME. OTHERWISE, I THINK WE'RE DONE.
SO YOUR PLAN IS TO REPOPULATE THE WORLD WITH MUTANTS? DRAWN FROM ALTERNATE EARTHS WHERE THEY'RE SUFFERING PERSECUTION?
I ALREADY COVERED THAT PART, DIDN'T I?
WHAT ABOUT THE MAN STAKED OUT IN THE DESERT? WHAT WAS HE FOR?
SALE INVENTED THE DIMENSIONAL GATES. AND THAT WAS THE ONLY THING HE INVENTED.
ALL THOSE OTHER PATENTS WERE FOR TECH HE STOLE FROM ALTERNATE WORLDS. WHICH IS WHY HE NAMED HIS COMPANY AFTER THE GOD OF THIEVES.
I ASKED WHAT HE WAS FOR. YOU WENT OUT OF YOUR WAY TO BRING HIM TO OUR ATTENTION. WHY?
BECAUSE YOU HAD TO SEE THIS. YOU HAD TO UNDERSTAND.
OTHERWISE YOU MIGHT THINK THERE WAS SOMETHING YOU COULD DO.

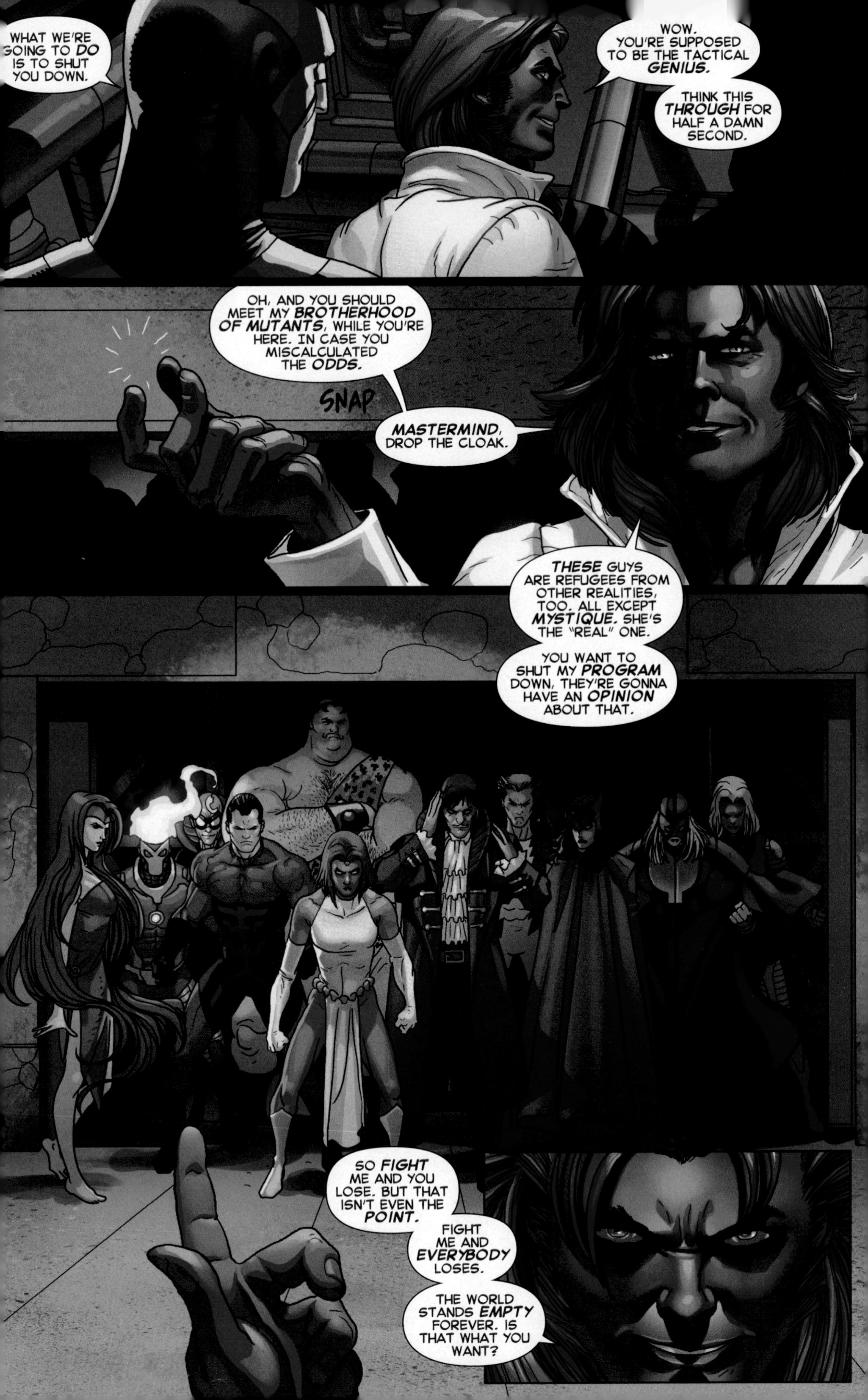
WHAT WE'RE GOING TO DO IS TO SHUT YOU DOWN.
WOW. YOU'RE SUPPOSED TO BE THE TACTICAL GENIUS.
THINK THIS THROUGH FOR HALF A DAMN SECOND.
OH, AND YOU SHOULD MEET MY BROTHERHOOD OF MUTANTS, WHILE YOU'RE HERE. IN CASE YOU MISCALCULATED THE ODDS.
SNAP
MASTERMIND, DROP THE CLOAK.
THESE GUYS ARE REFUGEES FROM OTHER REALITIES, TOO. ALL EXCEPT MYSTIQUE. SHE'S THE "REAL" ONE.
YOU WANT TO SHUT MY PROGRAM DOWN, THEY'RE GONNA HAVE AN OPINION ABOUT THAT.
SO FIGHT ME AND YOU LOSE. BUT THAT ISN'T EVEN THE POINT.
FIGHT ME AND EVERYBODY LOSES.
THE WORLD STANDS EMPTY FOREVER. IS THAT WHAT YOU WANT?

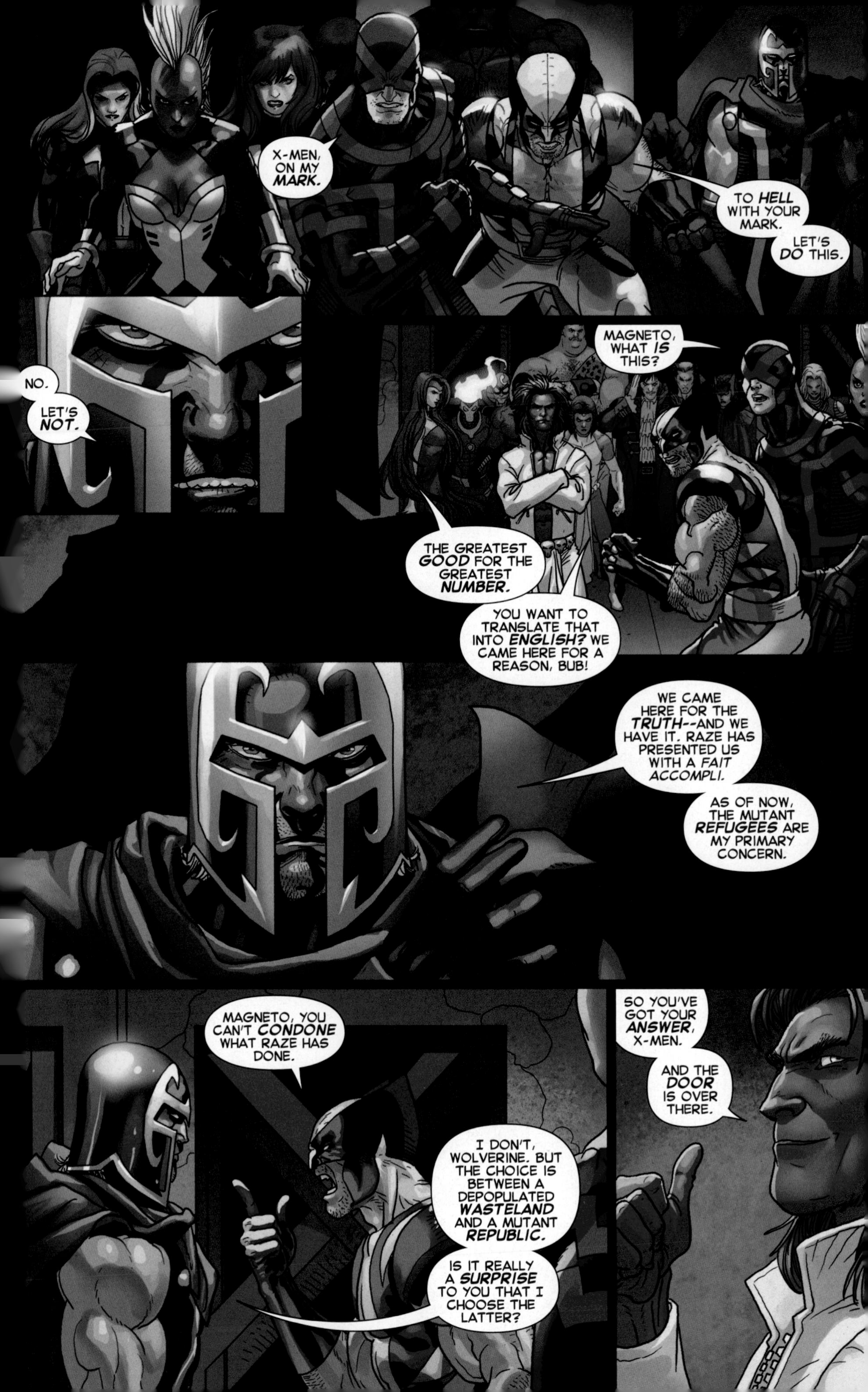
X-MEN, ON MY MARK.
TO HELL WITH YOUR MARK.
LET'S DO THIS.
NO.
LET'S NOT.
MAGNETO, WHAT IS THIS?
THE GREATEST GOOD FOR THE GREATEST NUMBER.
YOU WANT TO TRANSLATE THAT INTO ENGLISH? WE CAME HERE FOR A REASON, BUB!
WE CAME HERE FOR THE TRUTH--AND WE HAVE IT. RAZE HAS PRESENTED US WITH A FAIT ACCOMPLI.
AS OF NOW, THE MUTANT REFUGEES ARE MY PRIMARY CONCERN.
MAGNETO, YOU CAN'T CONDONE WHAT RAZE HAS DONE.
I DON'T, WOLVERINE. BUT THE CHOICE IS BETWEEN A DEPOPULATED WASTELAND AND A MUTANT REPUBLIC.
IS IT REALLY A SURPRISE TO YOU THAT I CHOOSE THE LATTER?
SO YOU'VE GOT YOUR ANSWER, X-MEN.
AND THE DOOR IS OVER THERE.

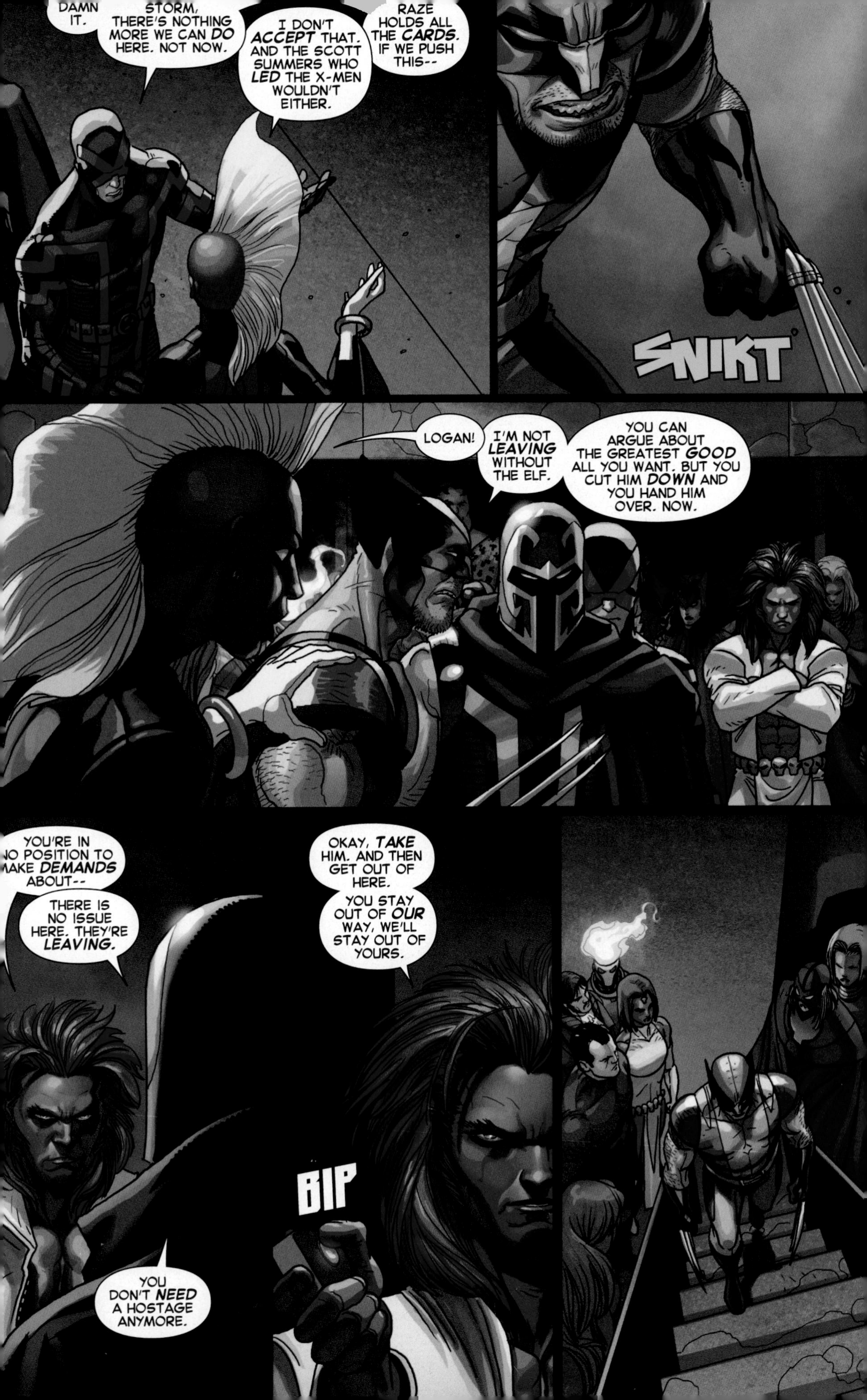
DAMN IT.
STORM, THERE'S NOTHING MORE WE CAN DO HERE. NOT NOW.
I DON'T ACCEPT THAT. AND THE SCOTT SUMMERS WHO LED THE X-MEN WOULDN'T EITHER.
RAZE HOLDS ALL THE CARDS. IF WE PUSH THIS--
SNIKT
LOGAN!
I'M NOT LEAVING WITHOUT THE ELF.
YOU CAN ARGUE ABOUT THE GREATEST GOOD ALL YOU WANT. BUT YOU CUT HIM DOWN AND YOU HAND HIM OVER. NOW.
YOU'RE IN NO POSITION TO MAKE DEMANDS ABOUT--
THERE IS NO ISSUE HERE. THEY'RE LEAVING.
YOU DON'T NEED A HOSTAGE ANYMORE.
BIP
OKAY, TAKE HIM. AND THEN GET OUT OF HERE.
YOU STAY OUT OF OUR WAY, WE'LL STAY OUT OF YOURS.

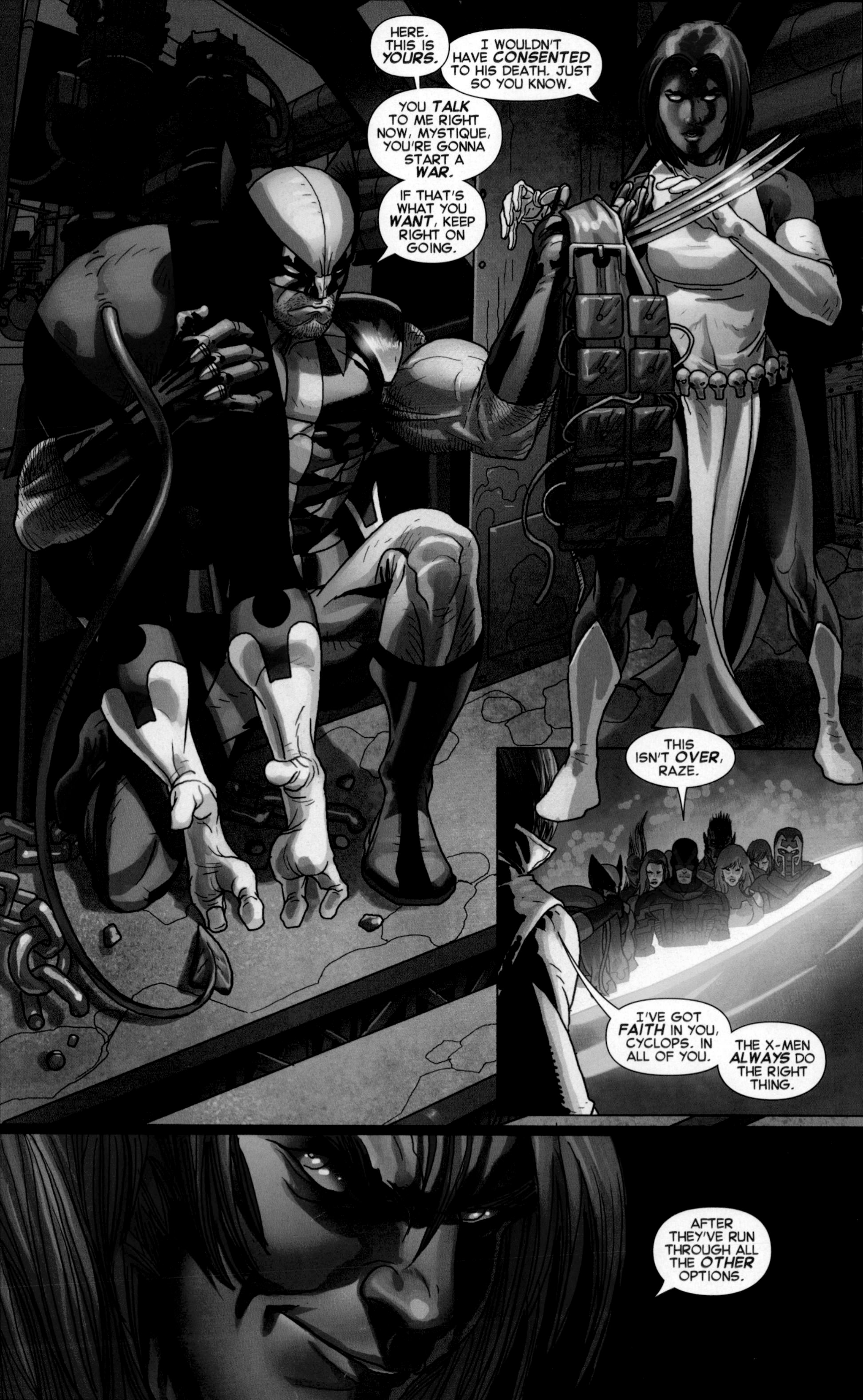

HERE. THIS IS YOURS.
I WOULDN'T HAVE CONSENTED TO HIS DEATH. JUST SO YOU KNOW.
YOU TALK TO ME RIGHT NOW, MYSTIQUE, YOU'RE GONNA START A WAR.
IF THAT'S WHAT YOU WANT, KEEP RIGHT ON GOING.
THIS ISN'T OVER, RAZE.
I'VE GOT FAITH IN YOU, CYCLOPS. IN ALL OF YOU.
THE X-MEN ALWAYS DO THE RIGHT THING.
AFTER THEY'VE RUN THROUGH ALL THE OTHER OPTIONS.

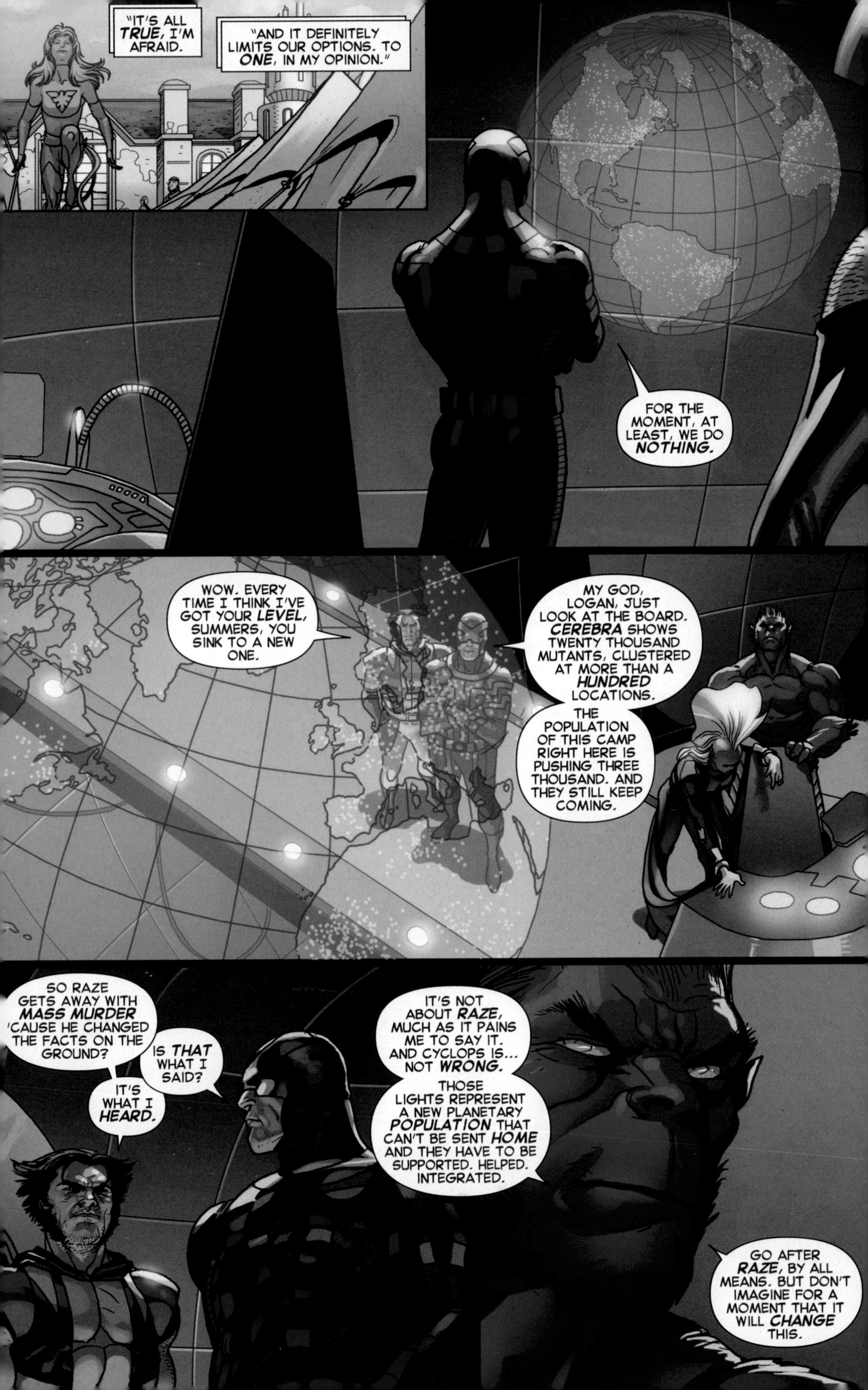
"IT'S ALL TRUE, I'M AFRAID.
"AND IT DEFINITELY LIMITS OUR OPTIONS. TO ONE, IN MY OPINION."
FOR THE MOMENT, AT LEAST, WE DO NOTHING.
WOW. EVERY TIME I THINK I'VE GOT YOUR LEVEL, SUMMERS, YOU SINK TO A NEW ONE.
MY GOD, LOGAN, JUST LOOK AT THE BOARD. CEREBRA SHOWS TWENTY THOUSAND MUTANTS, CLUSTERED AT MORE THAN A HUNDRED LOCATIONS.
THE POPULATION OF THIS CAMP RIGHT HERE IS PUSHING THREE THOUSAND. AND THEY STILL KEEP COMING.
SO RAZE GETS AWAY WITH MASS MURDER 'CAUSE HE CHANGED THE FACTS ON THE GROUND?
IS THAT WHAT I SAID?
IT'S WHAT I HEARD.
IT'S NOT ABOUT RAZE, MUCH AS IT PAINS ME TO SAY IT. AND CYCLOPS IS... NOT WRONG.
THOSE LIGHTS REPRESENT A NEW PLANETARY POPULATION THAT CAN'T BE SENT HOME AND THEY HAVE TO BE SUPPORTED. HELPED. INTEGRATED.
GO AFTER RAZE, BY ALL MEANS. BUT DON'T IMAGINE FOR A MOMENT THAT IT WILL CHANGE THIS.

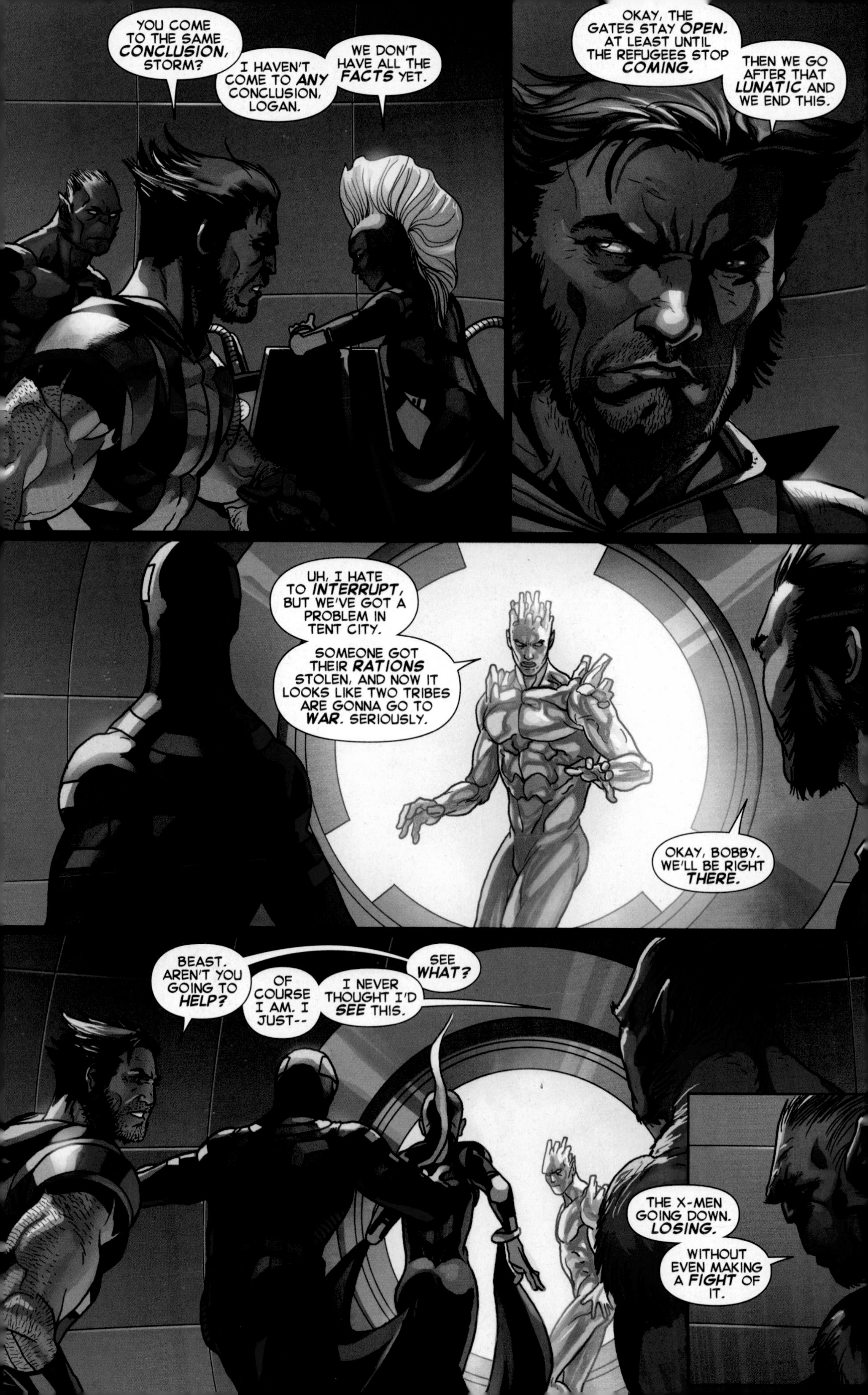
YOU COME TO THE SAME CONCLUSION, STORM?
I HAVEN'T COME TO ANY CONCLUSION, LOGAN.
WE DON'T HAVE ALL THE FACTS YET.
OKAY, THE GATES STAY OPEN. AT LEAST UNTIL THE REFUGEES STOP COMING.
THEN WE GO AFTER THAT LUNATIC AND WE END THIS.
UH, I HATE TO INTERRUPT, BUT WE'VE GOT A PROBLEM IN TENT CITY.
SOMEONE GOT THEIR RATIONS STOLEN, AND NOW IT LOOKS LIKE TWO TRIBES ARE GONNA GO TO WAR. SERIOUSLY.
OKAY, BOBBY. WE'LL BE RIGHT THERE.
BEAST. AREN'T YOU GOING TO HELP?
OF COURSE I AM. I JUST--
I NEVER THOUGHT I'D SEE THIS.
SEE WHAT?
THE X-MEN GOING DOWN. LOSING.
WITHOUT EVEN MAKING A FIGHT OF IT.

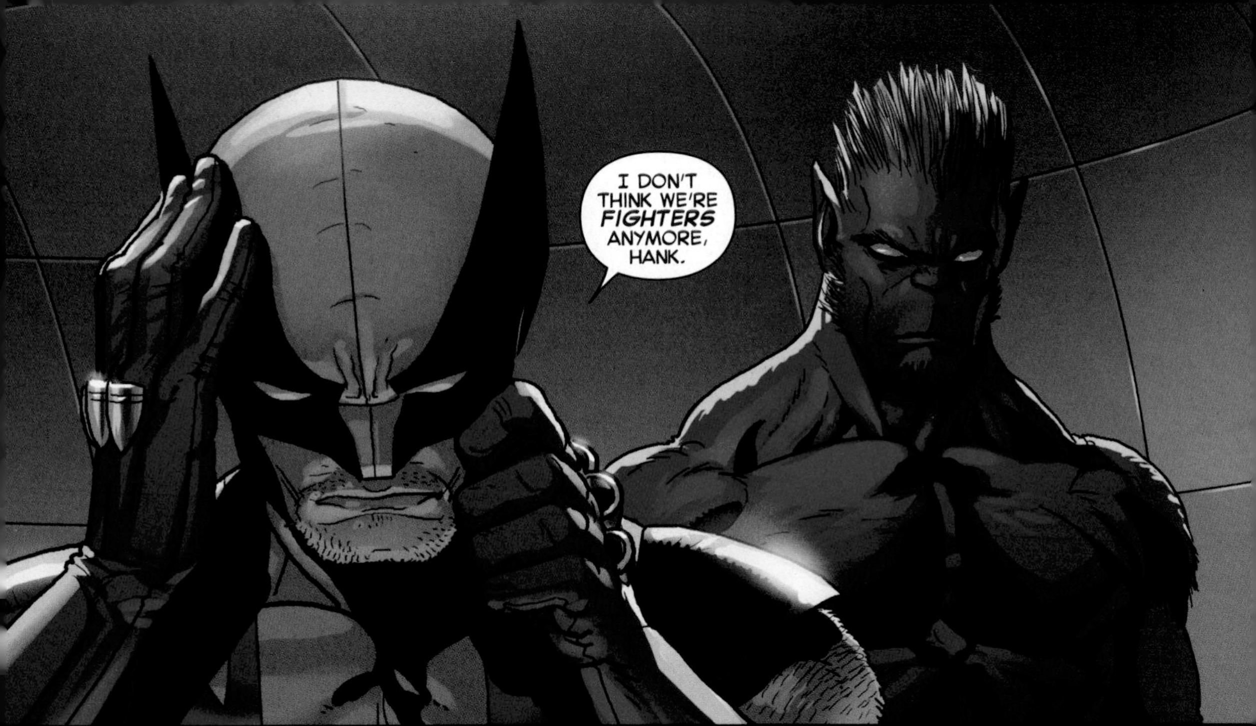
I DON'T THINK WE'RE FIGHTERS ANYMORE, HANK.

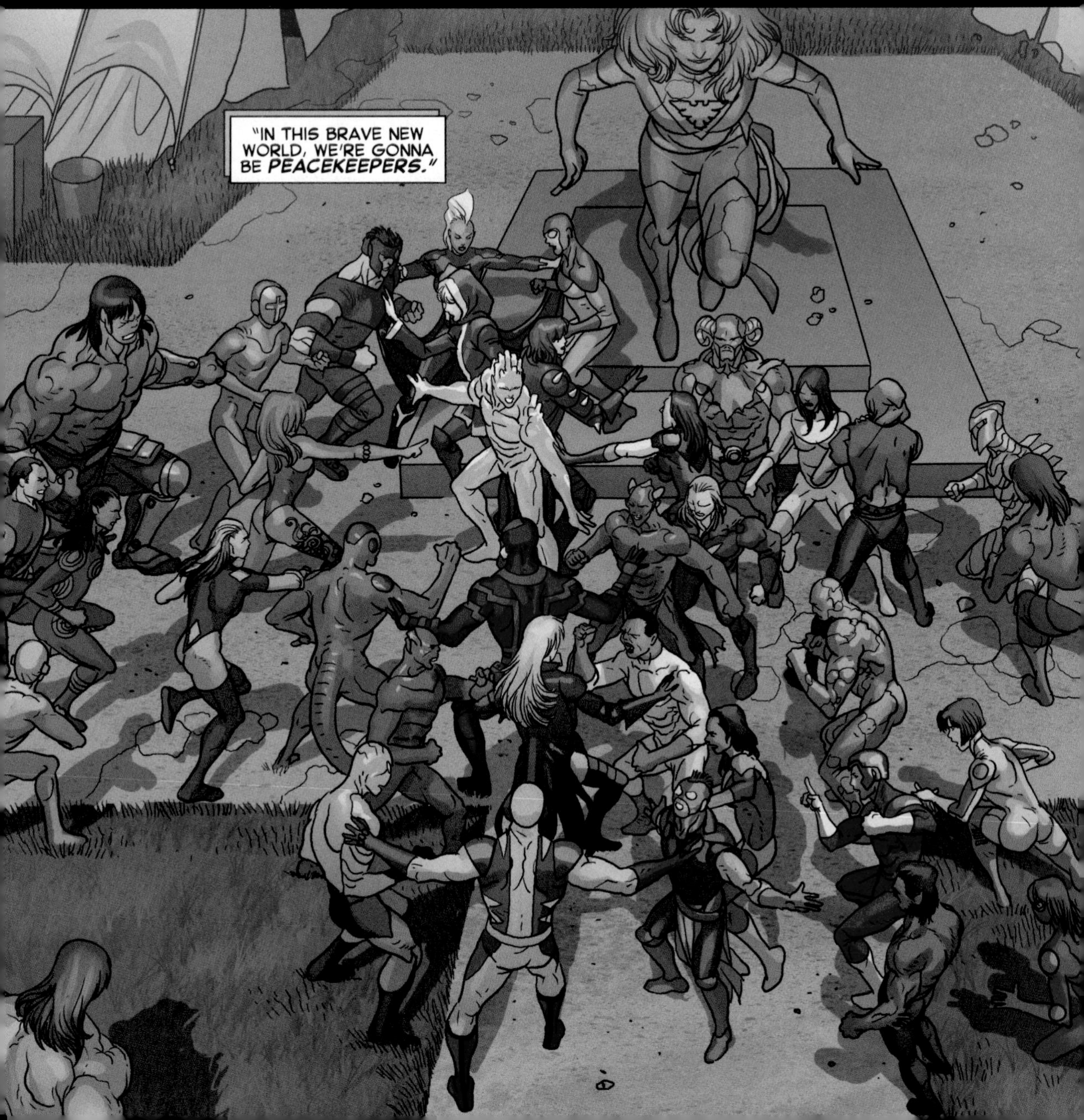
"IN THIS BRAVE NEW WORLD, WE'RE GONNA BE PEACEKEEPERS."

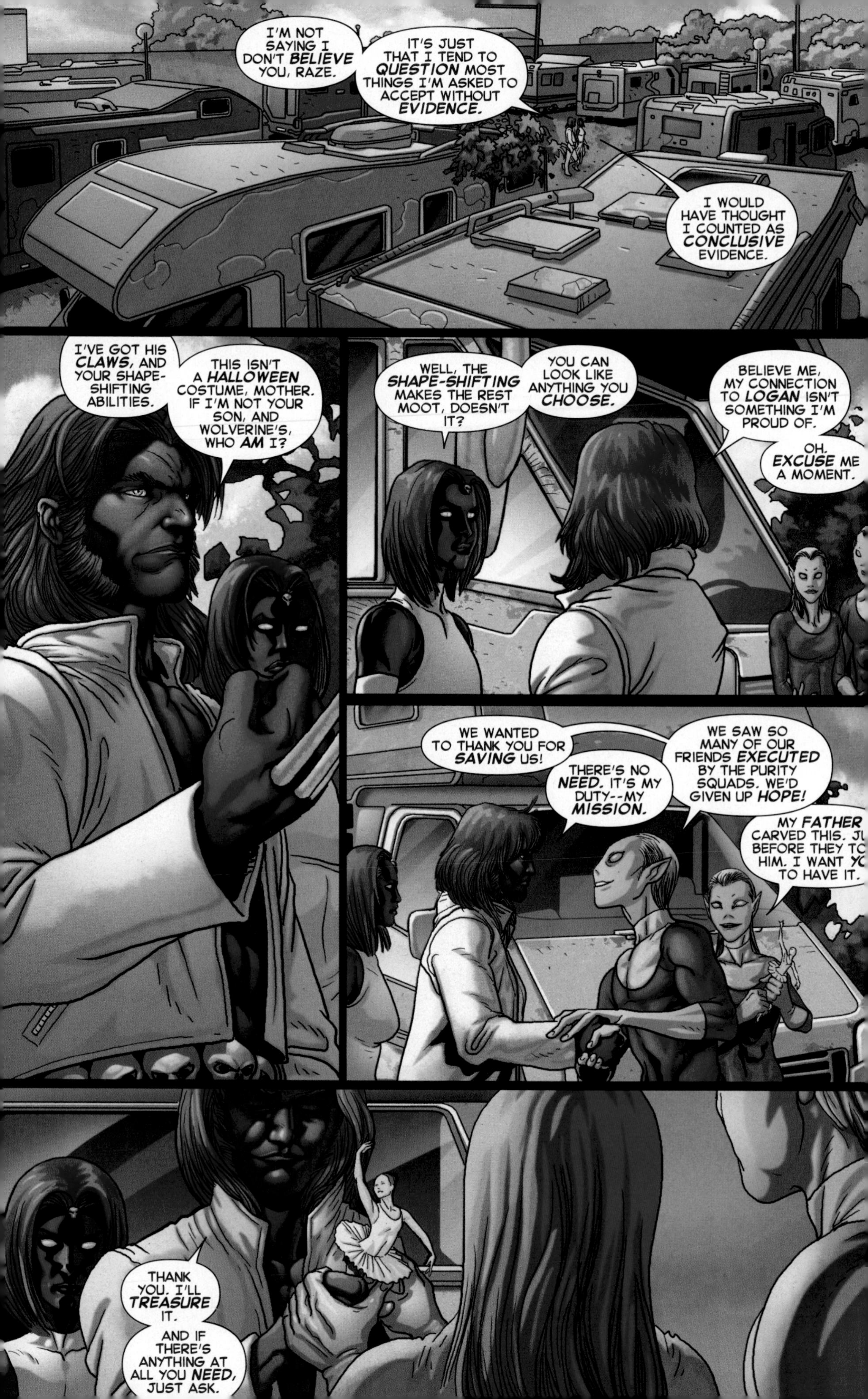
I'M NOT SAYING I DON'T BELIEVE YOU, RAZE.
IT'S JUST THAT I TEND TO QUESTION MOST THINGS I'M ASKED TO ACCEPT WITHOUT EVIDENCE.
I WOULD HAVE THOUGHT I COUNTED AS CONCLUSIVE EVIDENCE.
I'VE GOT HIS CLAWS, AND YOUR SHAPE-SHIFTING ABILITIES.
THIS ISN'T A HALLOWEEN COSTUME, MOTHER. IF I'M NOT YOUR SON, AND WOLVERINE'S, WHO AM I?
WELL, THE SHAPE-SHIFTING MAKES THE REST MOOT, DOESN'T IT?
YOU CAN LOOK LIKE ANYTHING YOU CHOOSE.
BELIEVE ME, MY CONNECTION TO LOGAN ISN'T SOMETHING I'M PROUD OF.
OH. EXCUSE ME A MOMENT.
WE WANTED TO THANK YOU FOR SAVING US!
WE SAW SO MANY OF OUR FRIENDS EXECUTED BY THE PURITY SQUADS. WE'D GIVEN UP HOPE!
THERE'S NO NEED. IT'S MY DUTY--MY MISSION.
THANK YOU. I'LL TREASURE IT.
AND IF THERE'S ANYTHING AT ALL YOU NEED, JUST ASK.

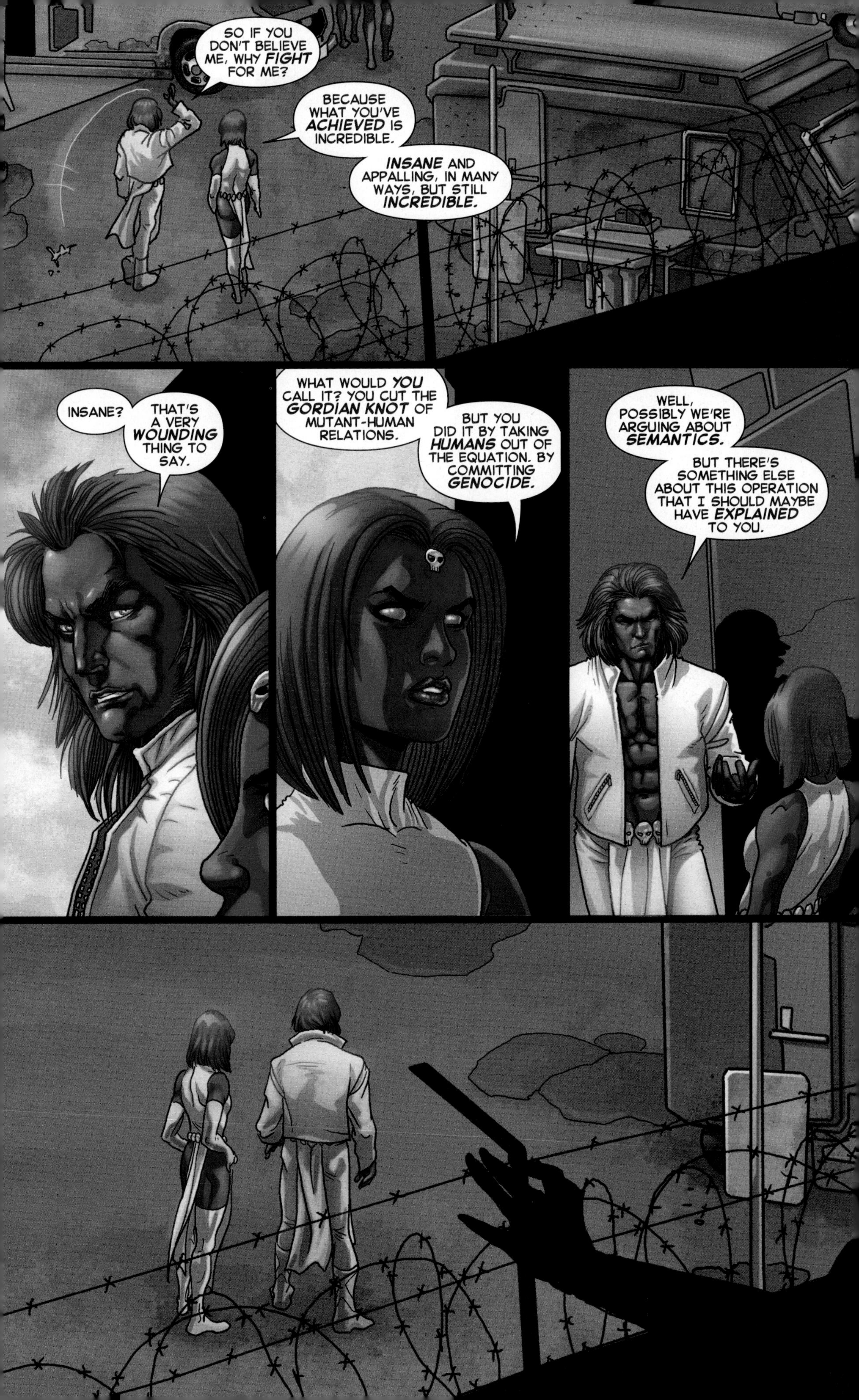
SO IF YOU DON'T BELIEVE ME, WHY FIGHT FOR ME?
BECAUSE WHAT YOU'VE ACHIEVED IS INCREDIBLE.
INSANE AND APPALLING, IN MANY WAYS, BUT STILL INCREDIBLE.
INSANE?
THAT'S A VERY WOUNDING THING TO SAY.
WHAT WOULD YOU CALL IT? YOU CUT THE GORDIAN KNOT OF MUTANT-HUMAN RELATIONS.
BUT YOU DID IT BY TAKING HUMANS OUT OF THE EQUATION. BY COMMITTING GENOCIDE.
WELL, POSSIBLY WE'RE ARGUING ABOUT SEMANTICS.
BUT THERE'S SOMETHING ELSE ABOUT THIS OPERATION THAT I SHOULD MAYBE HAVE EXPLAINED TO YOU.

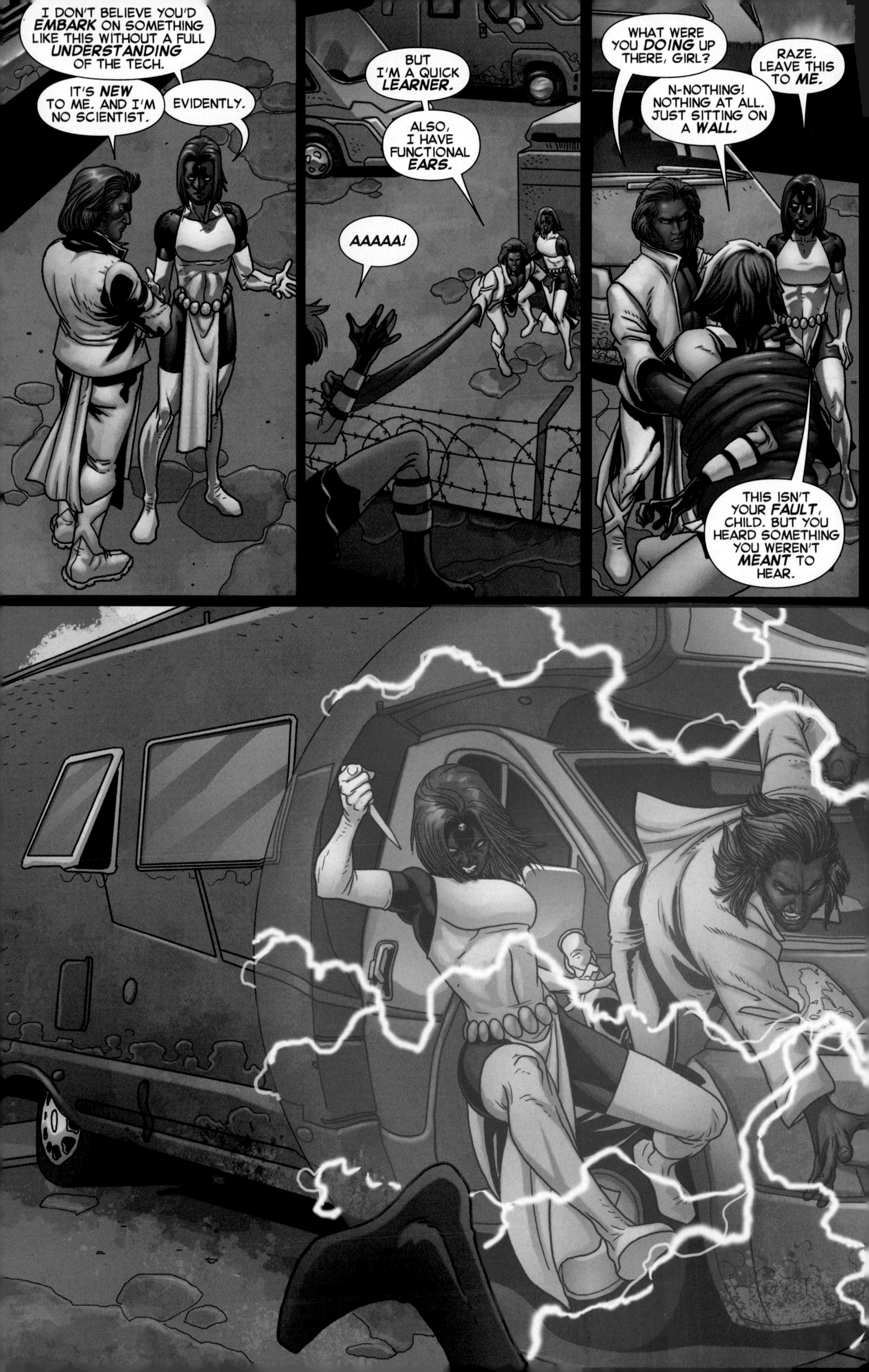
I DON'T BELIEVE YOU'D EMBARK ON SOMETHING LIKE THIS WITHOUT A FULL UNDERSTANDING OF THE TECH.
IT'S NEW TO ME. AND I'M NO SCIENTIST.
EVIDENTLY.
BUT I'M A QUICK LEARNER.
ALSO, I HAVE FUNCTIONAL EARS.
AAAAA!
WHAT WERE YOU DOING UP THERE, GIRL?
N-NOTHING! NOTHING AT ALL. JUST SITTING ON A WALL.
RAZE. LEAVE THIS TO ME.
THIS ISN'T YOUR FAULT, CHILD. BUT YOU HEARD SOMETHING YOU WEREN'T MEANT TO HEAR.

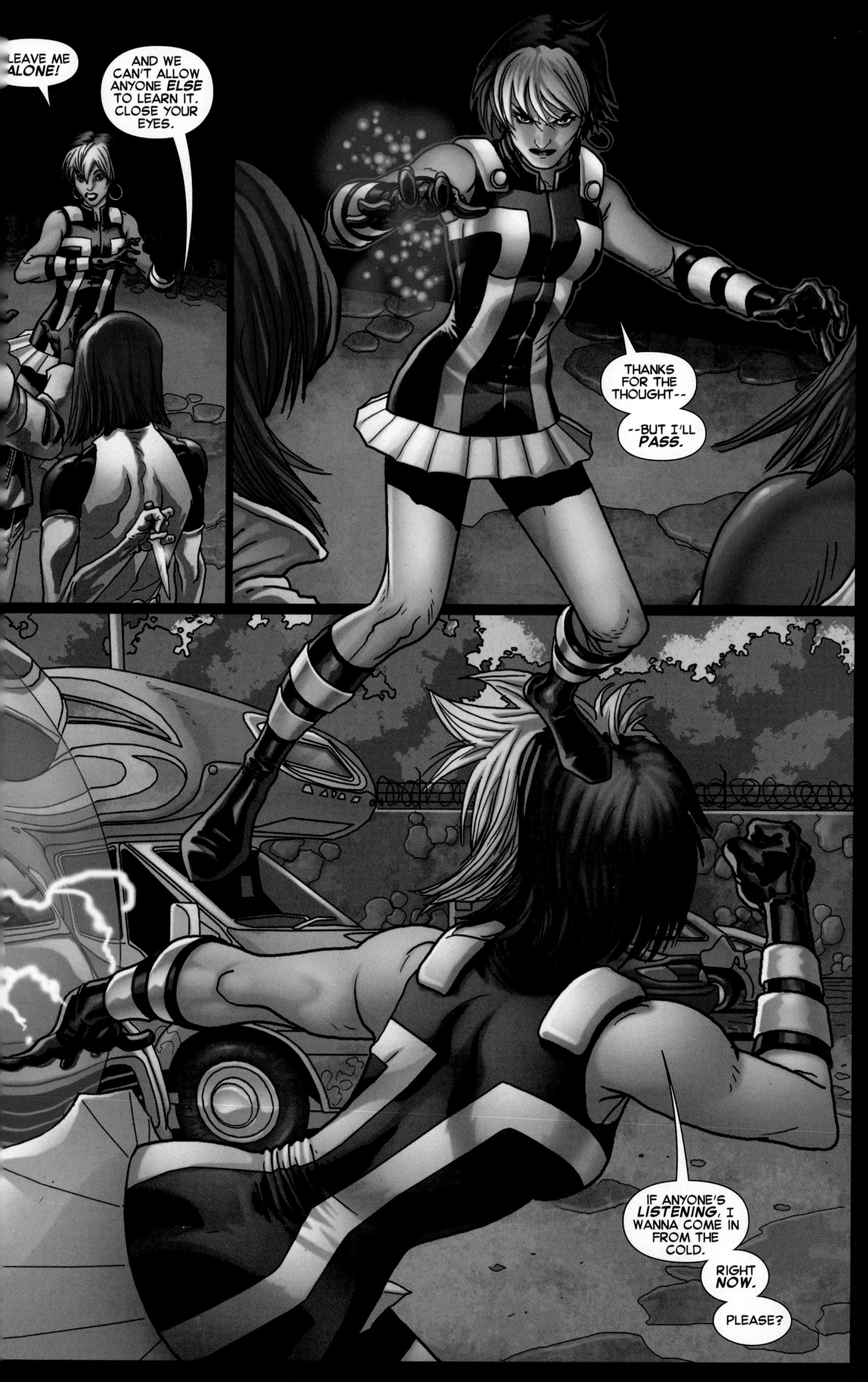
LEAVE ME ALONE!
AND WE CAN'T ALLOW ANYONE ELSE TO LEARN IT. CLOSE YOUR EYES.
THANKS FOR THE THOUGHT--
--BUT I'LL PASS.
IF ANYONE'S LISTENING, I WANNA COME IN FROM THE COLD.
RIGHT NOW.
PLEASE?

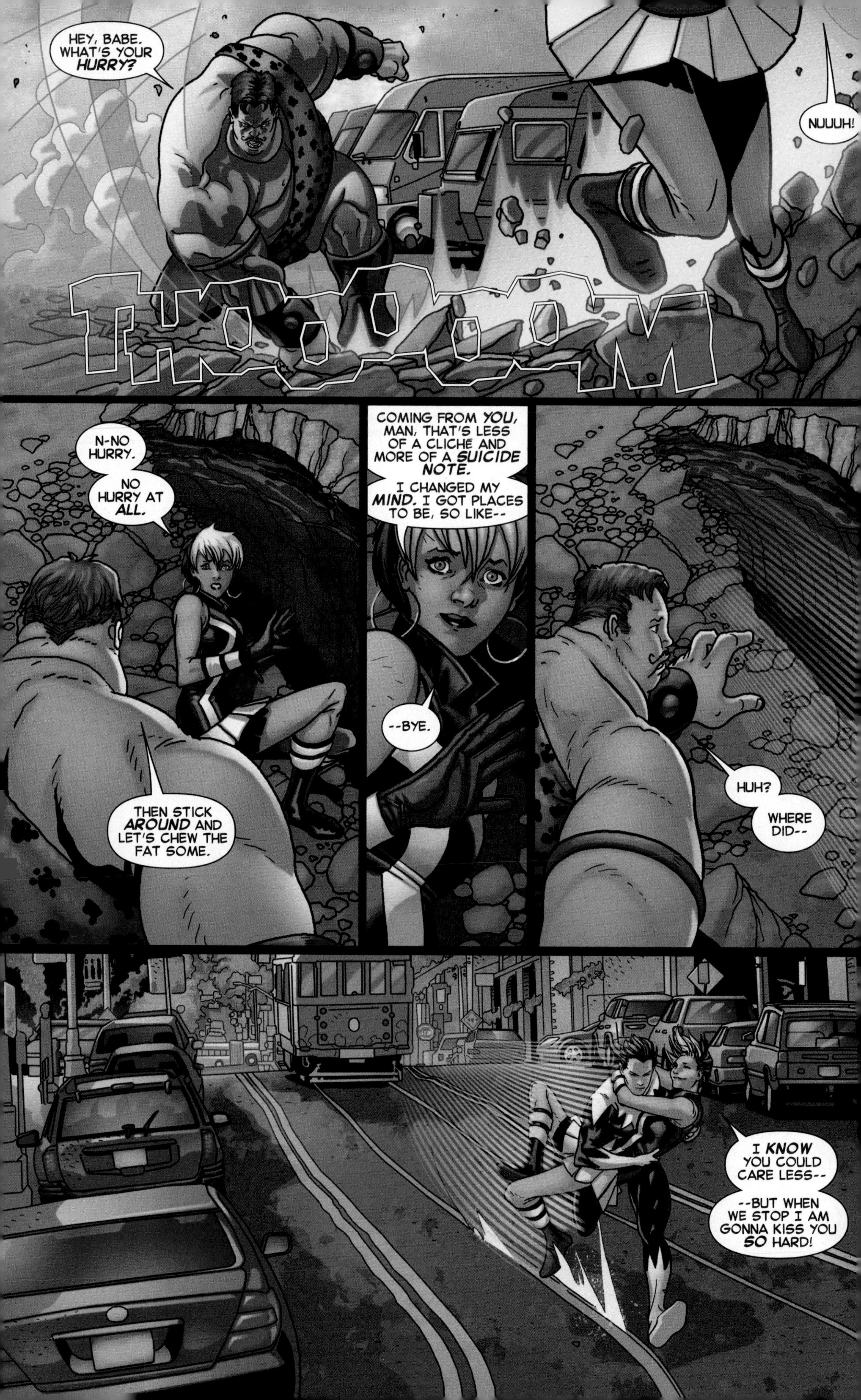
HEY, BABE. WHAT'S YOUR HURRY?
NUUUH!
THOOOOOM
N-NO HURRY.
NO HURRY AT ALL.
THEN STICK AROUND AND LET'S CHEW THE FAT SOME.
COMING FROM YOU, MAN, THAT'S LESS OF A CLICHE AND MORE OF A SUICIDE NOTE.
I CHANGED MY MIND. I GOT PLACES TO BE, SO LIKE--
--BYE.
HUH?
WHERE DID--
I KNOW YOU COULD CARE LESS--
--BUT WHEN WE STOP I AM GONNA KISS YOU SO HARD!

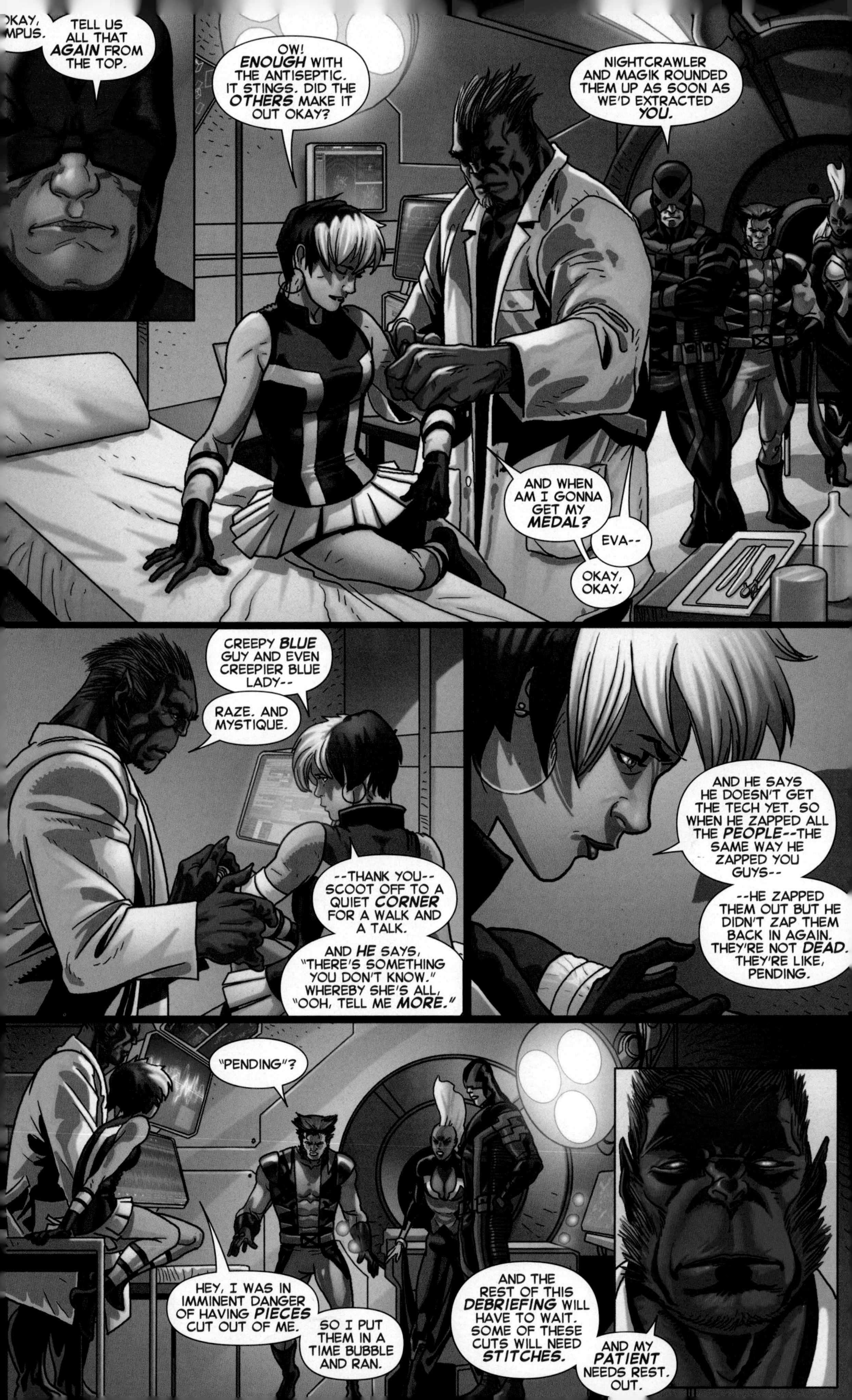

OKAY, ...MPUS.
TELL US ALL THAT AGAIN FROM THE TOP.
OW! ENOUGH WITH THE ANTISEPTIC. IT STINGS. DID THE OTHERS MAKE IT OUT OKAY?
NIGHTCRAWLER AND MAGIK ROUNDED THEM UP AS SOON AS WE'D EXTRACTED YOU.
AND WHEN AM I GONNA GET MY MEDAL?
EVA--
OKAY, OKAY.
CREEPY BLUE GUY AND EVEN CREEPIER BLUE LADY--
RAZE. AND MYSTIQUE.
--THANK YOU-- SCOOT OFF TO A QUIET CORNER FOR A WALK AND A TALK.
AND HE SAYS, "THERE'S SOMETHING YOU DON'T KNOW." WHEREBY SHE'S ALL, "OOH, TELL ME MORE."
AND HE SAYS HE DOESN'T GET THE TECH YET. SO WHEN HE ZAPPED ALL THE PEOPLE--THE SAME WAY HE ZAPPED YOU GUYS--
--HE ZAPPED THEM OUT BUT HE DIDN'T ZAP THEM BACK IN AGAIN. THEY'RE NOT DEAD. THEY'RE LIKE, PENDING.
"PENDING"?
HEY, I WAS IN IMMINENT DANGER OF HAVING PIECES CUT OUT OF ME.
SO I PUT THEM IN A TIME BUBBLE AND RAN.
AND THE REST OF THIS DEBRIEFING WILL HAVE TO WAIT. SOME OF THESE CUTS WILL NEED STITCHES.
AND MY PATIENT NEEDS REST. OUT.

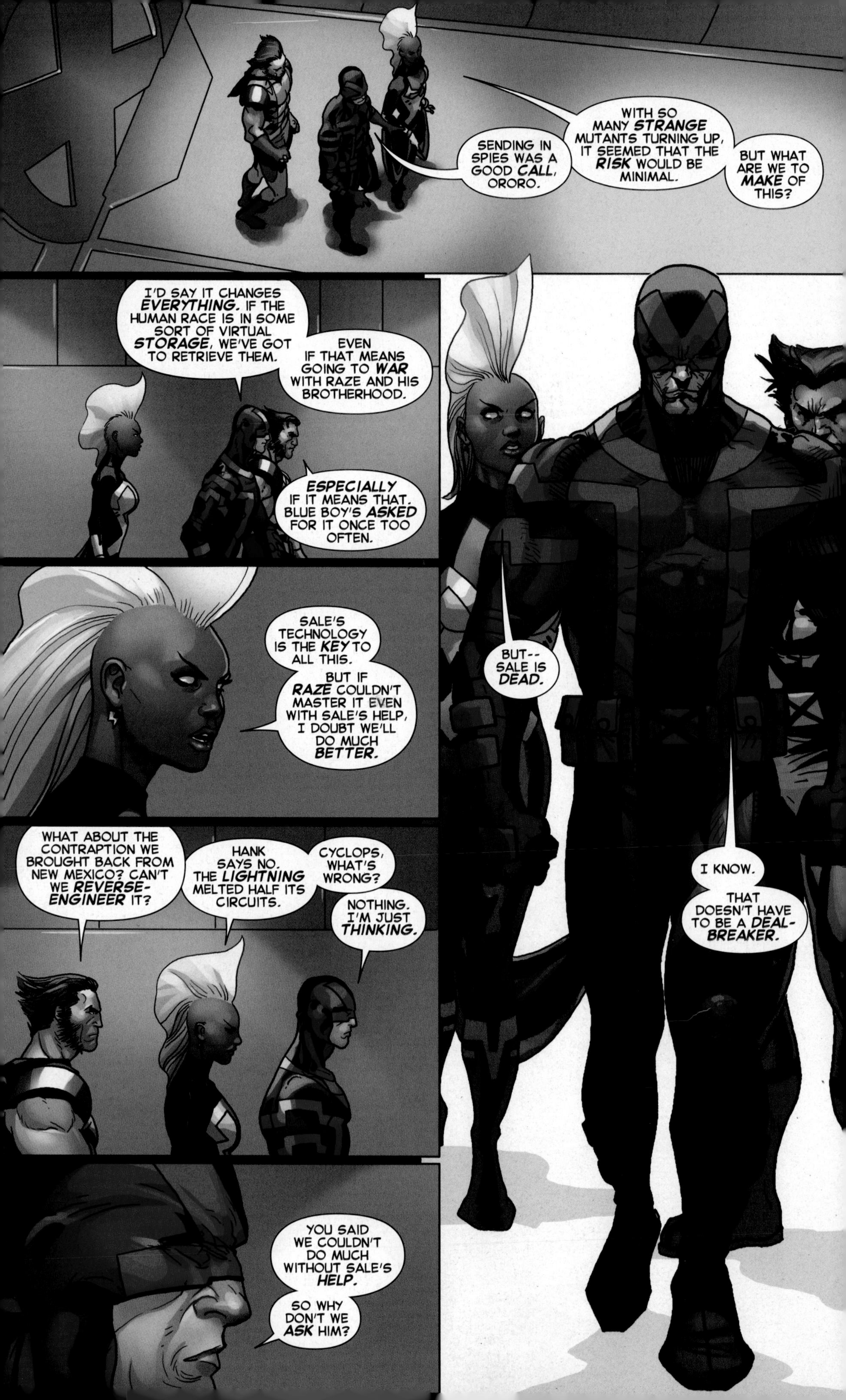
SENDING IN SPIES WAS A GOOD CALL, ORORO.
WITH SO MANY STRANGE MUTANTS TURNING UP, IT SEEMED THAT THE RISK WOULD BE MINIMAL.
BUT WHAT ARE WE TO MAKE OF THIS?
I'D SAY IT CHANGES EVERYTHING. IF THE HUMAN RACE IS IN SOME SORT OF VIRTUAL STORAGE, WE'VE GOT TO RETRIEVE THEM.
EVEN IF THAT MEANS GOING TO WAR WITH RAZE AND HIS BROTHERHOOD.
ESPECIALLY IF IT MEANS THAT. BLUE BOY'S ASKED FOR IT ONCE TOO OFTEN.
SALE'S TECHNOLOGY IS THE KEY TO ALL THIS.
BUT IF RAZE COULDN'T MASTER IT EVEN WITH SALE'S HELP, I DOUBT WE'LL DO MUCH BETTER.
WHAT ABOUT THE CONTRAPTION WE BROUGHT BACK FROM NEW MEXICO? CAN'T WE REVERSE-ENGINEER IT?
HANK SAYS NO. THE LIGHTNING MELTED HALF ITS CIRCUITS.
CYCLOPS, WHAT'S WRONG?
NOTHING. I'M JUST THINKING.
YOU SAID WE COULDN'T DO MUCH WITHOUT SALE'S HELP.
SO WHY DON'T WE ASK HIM?
BUT-- SALE IS DEAD.
I KNOW.
THAT DOESN'T HAVE TO BE A DEAL-BREAKER.

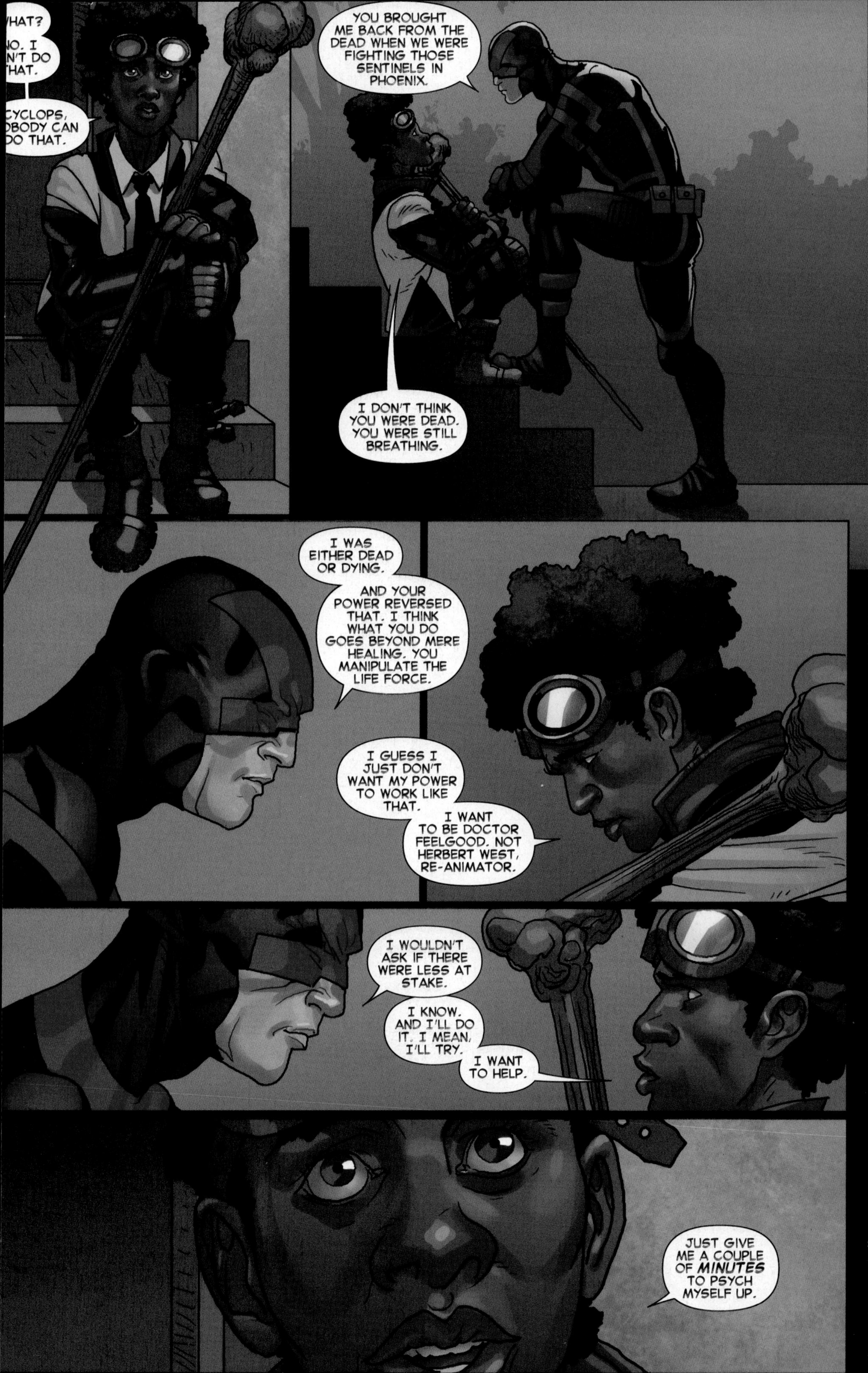

WHAT?
NO. I CAN'T DO THAT.
CYCLOPS, NOBODY CAN DO THAT.
YOU BROUGHT ME BACK FROM THE DEAD WHEN WE WERE FIGHTING THOSE SENTINELS IN PHOENIX.
I DON'T THINK YOU WERE DEAD. YOU WERE STILL BREATHING.
I WAS EITHER DEAD OR DYING.
AND YOUR POWER REVERSED THAT. I THINK WHAT YOU DO GOES BEYOND MERE HEALING. YOU MANIPULATE THE LIFE FORCE.
I GUESS I JUST DON'T WANT MY POWER TO WORK LIKE THAT.
I WANT TO BE DOCTOR FEELGOOD. NOT HERBERT WEST, RE-ANIMATOR.
I WOULDN'T ASK IF THERE WERE LESS AT STAKE.
I KNOW. AND I'LL DO IT. I MEAN, I'LL TRY.
I WANT TO HELP.
JUST GIVE ME A COUPLE OF MINUTES TO PSYCH MYSELF UP.

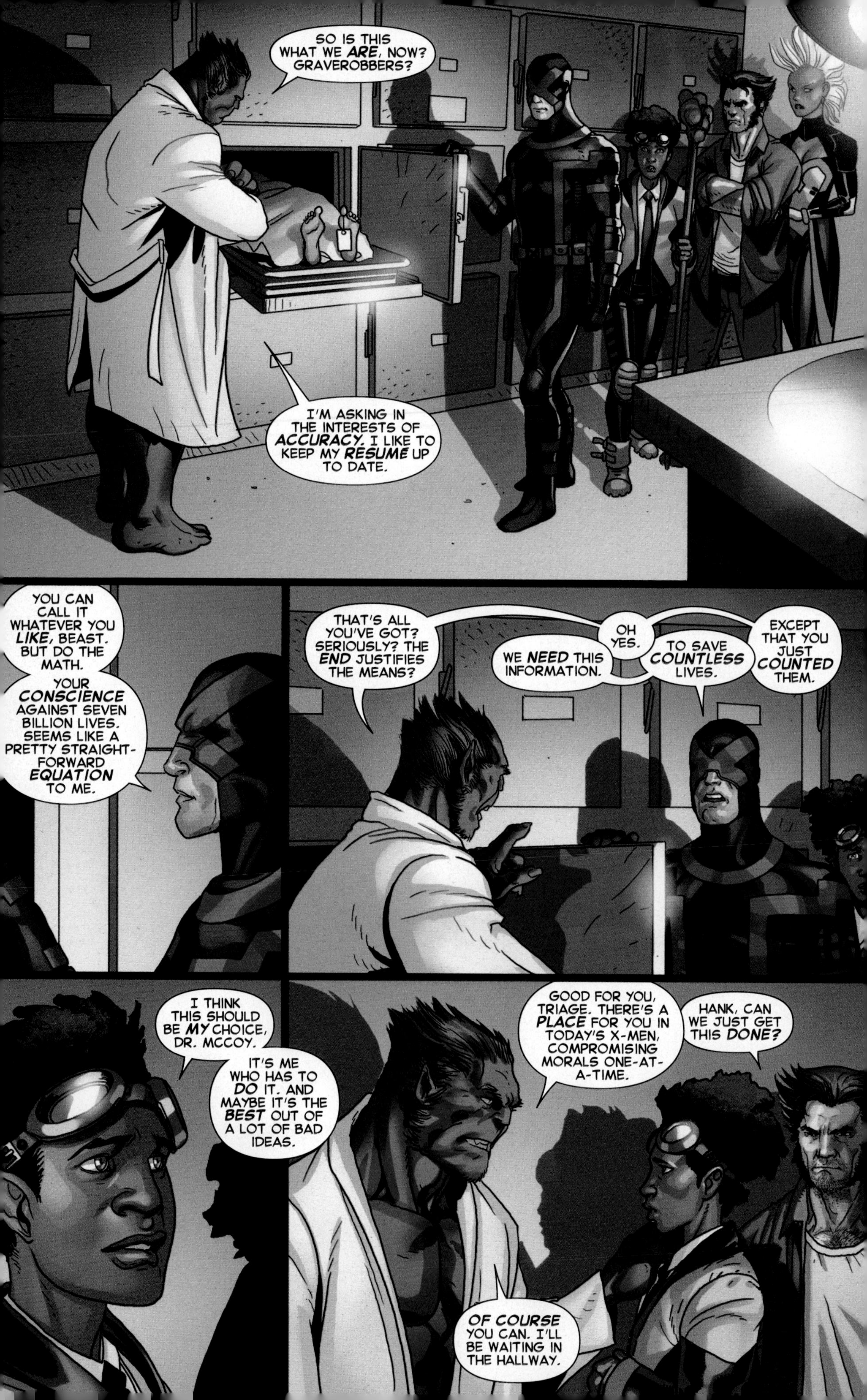
SO IS THIS WHAT WE ARE, NOW? GRAVEROBBERS?
I'M ASKING IN THE INTERESTS OF ACCURACY. I LIKE TO KEEP MY RESUME UP TO DATE.
YOU CAN CALL IT WHATEVER YOU LIKE, BEAST. BUT DO THE MATH.
YOUR CONSCIENCE AGAINST SEVEN BILLION LIVES. SEEMS LIKE A PRETTY STRAIGHT-FORWARD EQUATION TO ME.
THAT'S ALL YOU'VE GOT? SERIOUSLY? THE END JUSTIFIES THE MEANS?
WE NEED THIS INFORMATION.
OH YES.
TO SAVE COUNTLESS LIVES.
EXCEPT THAT YOU JUST COUNTED THEM.
I THINK THIS SHOULD BE MY CHOICE, DR. MCCOY.
IT'S ME WHO HAS TO DO IT. AND MAYBE IT'S THE BEST OUT OF A LOT OF BAD IDEAS.
GOOD FOR YOU, TRIAGE. THERE'S A PLACE FOR YOU IN TODAY'S X-MEN, COMPROMISING MORALS ONE-AT-A-TIME.
HANK, CAN WE JUST GET THIS DONE?
OF COURSE YOU CAN. I'LL BE WAITING IN THE HALLWAY.

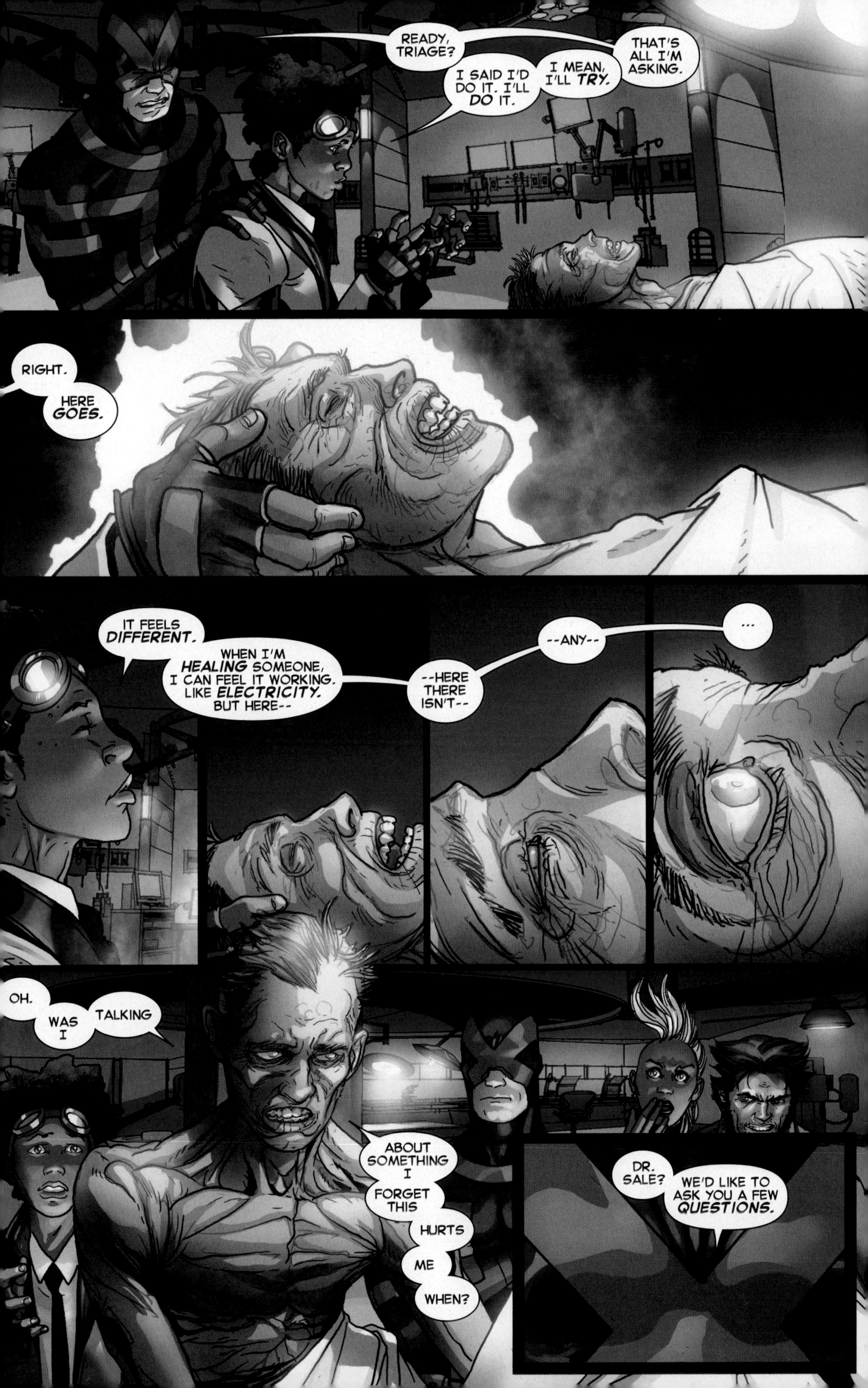
READY, TRIAGE?
I SAID I'D DO IT. I'LL DO IT.
I MEAN, I'LL TRY.
THAT'S ALL I'M ASKING.
RIGHT.
HERE GOES.
IT FEELS DIFFERENT.
WHEN I'M HEALING SOMEONE, I CAN FEEL IT WORKING. LIKE ELECTRICITY. BUT HERE--
--HERE THERE ISN'T--
--ANY--
...
OH.
WAS I
TALKING
ABOUT SOMETHING I
FORGET THIS
HURTS
ME
WHEN?
DR. SALE?
WE'D LIKE TO ASK YOU A FEW QUESTIONS.

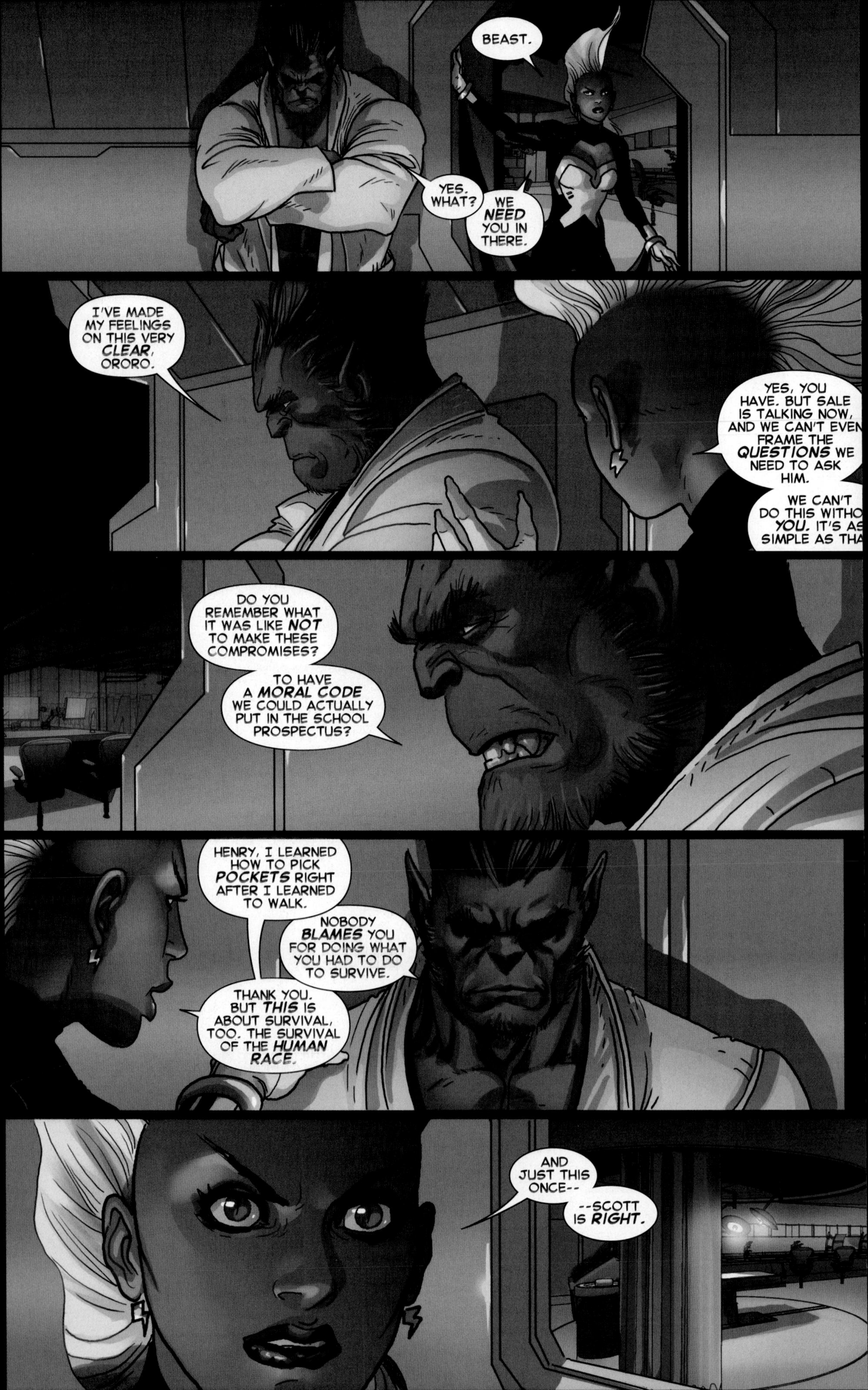
BEAST.
YES. WHAT?
WE NEED YOU IN THERE.
I'VE MADE MY FEELINGS ON THIS VERY CLEAR, ORORO.
YES, YOU HAVE. BUT SALE IS TALKING NOW, AND WE CAN'T EVEN FRAME THE QUESTIONS WE NEED TO ASK HIM.
WE CAN'T DO THIS WITHO YOU. IT'S AS SIMPLE AS THA
DO YOU REMEMBER WHAT IT WAS LIKE NOT TO MAKE THESE COMPROMISES?
TO HAVE A MORAL CODE WE COULD ACTUALLY PUT IN THE SCHOOL PROSPECTUS?
HENRY, I LEARNED HOW TO PICK POCKETS RIGHT AFTER I LEARNED TO WALK.
NOBODY BLAMES YOU FOR DOING WHAT YOU HAD TO DO TO SURVIVE.
THANK YOU. BUT THIS IS ABOUT SURVIVAL, TOO. THE SURVIVAL OF THE HUMAN RACE.
AND JUST THIS ONCE--
--SCOTT IS RIGHT.

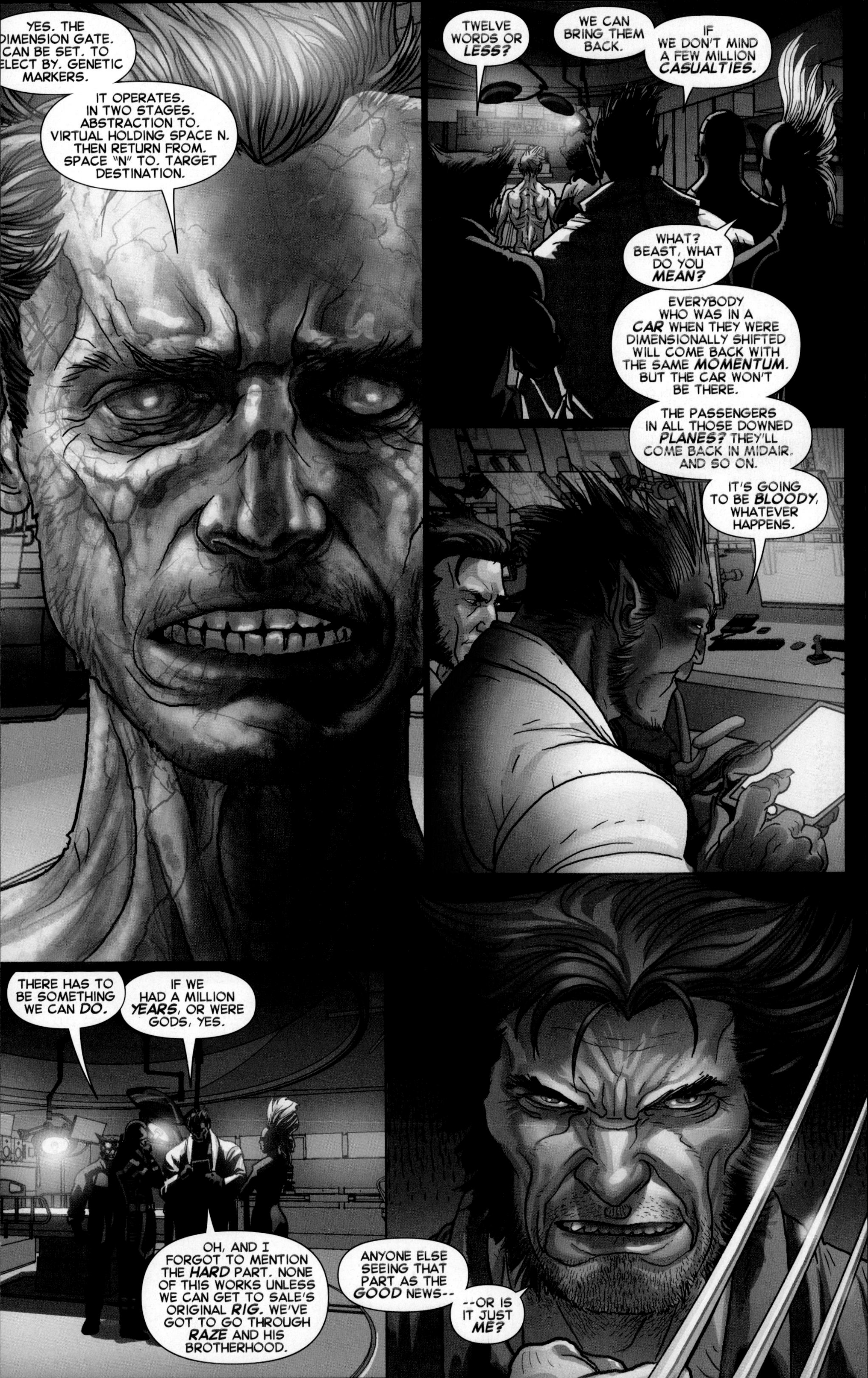
YES. THE DIMENSION GATE. CAN BE SET. TO SELECT BY. GENETIC MARKERS.
IT OPERATES. IN TWO STAGES. ABSTRACTION TO. VIRTUAL HOLDING SPACE N. THEN RETURN FROM. SPACE "N" TO. TARGET DESTINATION.
TWELVE WORDS OR *LESS?*
WE CAN BRING THEM BACK.
IF WE DON'T MIND A FEW MILLION *CASUALTIES.*
WHAT? BEAST, WHAT DO YOU *MEAN?*
EVERYBODY WHO WAS IN A *CAR* WHEN THEY WERE DIMENSIONALLY SHIFTED WILL COME BACK WITH THE SAME *MOMENTUM.* BUT THE CAR WON'T BE THERE.
THE PASSENGERS IN ALL THOSE DOWNED *PLANES?* THEY'LL COME BACK IN MIDAIR. AND SO ON.
IT'S GOING TO BE *BLOODY,* WHATEVER HAPPENS.
THERE HAS TO BE SOMETHING WE CAN *DO.*
IF WE HAD A MILLION *YEARS,* OR WERE GODS, YES.
OH, AND I FORGOT TO MENTION THE *HARD* PART. NONE OF THIS WORKS UNLESS WE CAN GET TO SALE'S ORIGINAL *RIG.* WE'VE GOT TO GO THROUGH *RAZE* AND HIS BROTHERHOOD.
ANYONE ELSE SEEING THAT PART AS THE *GOOD* NEWS--
--OR IS IT JUST *ME?*

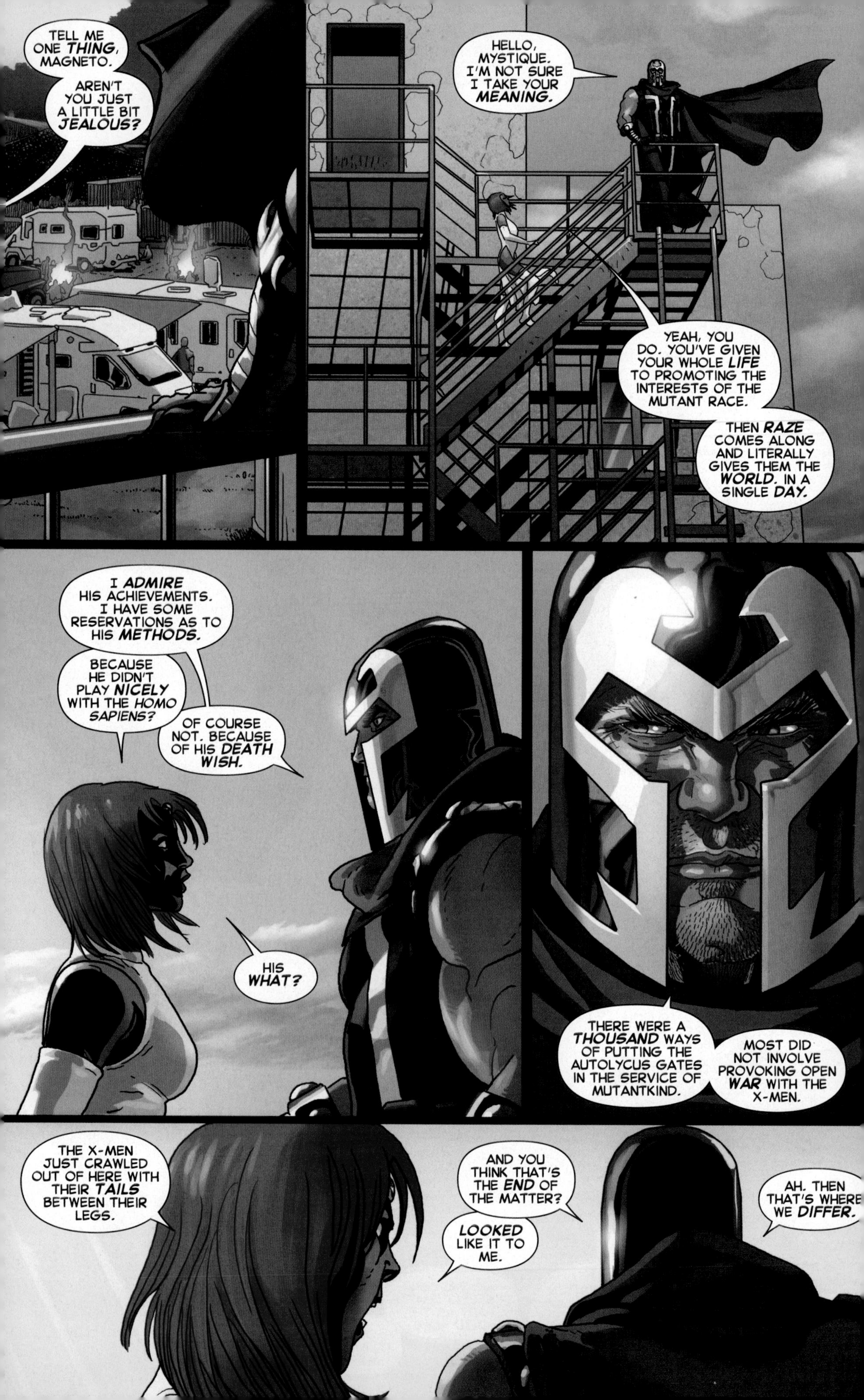
TELL ME ONE THING, MAGNETO.
AREN'T YOU JUST A LITTLE BIT JEALOUS?
HELLO, MYSTIQUE. I'M NOT SURE I TAKE YOUR MEANING.
YEAH, YOU DO. YOU'VE GIVEN YOUR WHOLE LIFE TO PROMOTING THE INTERESTS OF THE MUTANT RACE.
THEN RAZE COMES ALONG AND LITERALLY GIVES THEM THE WORLD. IN A SINGLE DAY.
I ADMIRE HIS ACHIEVEMENTS. I HAVE SOME RESERVATIONS AS TO HIS METHODS.
BECAUSE HE DIDN'T PLAY NICELY WITH THE HOMO SAPIENS?
OF COURSE NOT. BECAUSE OF HIS DEATH WISH.
HIS WHAT?
THERE WERE A THOUSAND WAYS OF PUTTING THE AUTOLYCUS GATES IN THE SERVICE OF MUTANTKIND.
MOST DID NOT INVOLVE PROVOKING OPEN WAR WITH THE X-MEN.
THE X-MEN JUST CRAWLED OUT OF HERE WITH THEIR TAILS BETWEEN THEIR LEGS.
AND YOU THINK THAT'S THE END OF THE MATTER?
LOOKED LIKE IT TO ME.
AH. THEN THAT'S WHERE WE DIFFER.

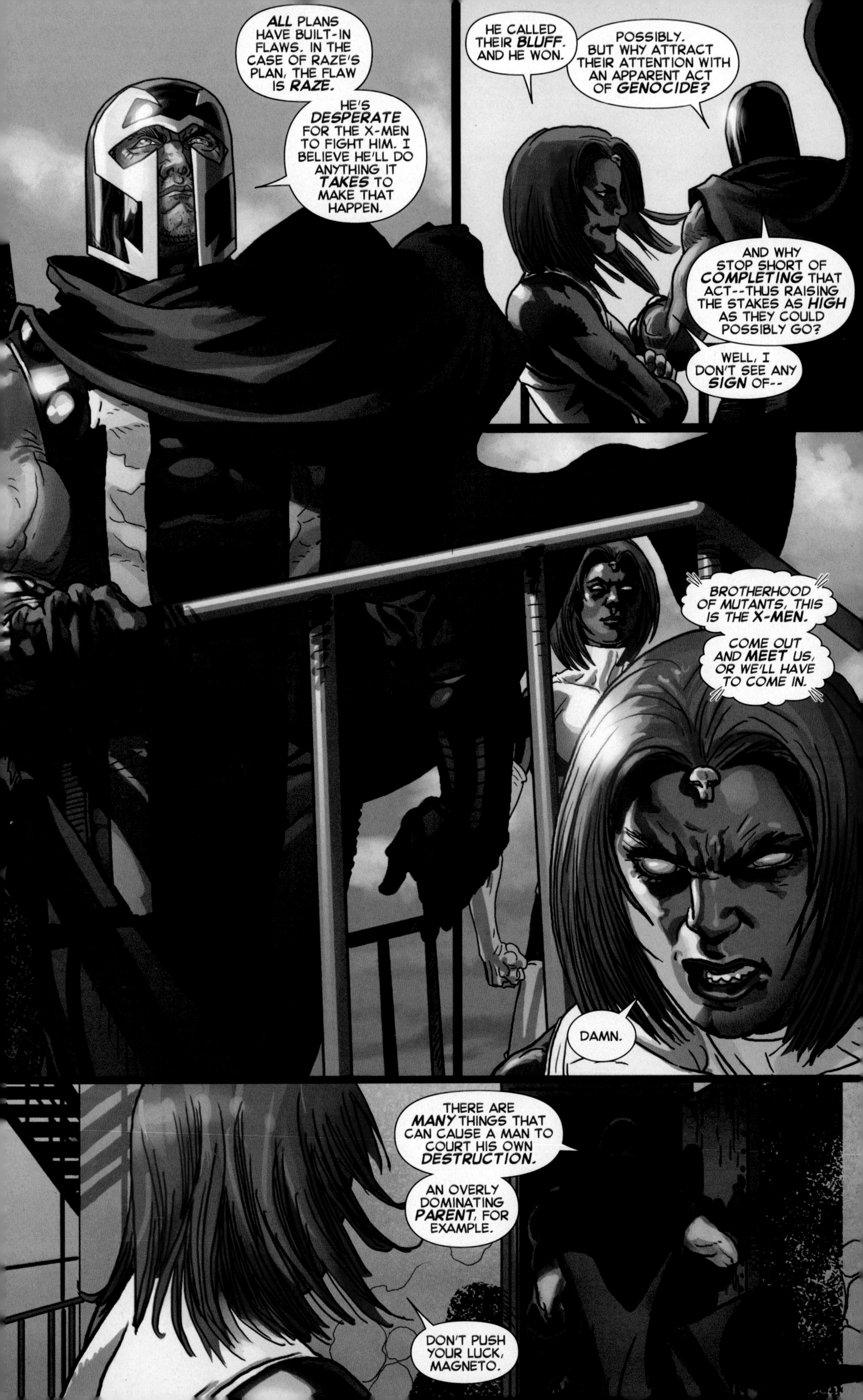
ALL PLANS HAVE BUILT-IN FLAWS. IN THE CASE OF RAZE'S PLAN, THE FLAW IS RAZE.
HE'S DESPERATE FOR THE X-MEN TO FIGHT HIM. I BELIEVE HE'LL DO ANYTHING IT TAKES TO MAKE THAT HAPPEN.
HE CALLED THEIR BLUFF. AND HE WON.
POSSIBLY. BUT WHY ATTRACT THEIR ATTENTION WITH AN APPARENT ACT OF GENOCIDE?
AND WHY STOP SHORT OF COMPLETING THAT ACT--THUS RAISING THE STAKES AS HIGH AS THEY COULD POSSIBLY GO?
WELL, I DON'T SEE ANY SIGN OF--
BROTHERHOOD OF MUTANTS, THIS IS THE X-MEN.
COME OUT AND MEET US, OR WE'LL HAVE TO COME IN.
DAMN.
THERE ARE MANY THINGS THAT CAN CAUSE A MAN TO COURT HIS OWN DESTRUCTION.
AN OVERLY DOMINATING PARENT, FOR EXAMPLE.
DON'T PUSH YOUR LUCK, MAGNETO.

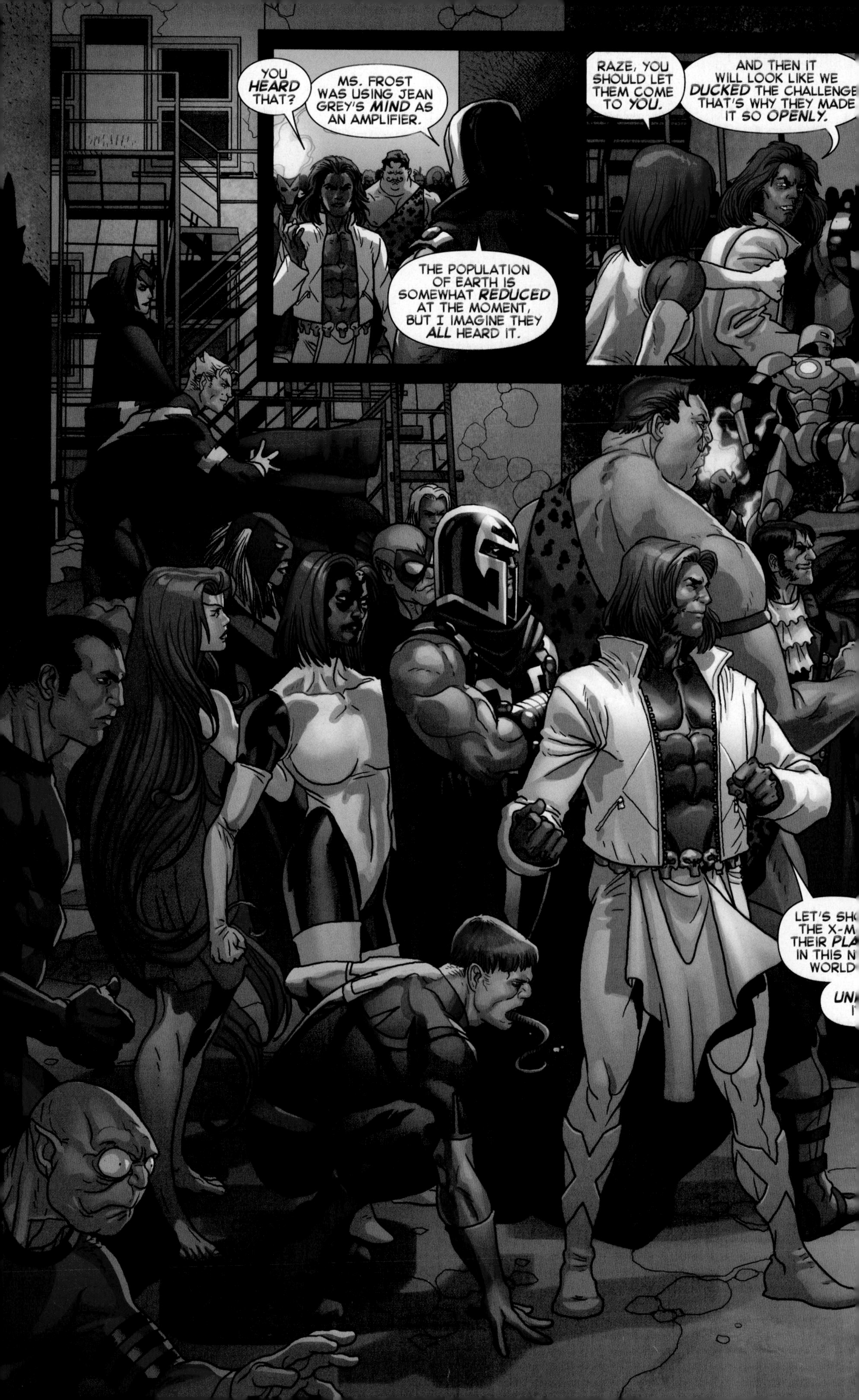
YOU HEARD THAT?
MS. FROST WAS USING JEAN GREY'S MIND AS AN AMPLIFIER.
THE POPULATION OF EARTH IS SOMEWHAT REDUCED AT THE MOMENT, BUT I IMAGINE THEY ALL HEARD IT.
RAZE, YOU SHOULD LET THEM COME TO YOU.
AND THEN IT WILL LOOK LIKE WE DUCKED THE CHALLENGE THAT'S WHY THEY MADE IT SO OPENLY.
LET'S SH THE X-M THEIR PLA IN THIS N WORLD

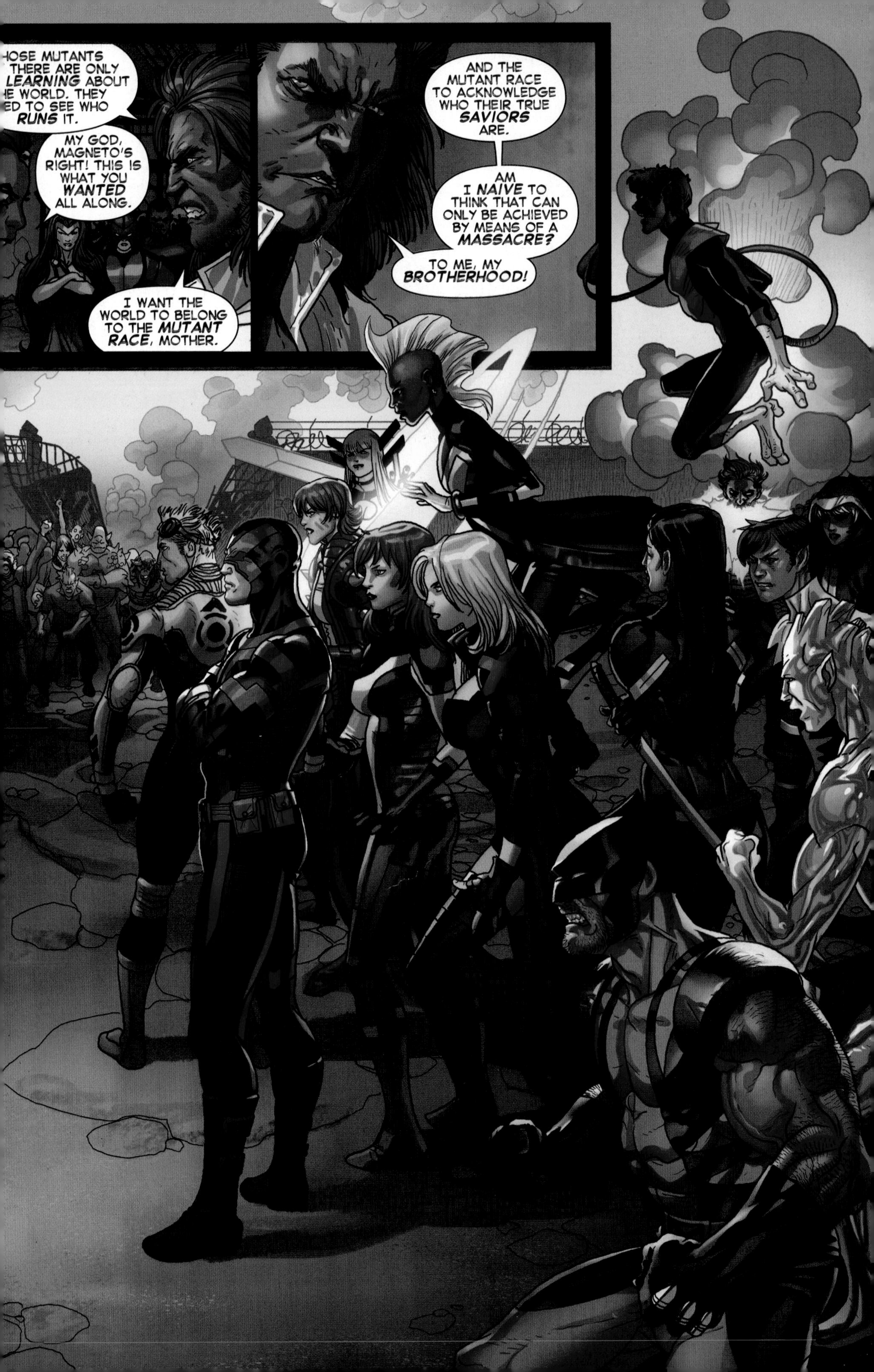

HOSE MUTANTS THERE ARE ONLY LEARNING ABOUT HE WORLD. THEY ED TO SEE WHO RUNS IT.
MY GOD, MAGNETO'S RIGHT! THIS IS WHAT YOU WANTED ALL ALONG.
I WANT THE WORLD TO BELONG TO THE MUTANT RACE, MOTHER.
AND THE MUTANT RACE TO ACKNOWLEDGE WHO THEIR TRUE SAVIORS ARE.
AM I NAIVE TO THINK THAT CAN ONLY BE ACHIEVED BY MEANS OF A MASSACRE?
TO ME, MY BROTHERHOOD!

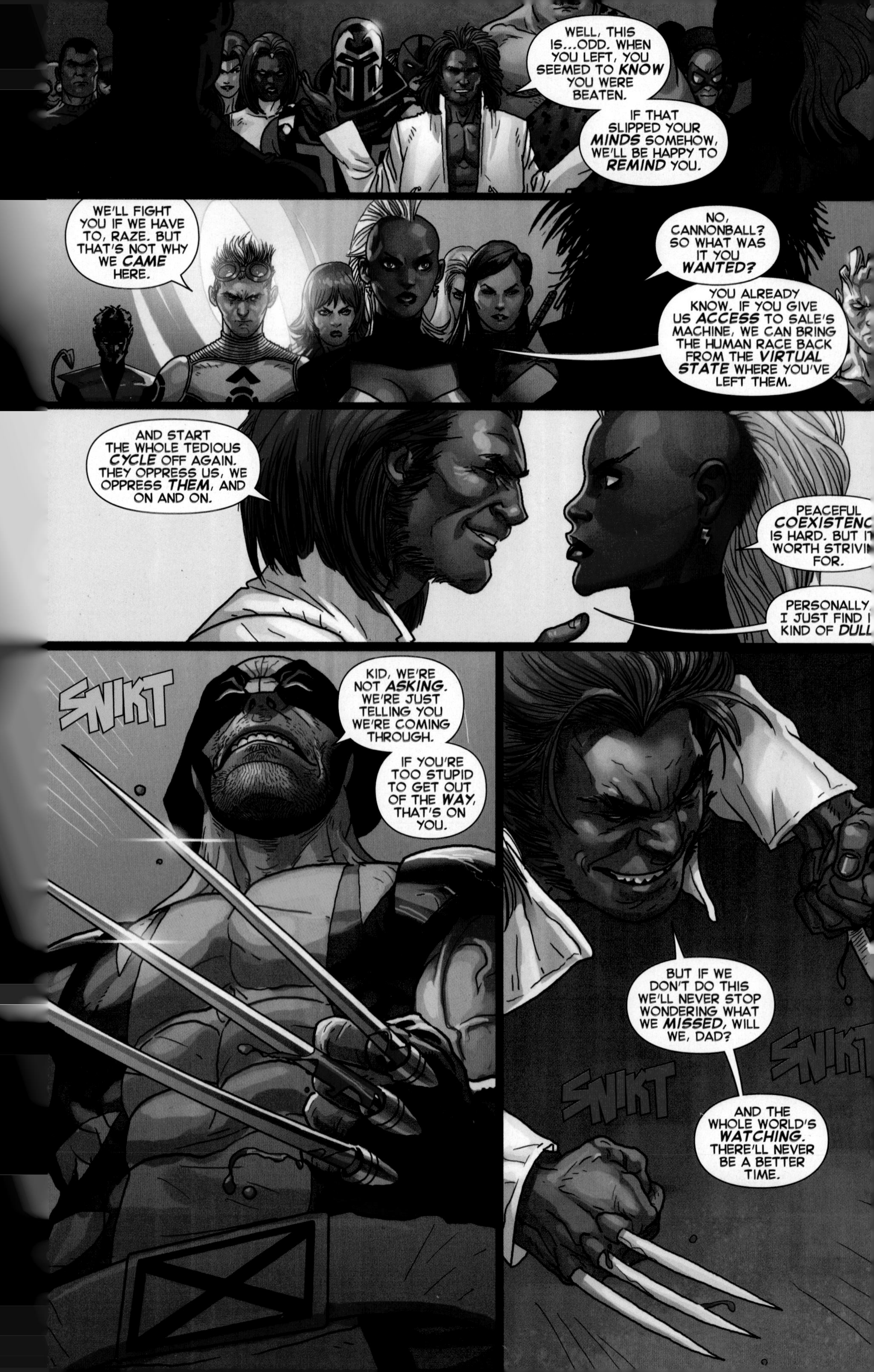
WELL, THIS IS...ODD. WHEN YOU LEFT, YOU SEEMED TO KNOW YOU WERE BEATEN.
IF THAT SLIPPED YOUR MINDS SOMEHOW, WE'LL BE HAPPY TO REMIND YOU.
WE'LL FIGHT YOU IF WE HAVE TO, RAZE. BUT THAT'S NOT WHY WE CAME HERE.
NO, CANNONBALL? SO WHAT WAS IT YOU WANTED?
YOU ALREADY KNOW. IF YOU GIVE US ACCESS TO SALE'S MACHINE, WE CAN BRING THE HUMAN RACE BACK FROM THE VIRTUAL STATE WHERE YOU'VE LEFT THEM.
AND START THE WHOLE TEDIOUS CYCLE OFF AGAIN. THEY OPPRESS US, WE OPPRESS THEM, AND ON AND ON.
PEACEFUL COEXISTENC IS HARD. BUT IT WORTH STRIVI FOR.
PERSONALLY I JUST FIND I KIND OF DULL
SNIKT
KID, WE'RE NOT ASKING. WE'RE JUST TELLING YOU WE'RE COMING THROUGH.
IF YOU'RE TOO STUPID TO GET OUT OF THE WAY, THAT'S ON YOU.
BUT IF WE DON'T DO THIS WE'LL NEVER STOP WONDERING WHAT WE MISSED, WILL WE, DAD?
SNIKT
SNIKT
AND THE WHOLE WORLD'S WATCHING. THERE'LL NEVER BE A BETTER TIME.

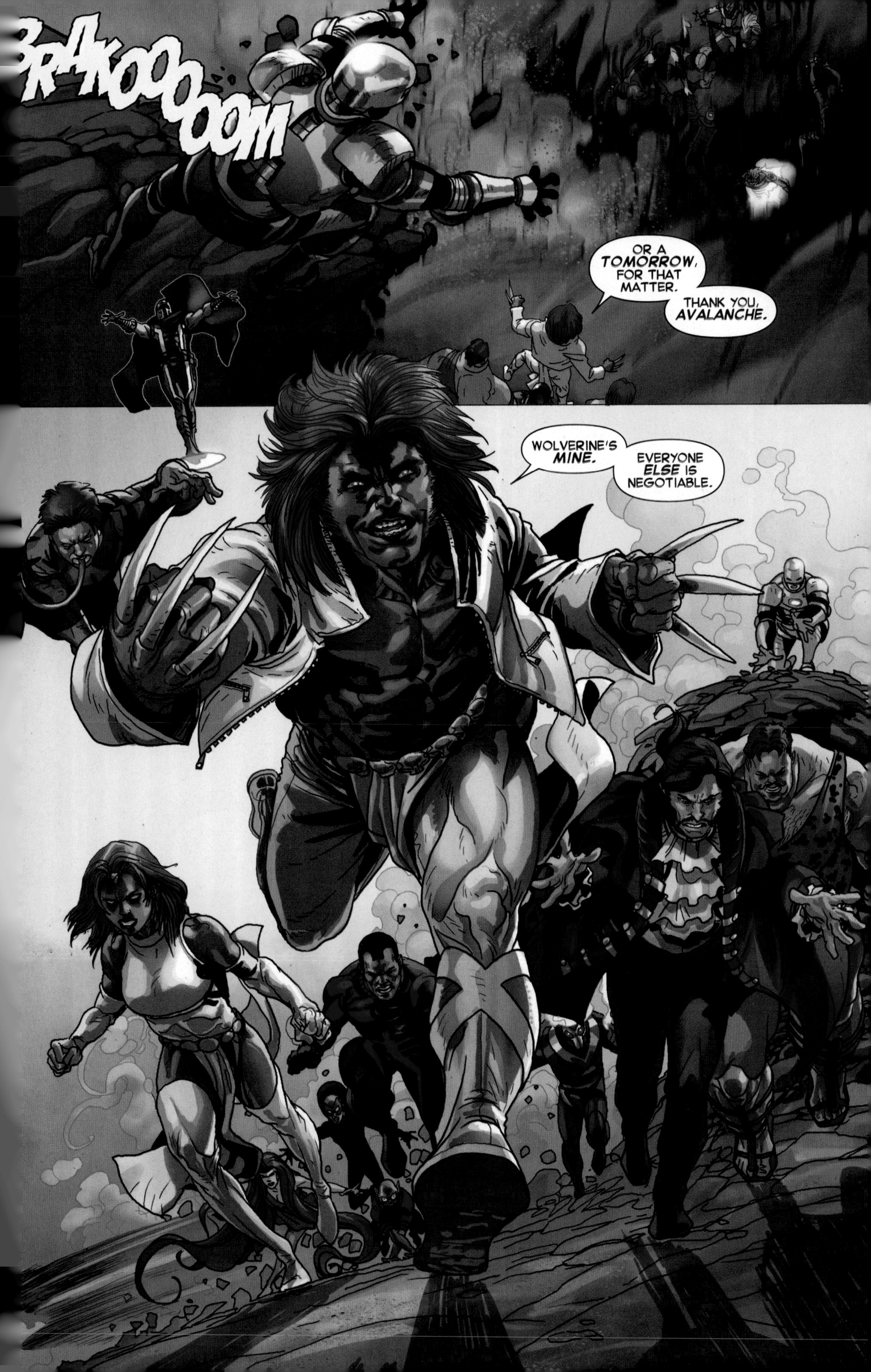
BRAKOOOOOM
OR A TOMORROW, FOR THAT MATTER.
THANK YOU, AVALANCHE.
WOLVERINE'S MINE.
EVERYONE ELSE IS NEGOTIABLE.

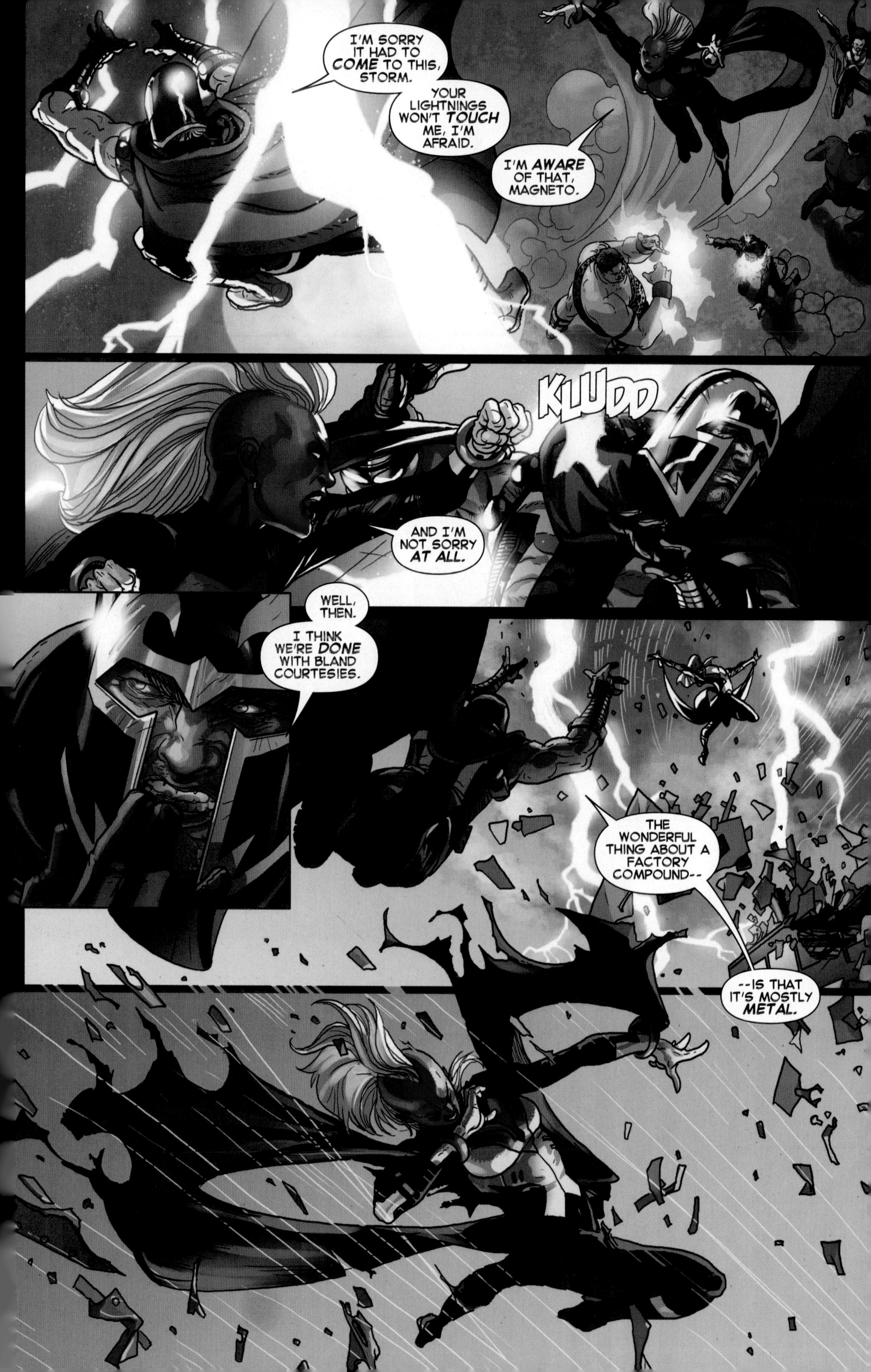
I'M SORRY IT HAD TO COME TO THIS, STORM.
YOUR LIGHTNINGS WON'T TOUCH ME, I'M AFRAID.
I'M AWARE OF THAT, MAGNETO.
KLUDD
AND I'M NOT SORRY AT ALL.
WELL, THEN.
I THINK WE'RE DONE WITH BLAND COURTESIES.
THE WONDERFUL THING ABOUT A FACTORY COMPOUND--
--IS THAT IT'S MOSTLY METAL.

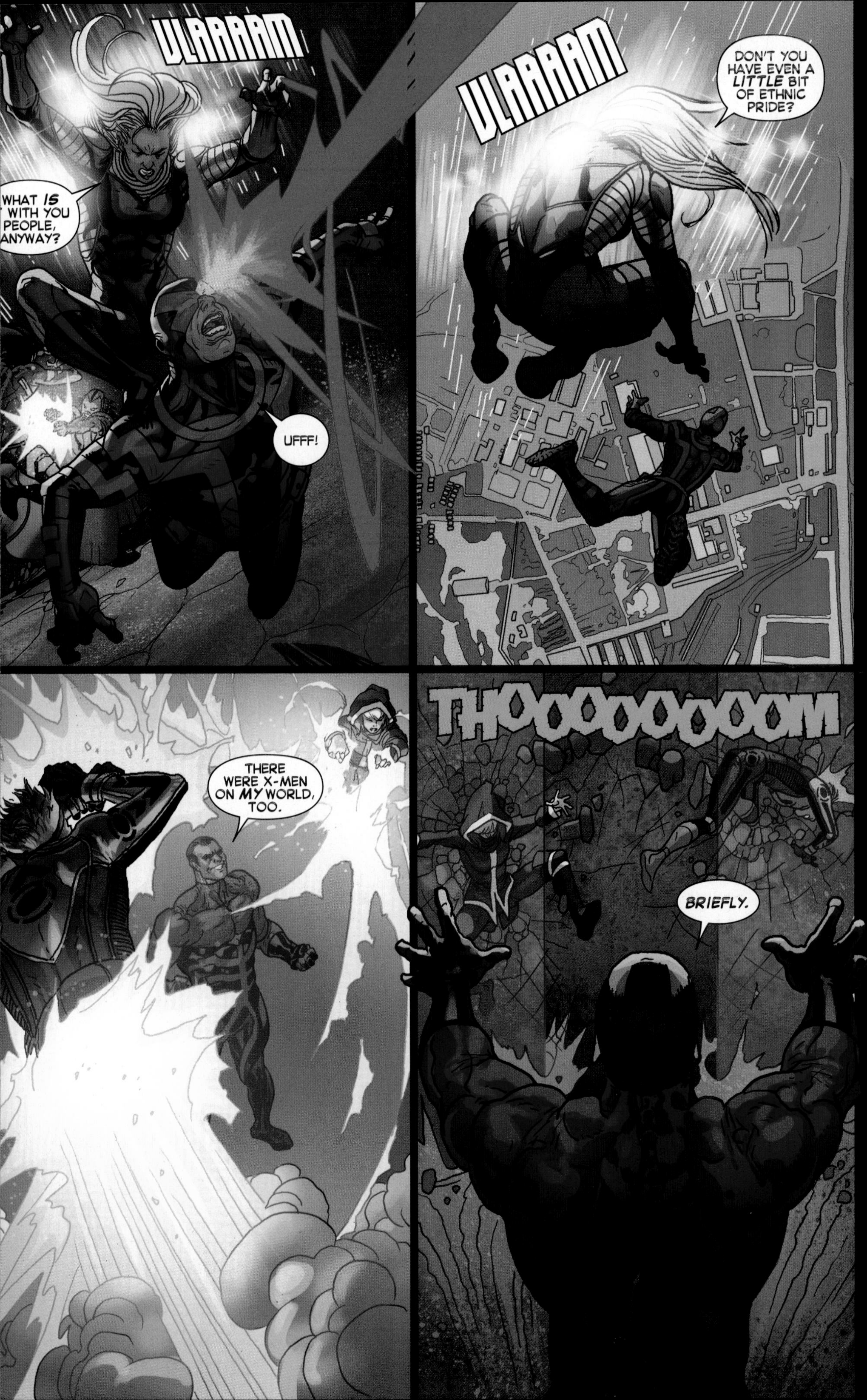
VLAAAAM
WHAT IS WITH YOU PEOPLE, ANYWAY?
UFFF!
VLAAAAM
DON'T YOU HAVE EVEN A LITTLE BIT OF ETHNIC PRIDE?
THERE WERE X-MEN ON MY WORLD, TOO.
THOOOOOOOOOM
BRIEFLY.

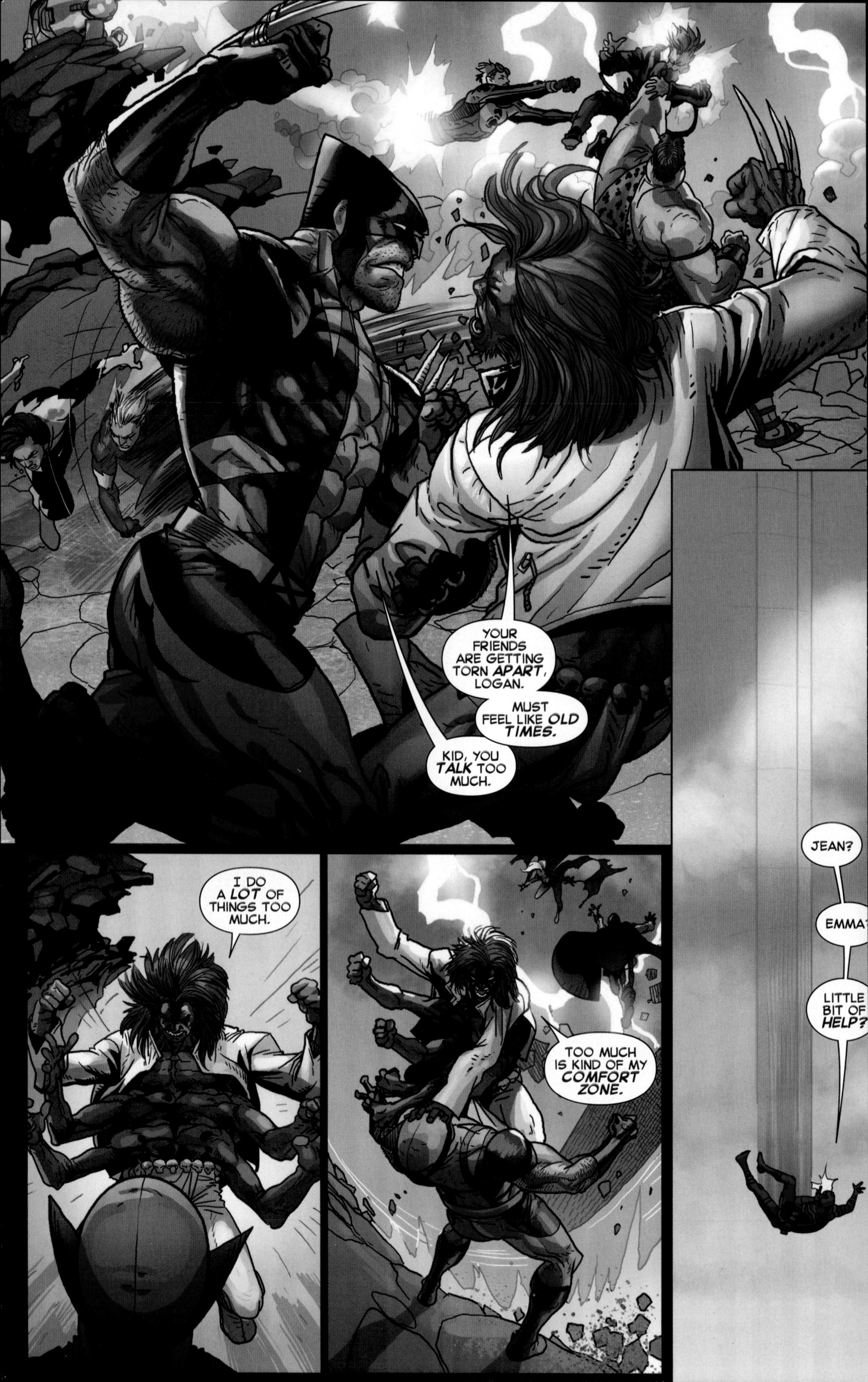
YOUR FRIENDS ARE GETTING TORN APART, LOGAN.
MUST FEEL LIKE OLD TIMES.
KID, YOU TALK TOO MUCH.
I DO A LOT OF THINGS TOO MUCH.
TOO MUCH IS KIND OF MY COMFORT ZONE.
JEAN?
EMMA?
LITTLE BIT OF HELP?

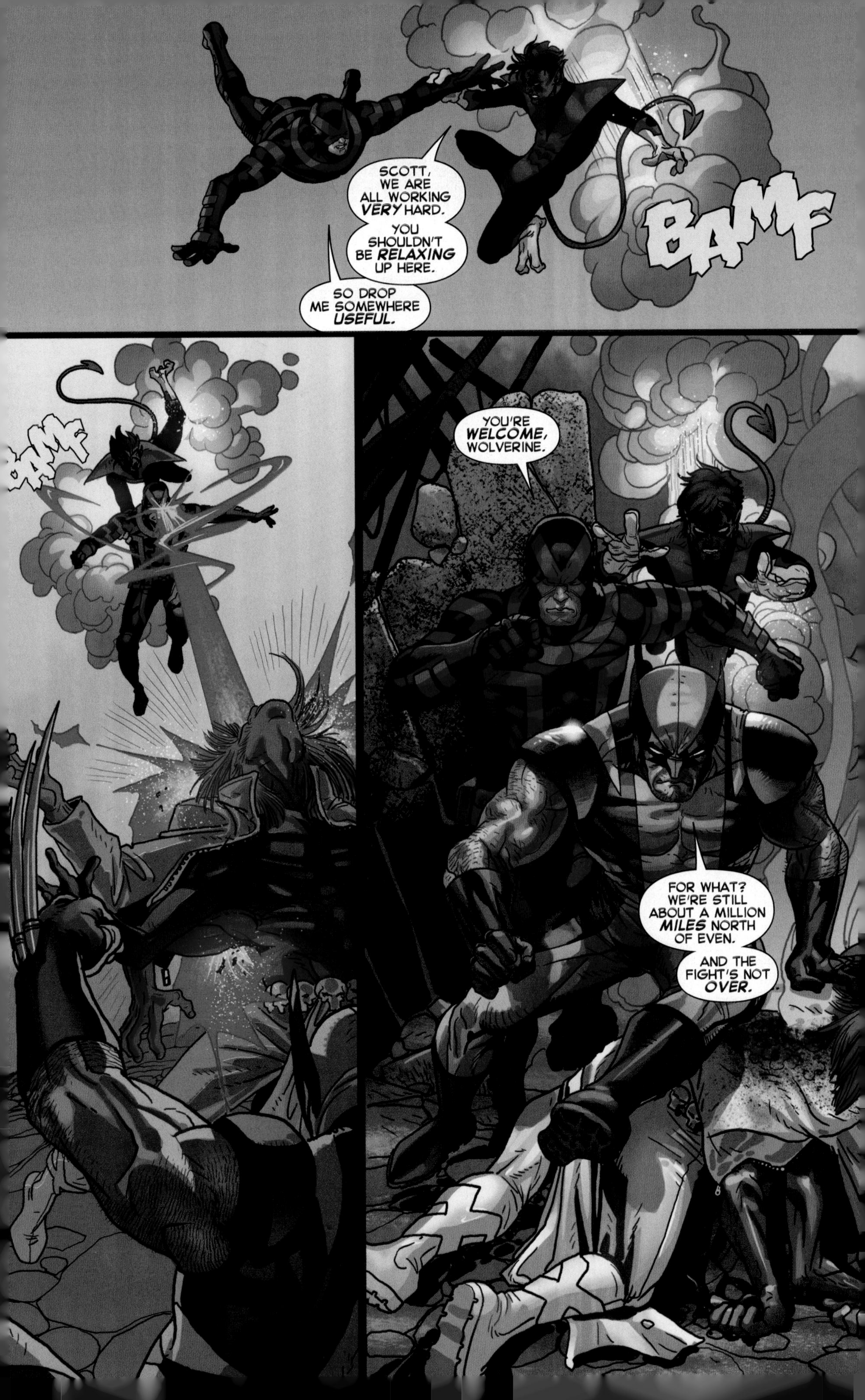
SCOTT, WE ARE ALL WORKING VERY HARD.
YOU SHOULDN'T BE RELAXING UP HERE.
SO DROP ME SOMEWHERE USEFUL.
BAMF
BAMF
YOU'RE WELCOME, WOLVERINE.
FOR WHAT? WE'RE STILL ABOUT A MILLION MILES NORTH OF EVEN.
AND THE FIGHT'S NOT OVER.

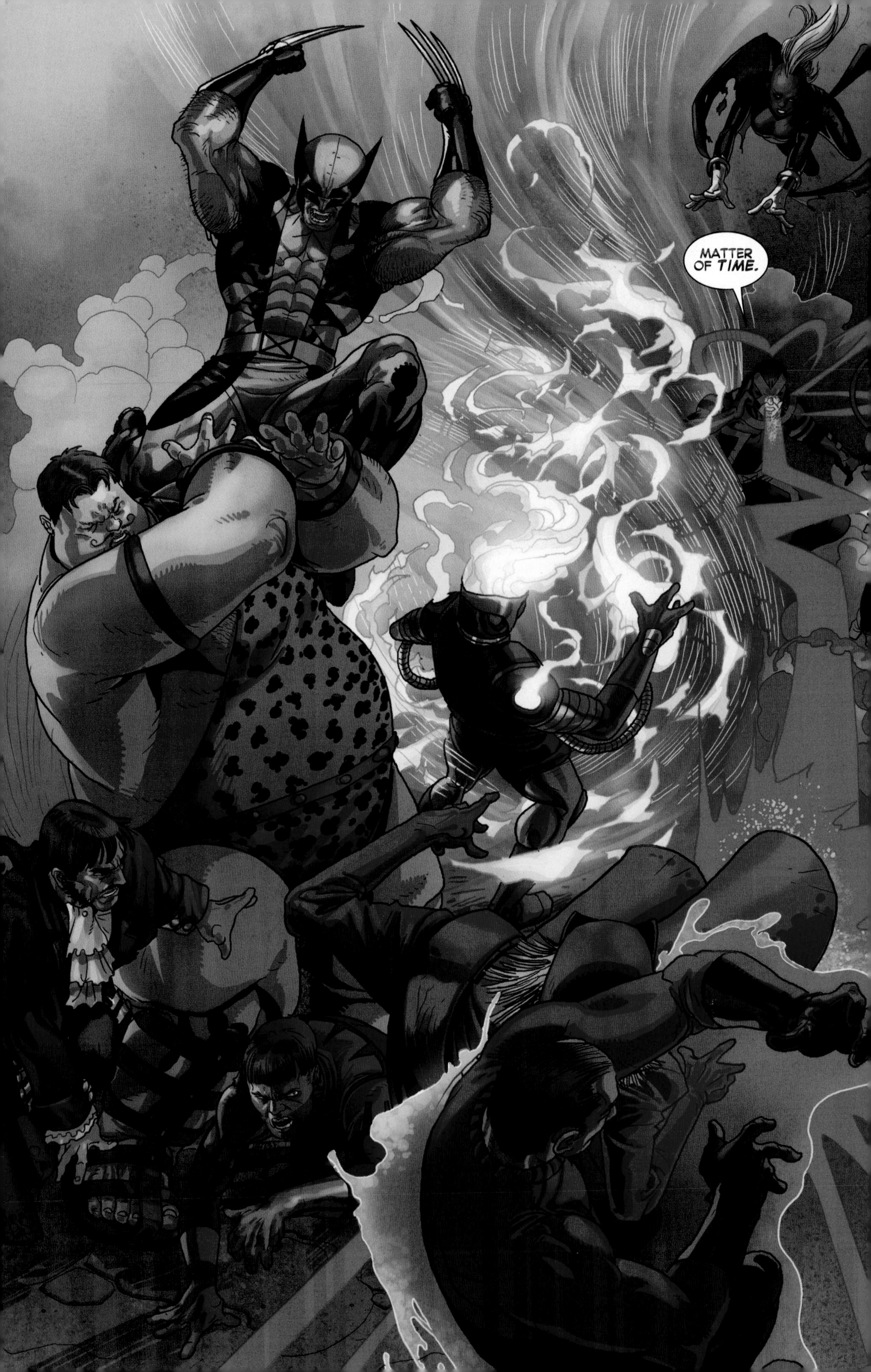
MATTER OF TIME.

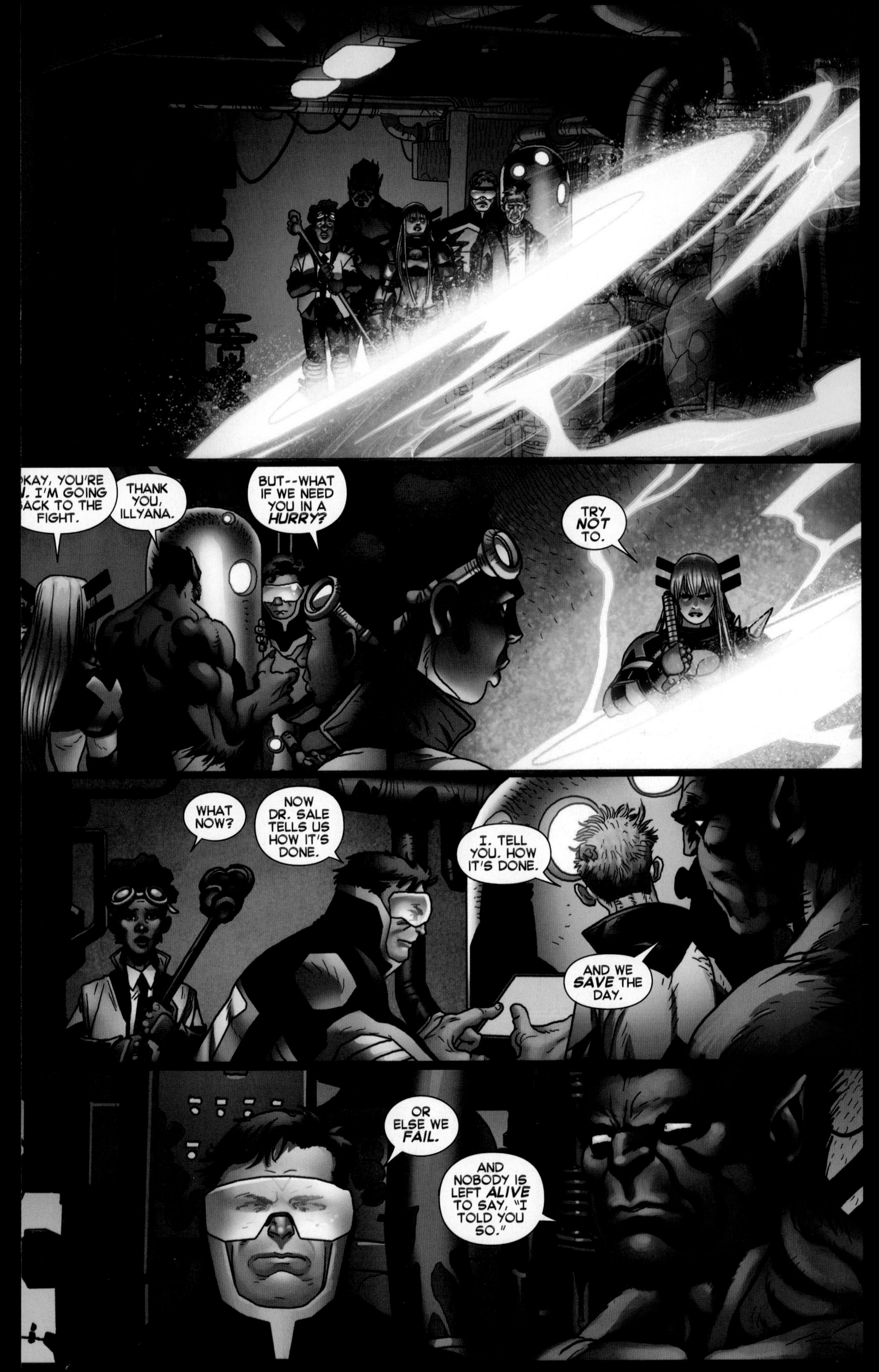

OKAY, YOU'RE IN. I'M GOING BACK TO THE FIGHT.
THANK YOU, ILLYANA.
BUT--WHAT IF WE NEED YOU IN A HURRY?
TRY NOT TO.
WHAT NOW?
NOW DR. SALE TELLS US HOW IT'S DONE.
I. TELL YOU. HOW IT'S DONE.
AND WE SAVE THE DAY.
OR ELSE WE FAIL.
AND NOBODY IS LEFT ALIVE TO SAY, "I TOLD YOU SO."

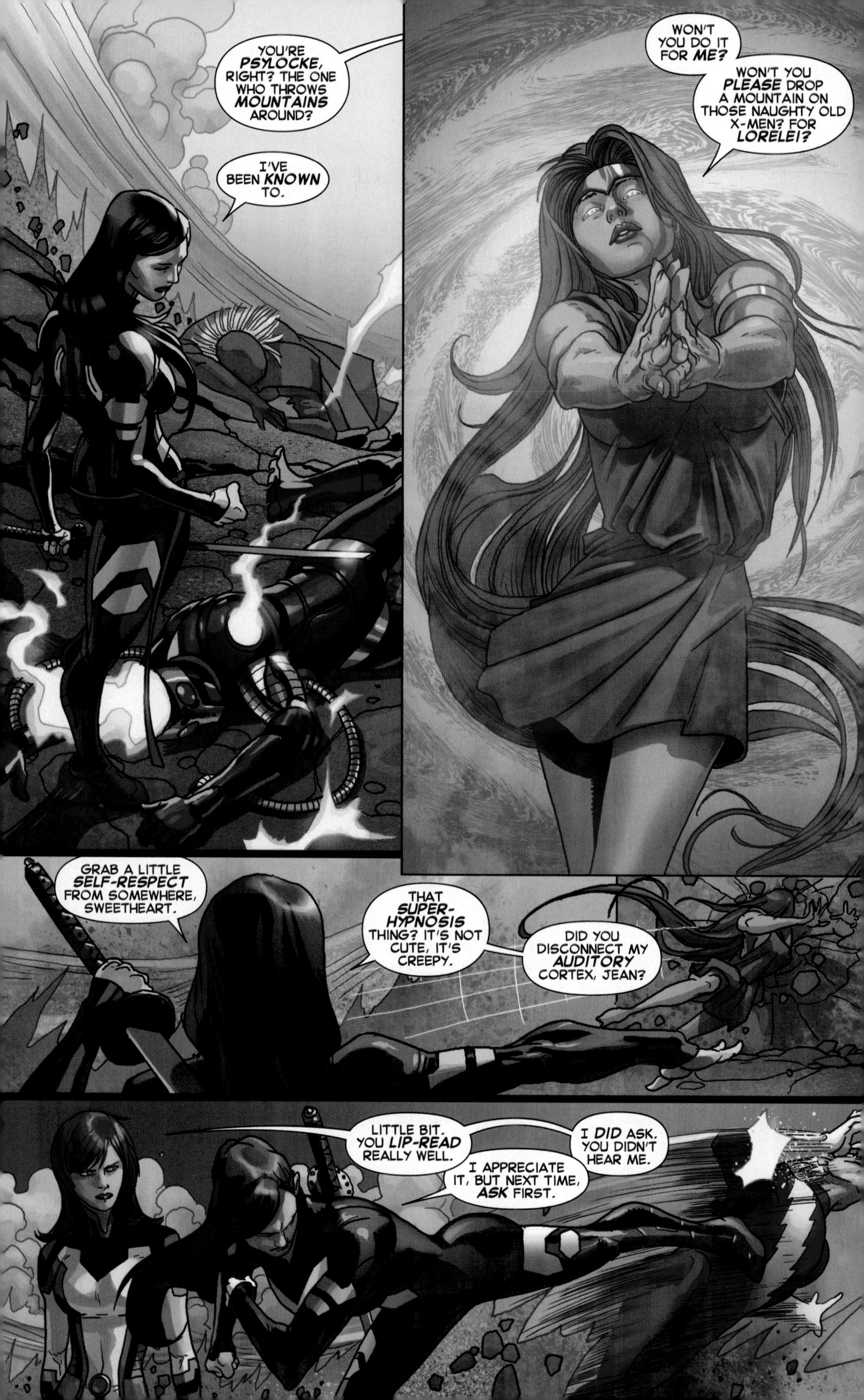
YOU'RE PSYLOCKE, RIGHT? THE ONE WHO THROWS MOUNTAINS AROUND?
I'VE BEEN KNOWN TO.
WON'T YOU DO IT FOR ME?
WON'T YOU PLEASE DROP A MOUNTAIN ON THOSE NAUGHTY OLD X-MEN? FOR LORELEI?
GRAB A LITTLE SELF-RESPECT FROM SOMEWHERE, SWEETHEART.
THAT SUPER-HYPNOSIS THING? IT'S NOT CUTE, IT'S CREEPY.
DID YOU DISCONNECT MY AUDITORY CORTEX, JEAN?
LITTLE BIT. YOU LIP-READ REALLY WELL.
I APPRECIATE IT, BUT NEXT TIME, ASK FIRST.
I DID ASK. YOU DIDN'T HEAR ME.

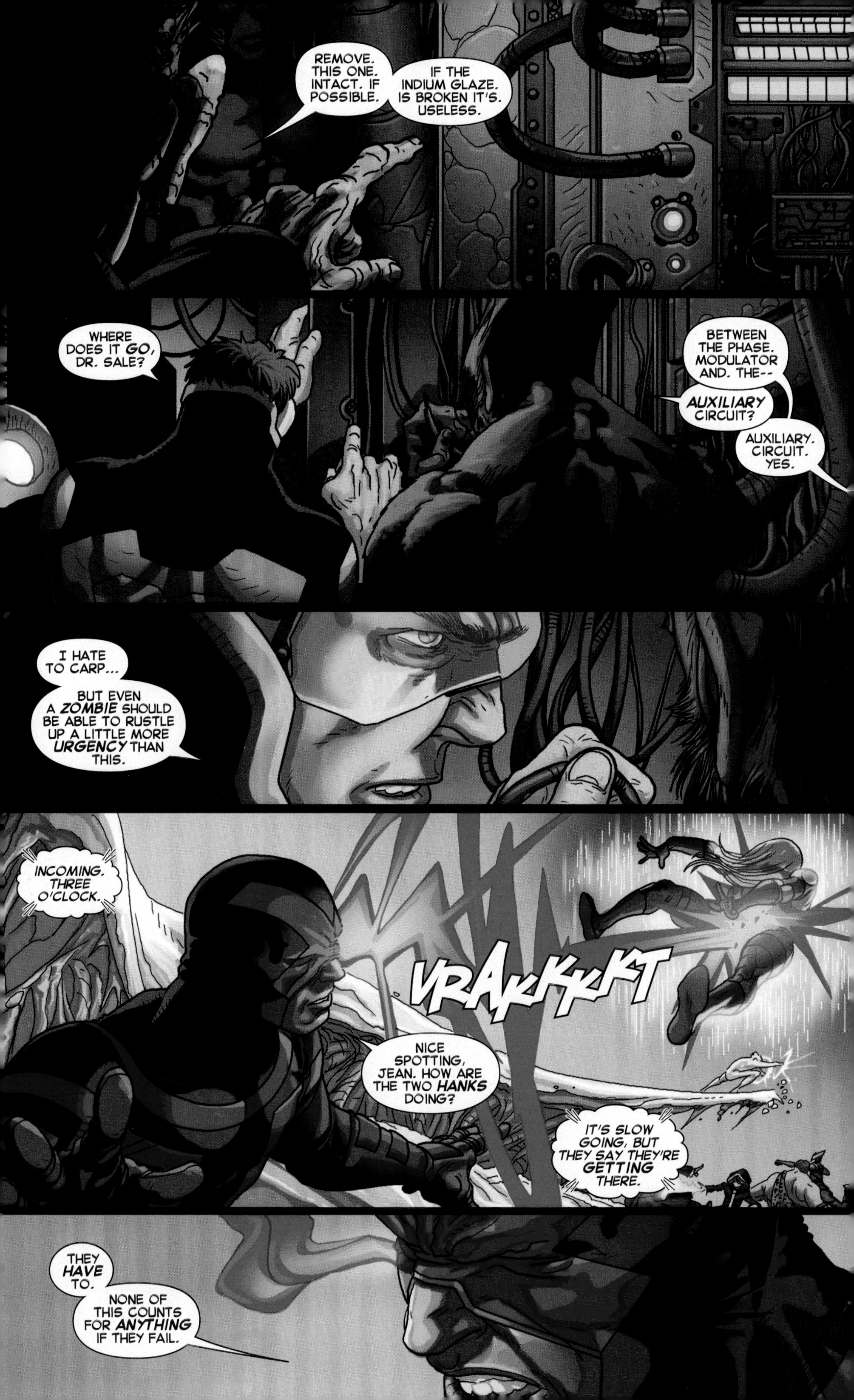
REMOVE. THIS ONE. INTACT. IF POSSIBLE.
IF THE INDIUM GLAZE. IS BROKEN IT'S. USELESS.
WHERE DOES IT GO, DR. SALE?
BETWEEN THE PHASE. MODULATOR AND. THE--
AUXILIARY CIRCUIT?
AUXILIARY. CIRCUIT. YES.
I HATE TO CARP...
BUT EVEN A ZOMBIE SHOULD BE ABLE TO RUSTLE UP A LITTLE MORE URGENCY THAN THIS.
INCOMING. THREE O'CLOCK.
VRAKKKKT
NICE SPOTTING, JEAN. HOW ARE THE TWO HANKS DOING?
IT'S SLOW GOING, BUT THEY SAY THEY'RE GETTING THERE.
THEY HAVE TO.
NONE OF THIS COUNTS FOR ANYTHING IF THEY FAIL.

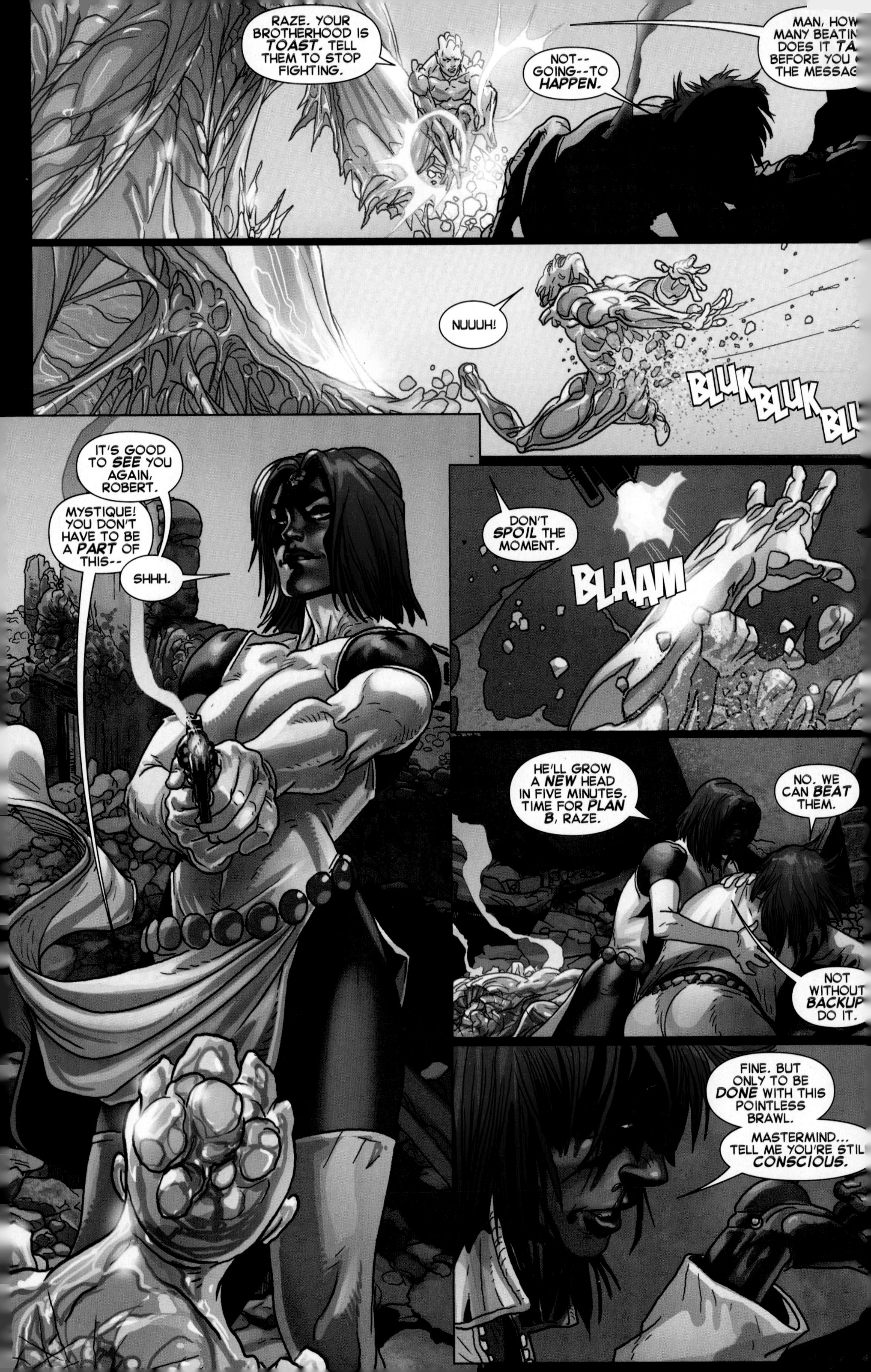
RAZE. YOUR BROTHERHOOD IS TOAST. TELL THEM TO STOP FIGHTING.
NOT-- GOING--TO HAPPEN.
MAN, HOW MANY BEATIN DOES IT TA BEFORE YOU THE MESSAG
NUUUH!
BLUK BLUK BL
IT'S GOOD TO SEE YOU AGAIN, ROBERT.
MYSTIQUE! YOU DON'T HAVE TO BE A PART OF THIS--
SHHH.
DON'T SPOIL THE MOMENT.
BLAAM
HE'LL GROW A NEW HEAD IN FIVE MINUTES. TIME FOR PLAN B, RAZE.
NO. WE CAN BEAT THEM.
NOT WITHOUT BACKUP DO IT.
FINE. BUT ONLY TO BE DONE WITH THIS POINTLESS BRAWL.
MASTERMIND... TELL ME YOU'RE STIL CONSCIOUS.

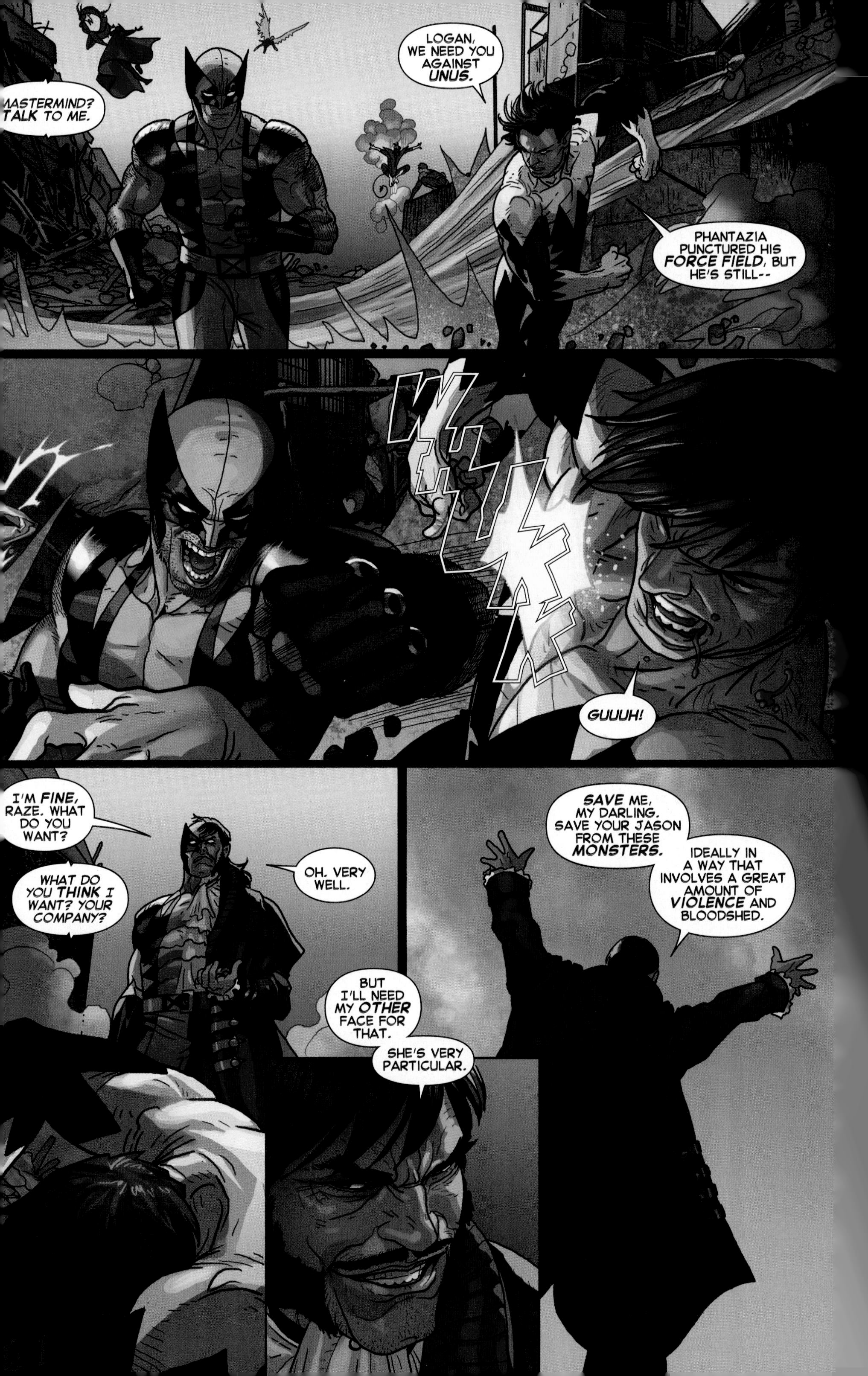
MASTERMIND? TALK TO ME.
LOGAN, WE NEED YOU AGAINST UNUS.
PHANTAZIA PUNCTURED HIS FORCE FIELD, BUT HE'S STILL--
WHAK
GUUUH!
I'M FINE, RAZE. WHAT DO YOU WANT?
WHAT DO YOU THINK I WANT? YOUR COMPANY?
OH. VERY WELL.
SAVE ME, MY DARLING. SAVE YOUR JASON FROM THESE MONSTERS.
IDEALLY IN A WAY THAT INVOLVES A GREAT AMOUNT OF VIOLENCE AND BLOODSHED.
BUT I'LL NEED MY OTHER FACE FOR THAT.
SHE'S VERY PARTICULAR.

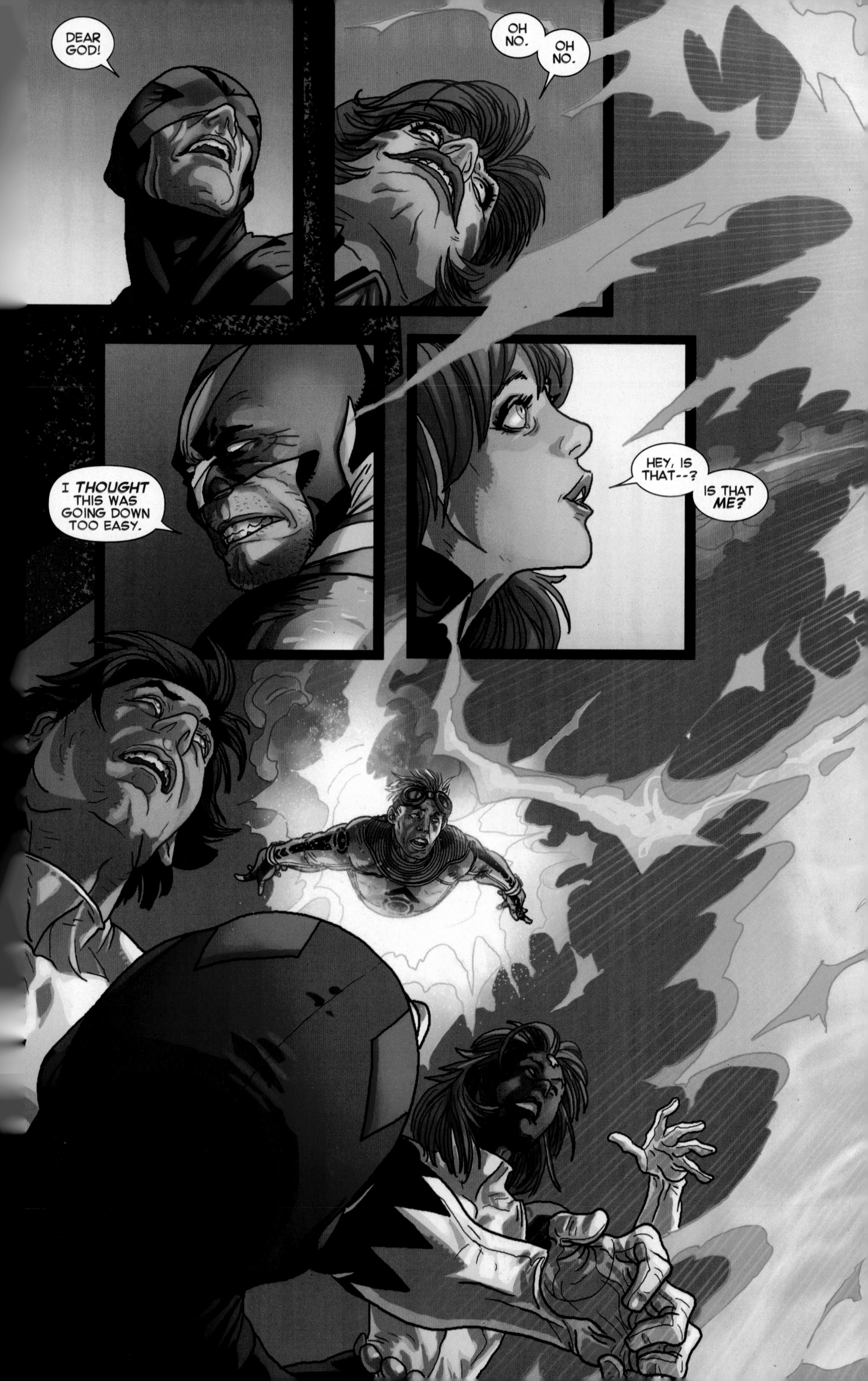
DEAR GOD!
OH NO.
OH NO.
I *THOUGHT* THIS WAS GOING DOWN TOO EASY.
HEY, IS THAT--?
IS THAT *ME?*

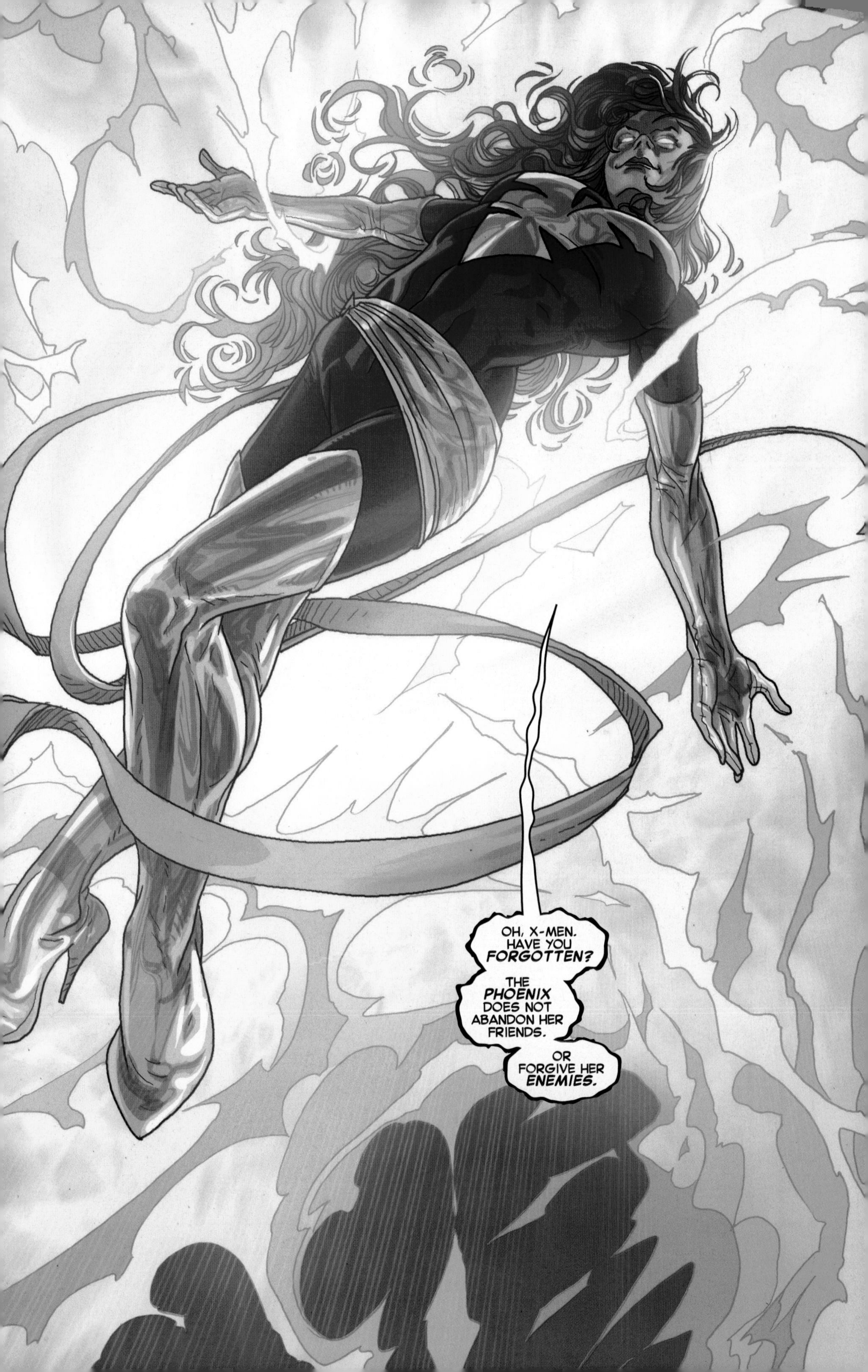
OH, X-MEN. HAVE YOU FORGOTTEN?
THE PHOENIX DOES NOT ABANDON HER FRIENDS.
OR FORGIVE HER ENEMIES.

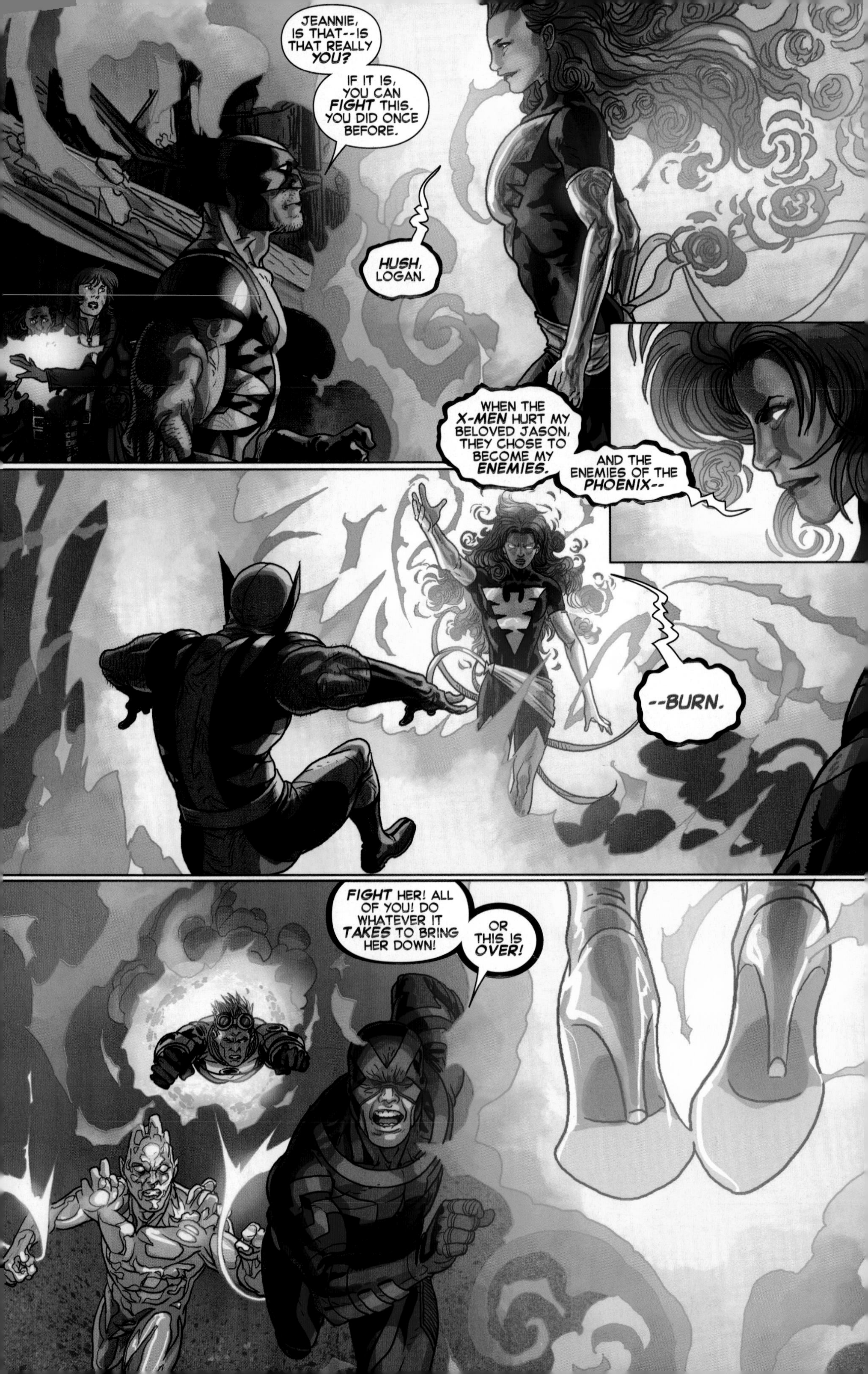
JEANNIE, IS THAT--IS THAT REALLY YOU?
IF IT IS, YOU CAN FIGHT THIS. YOU DID ONCE BEFORE.
HUSH, LOGAN.
WHEN THE X-MEN HURT MY BELOVED JASON, THEY CHOSE TO BECOME MY ENEMIES.
AND THE ENEMIES OF THE PHOENIX--
--BURN.
FIGHT HER! ALL OF YOU! DO WHATEVER IT TAKES TO BRING HER DOWN!
OR THIS IS OVER!

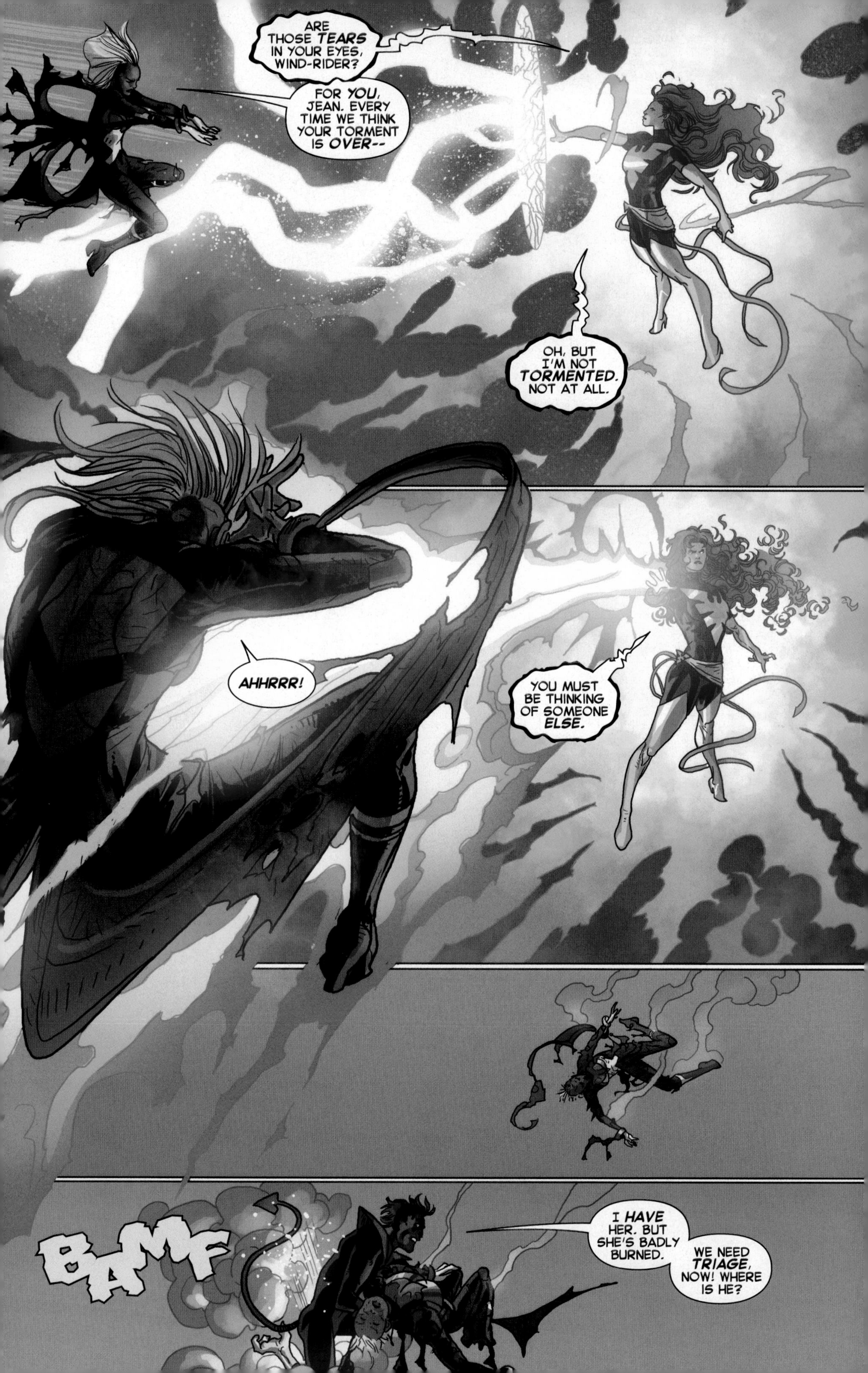
ARE THOSE TEARS IN YOUR EYES, WIND-RIDER?
FOR YOU, JEAN. EVERY TIME WE THINK YOUR TORMENT IS OVER--
OH, BUT I'M NOT TORMENTED. NOT AT ALL.
AHHRRR!
YOU MUST BE THINKING OF SOMEONE ELSE.
BAMF
I HAVE HER. BUT SHE'S BADLY BURNED.
WE NEED TRIAGE, NOW! WHERE IS HE?

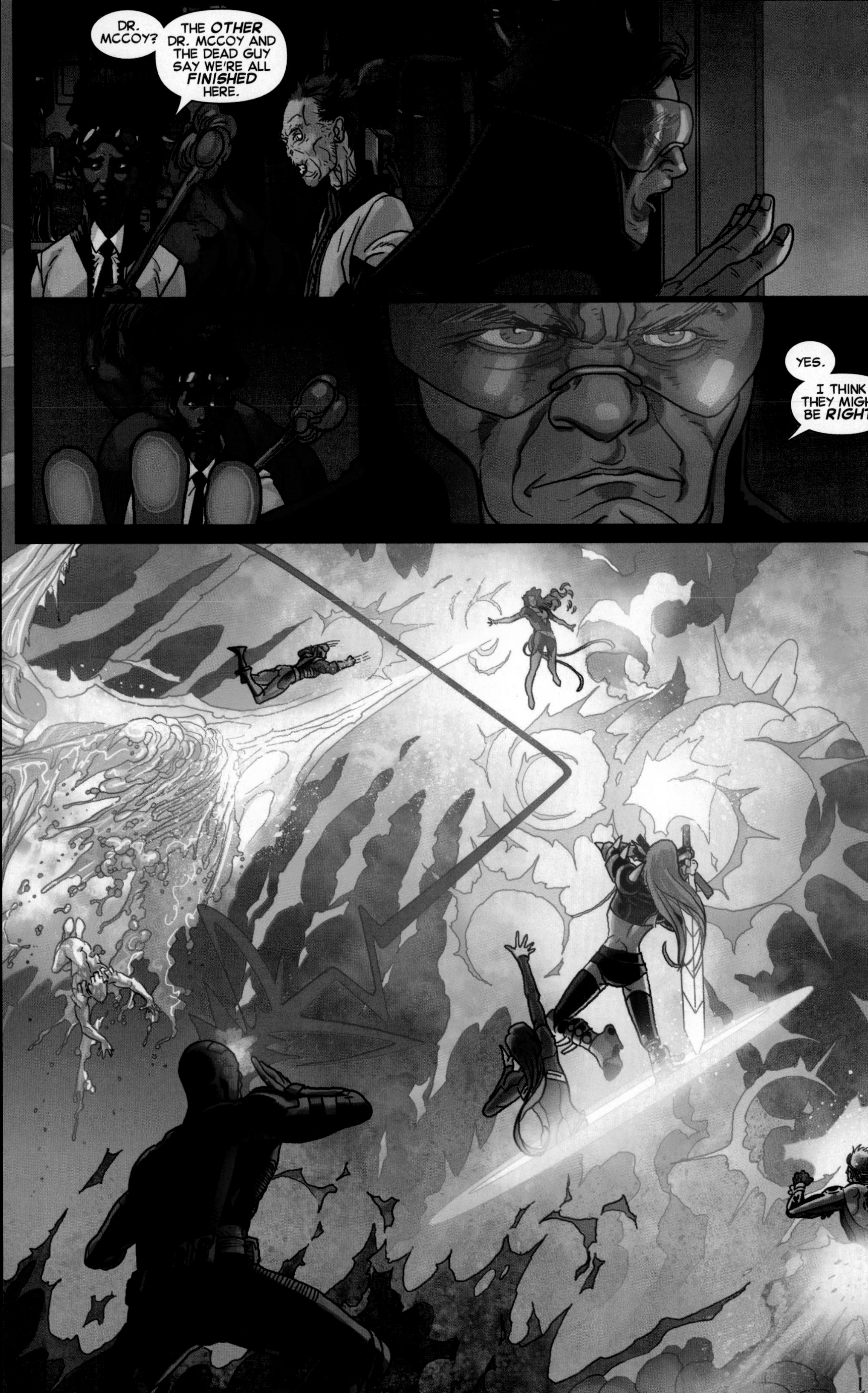
DR. MCCOY?
THE OTHER DR. MCCOY AND THE DEAD GUY SAY WE'RE ALL FINISHED HERE.
YES.
I THINK THEY MIGH BE RIGHT

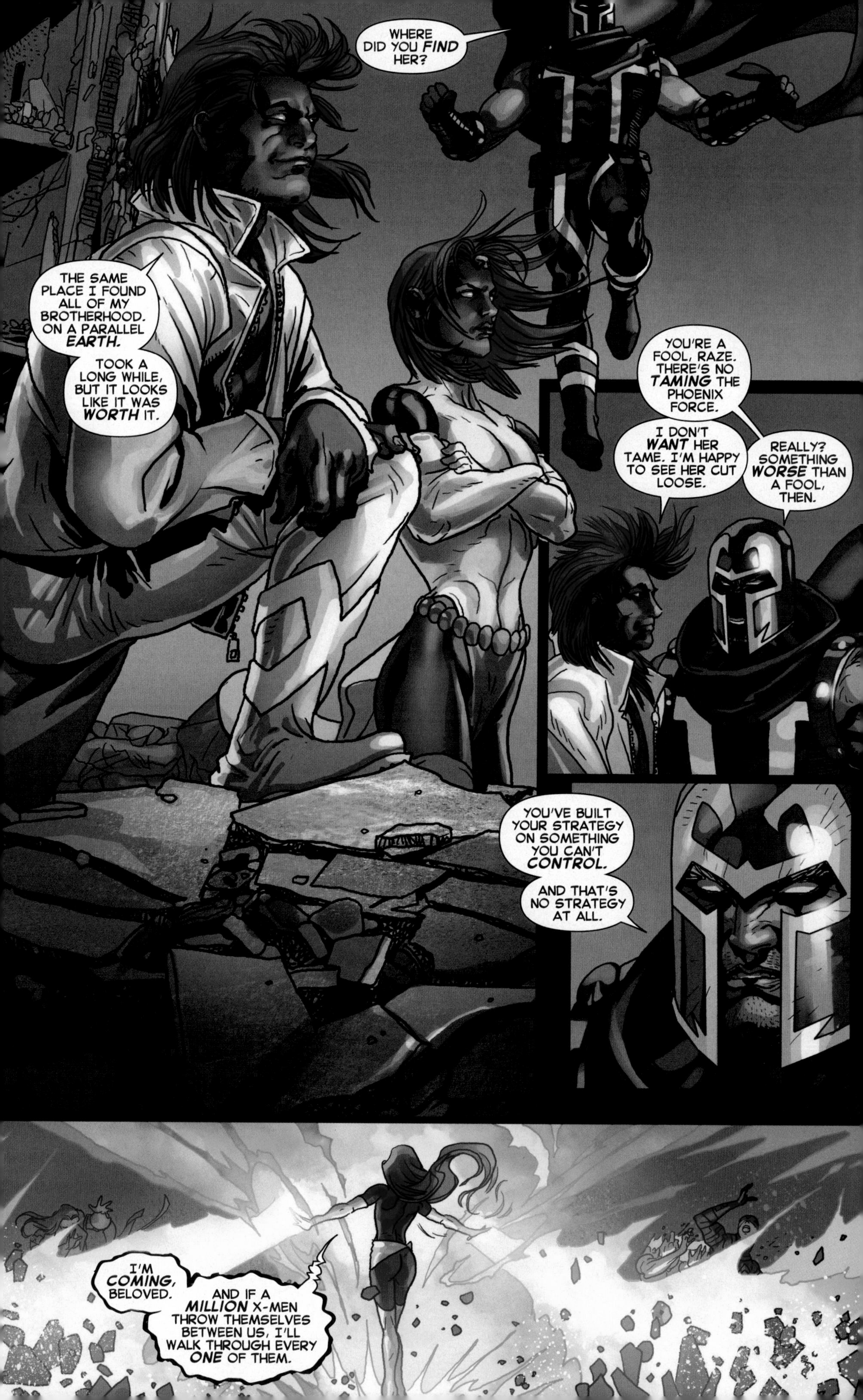
WHERE DID YOU FIND HER?
THE SAME PLACE I FOUND ALL OF MY BROTHERHOOD. ON A PARALLEL EARTH.
TOOK A LONG WHILE, BUT IT LOOKS LIKE IT WAS WORTH IT.
YOU'RE A FOOL, RAZE. THERE'S NO TAMING THE PHOENIX FORCE.
I DON'T WANT HER TAME. I'M HAPPY TO SEE HER CUT LOOSE.
REALLY? SOMETHING WORSE THAN A FOOL, THEN.
YOU'VE BUILT YOUR STRATEGY ON SOMETHING YOU CAN'T CONTROL.
AND THAT'S NO STRATEGY AT ALL.
I'M COMING, BELOVED.
AND IF A MILLION X-MEN THROW THEMSELVES BETWEEN US, I'LL WALK THROUGH EVERY ONE OF THEM.

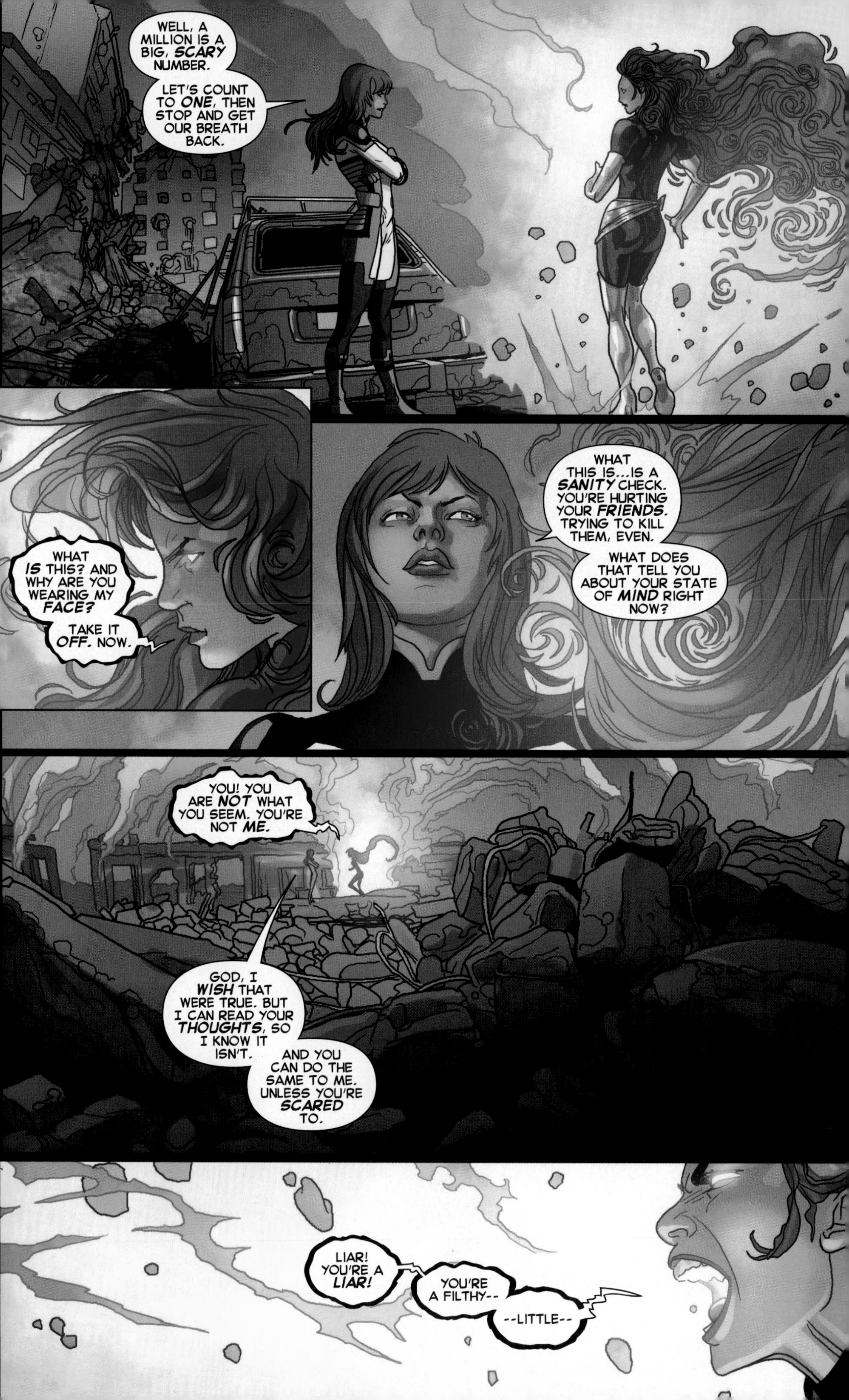
WELL, A MILLION IS A BIG, SCARY NUMBER.
LET'S COUNT TO ONE, THEN STOP AND GET OUR BREATH BACK.
WHAT IS THIS? AND WHY ARE YOU WEARING MY FACE?
TAKE IT OFF. NOW.
WHAT THIS IS...IS A SANITY CHECK. YOU'RE HURTING YOUR FRIENDS. TRYING TO KILL THEM, EVEN.
WHAT DOES THAT TELL YOU ABOUT YOUR STATE OF MIND RIGHT NOW?
YOU! YOU ARE NOT WHAT YOU SEEM. YOU'RE NOT ME.
GOD, I WISH THAT WERE TRUE. BUT I CAN READ YOUR THOUGHTS, SO I KNOW IT ISN'T.
AND YOU CAN DO THE SAME TO ME. UNLESS YOU'RE SCARED TO.
LIAR! YOU'RE A LIAR!
YOU'RE A FILTHY--
--LITTLE--

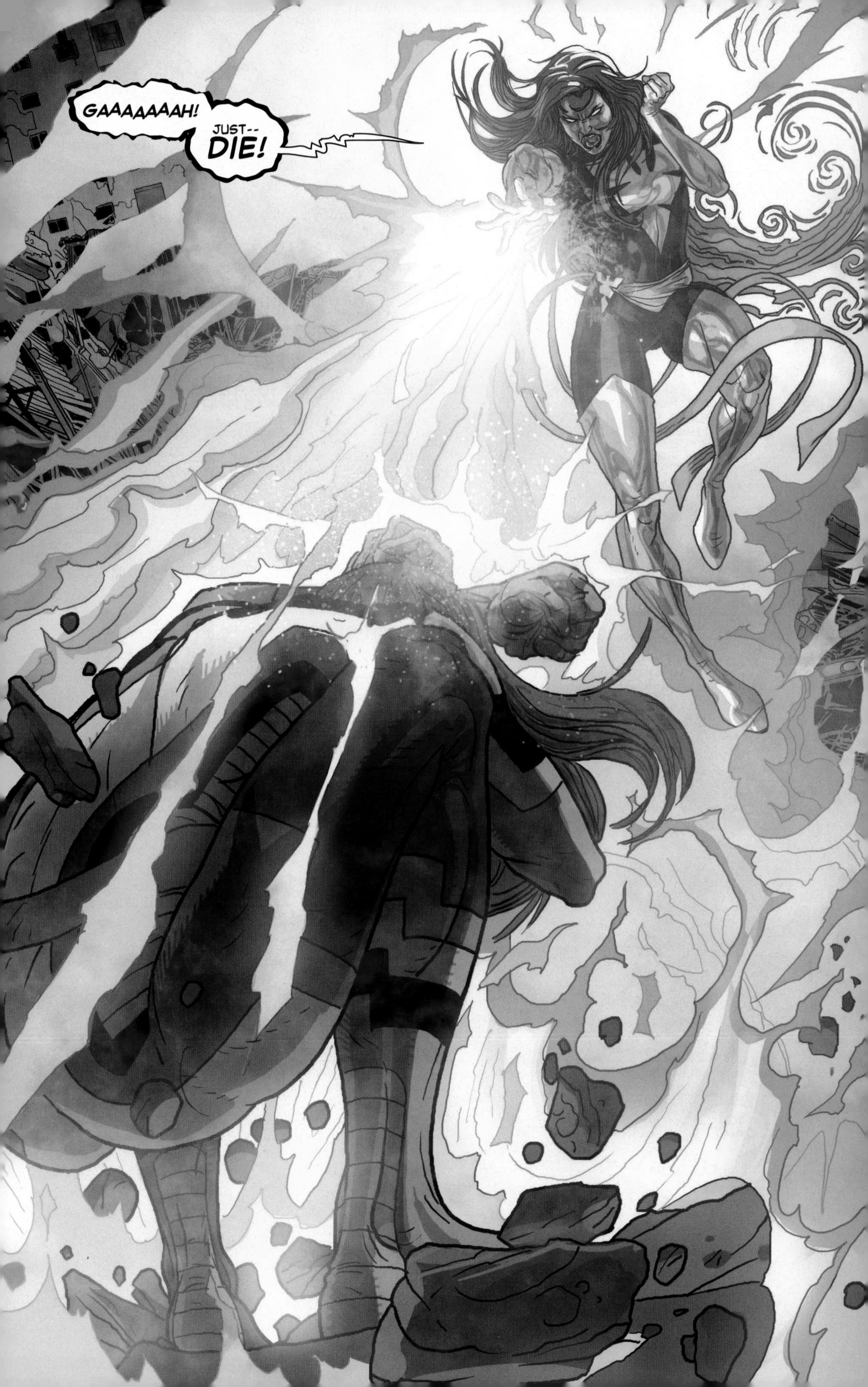
GAAAAAAAH!
JUST--
DIE!

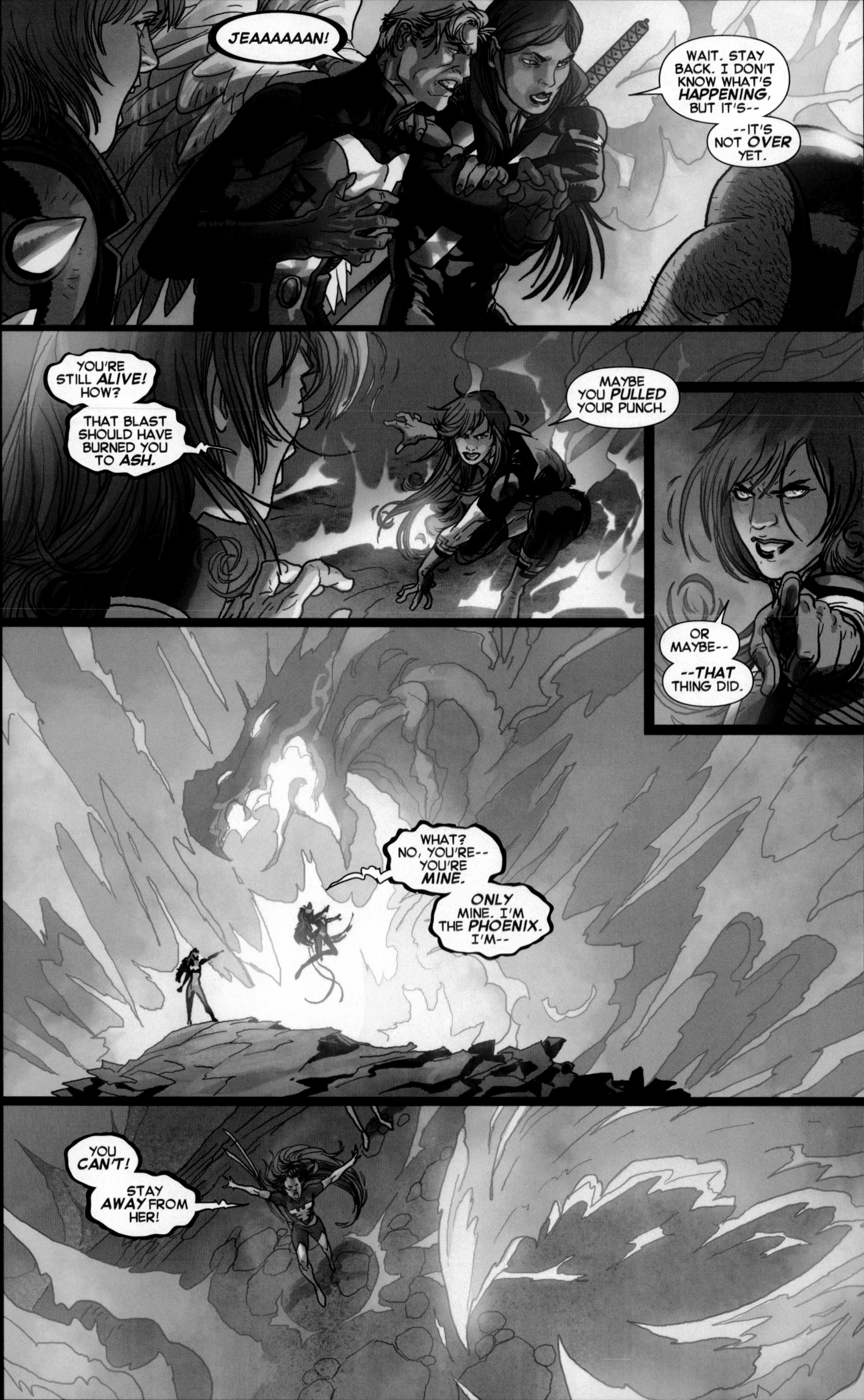
JEAAAAAAN!
WAIT. STAY BACK. I DON'T KNOW WHAT'S HAPPENING, BUT IT'S--
--IT'S NOT OVER YET.
YOU'RE STILL ALIVE! HOW?
THAT BLAST SHOULD HAVE BURNED YOU TO ASH.
MAYBE YOU PULLED YOUR PUNCH.
OR MAYBE--
--THAT THING DID.
WHAT? NO, YOU'RE-- YOU'RE MINE.
ONLY MINE. I'M THE PHOENIX. I'M--
YOU CAN'T!
STAY AWAY FROM HER!

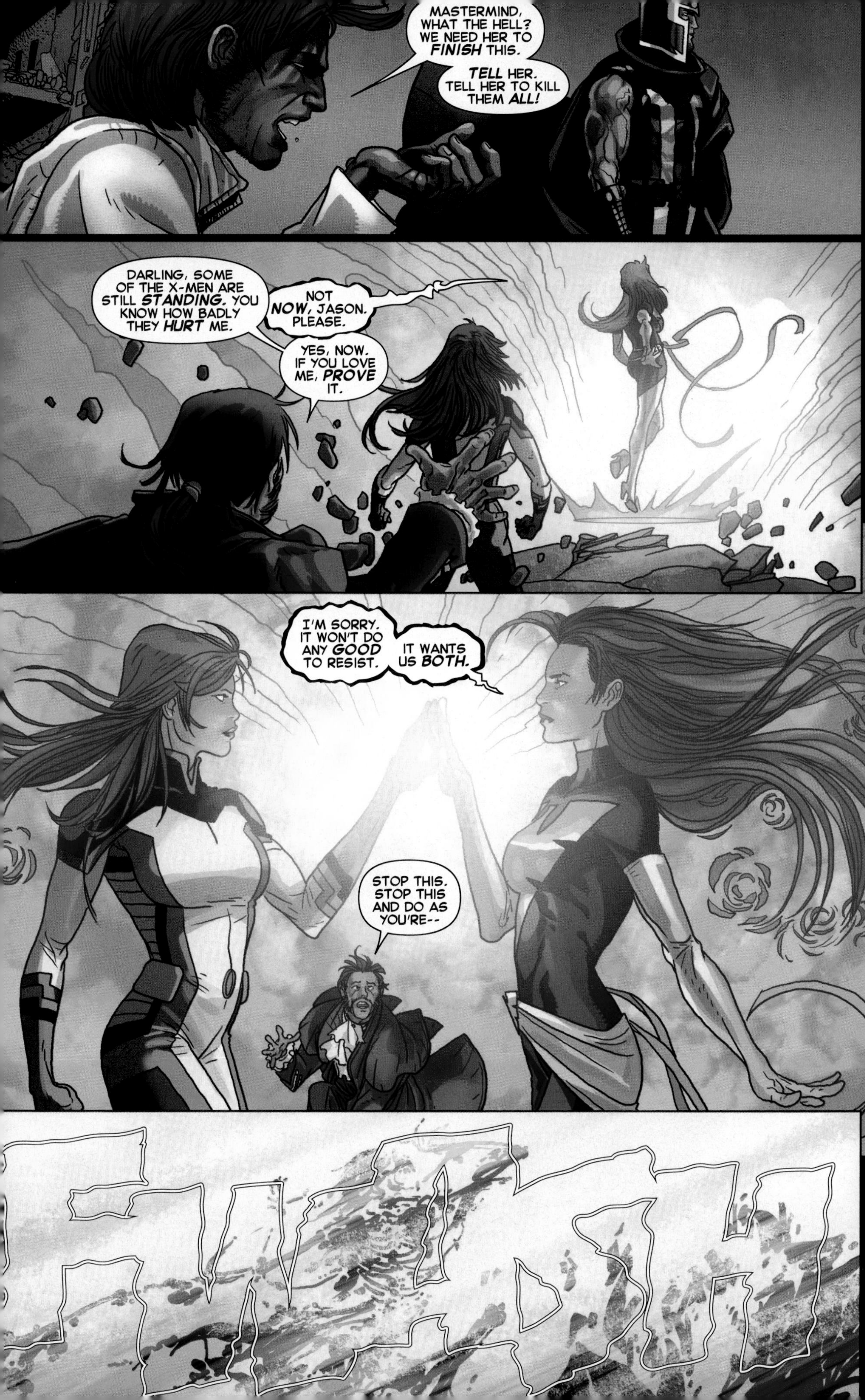
MASTERMIND, WHAT THE HELL? WE NEED HER TO FINISH THIS.
TELL HER. TELL HER TO KILL THEM ALL!
DARLING, SOME OF THE X-MEN ARE STILL STANDING. YOU KNOW HOW BADLY THEY HURT ME.
NOT NOW, JASON. PLEASE.
YES, NOW. IF YOU LOVE ME, PROVE IT.
I'M SORRY. IT WON'T DO ANY GOOD TO RESIST.
IT WANTS US BOTH.
STOP THIS. STOP THIS AND DO AS YOU'RE--

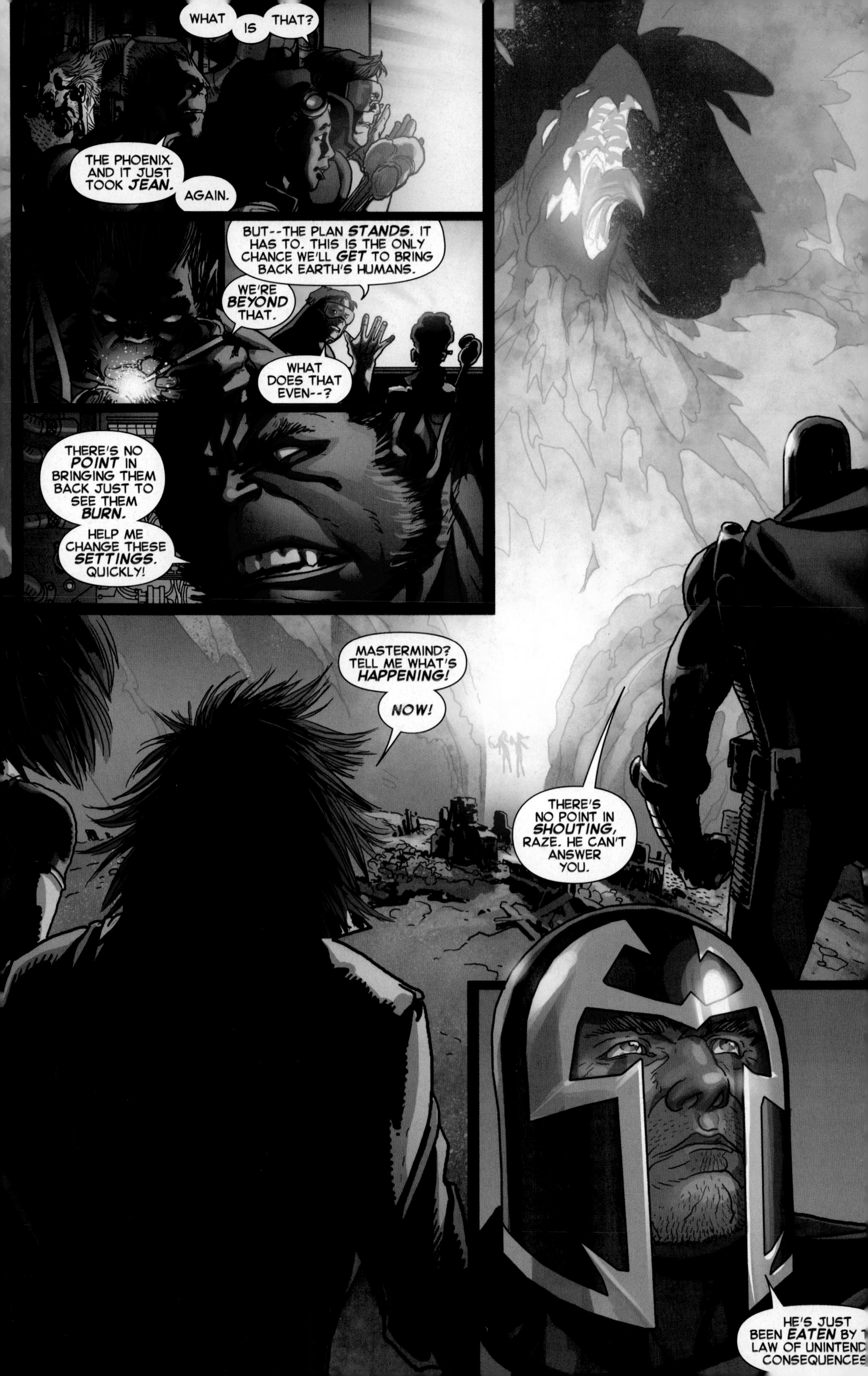
WHAT IS THAT?
THE PHOENIX. AND IT JUST TOOK JEAN.
AGAIN.
BUT--THE PLAN STANDS. IT HAS TO. THIS IS THE ONLY CHANCE WE'LL GET TO BRING BACK EARTH'S HUMANS.
WE'RE BEYOND THAT.
WHAT DOES THAT EVEN--?
THERE'S NO POINT IN BRINGING THEM BACK JUST TO SEE THEM BURN.
HELP ME CHANGE THESE SETTINGS. QUICKLY!
MASTERMIND? TELL ME WHAT'S HAPPENING!
NOW!
THERE'S NO POINT IN SHOUTING, RAZE. HE CAN'T ANSWER YOU.
HE'S JUST BEEN EATEN BY T
LAW OF UNINTEND
CONSEQUENCES

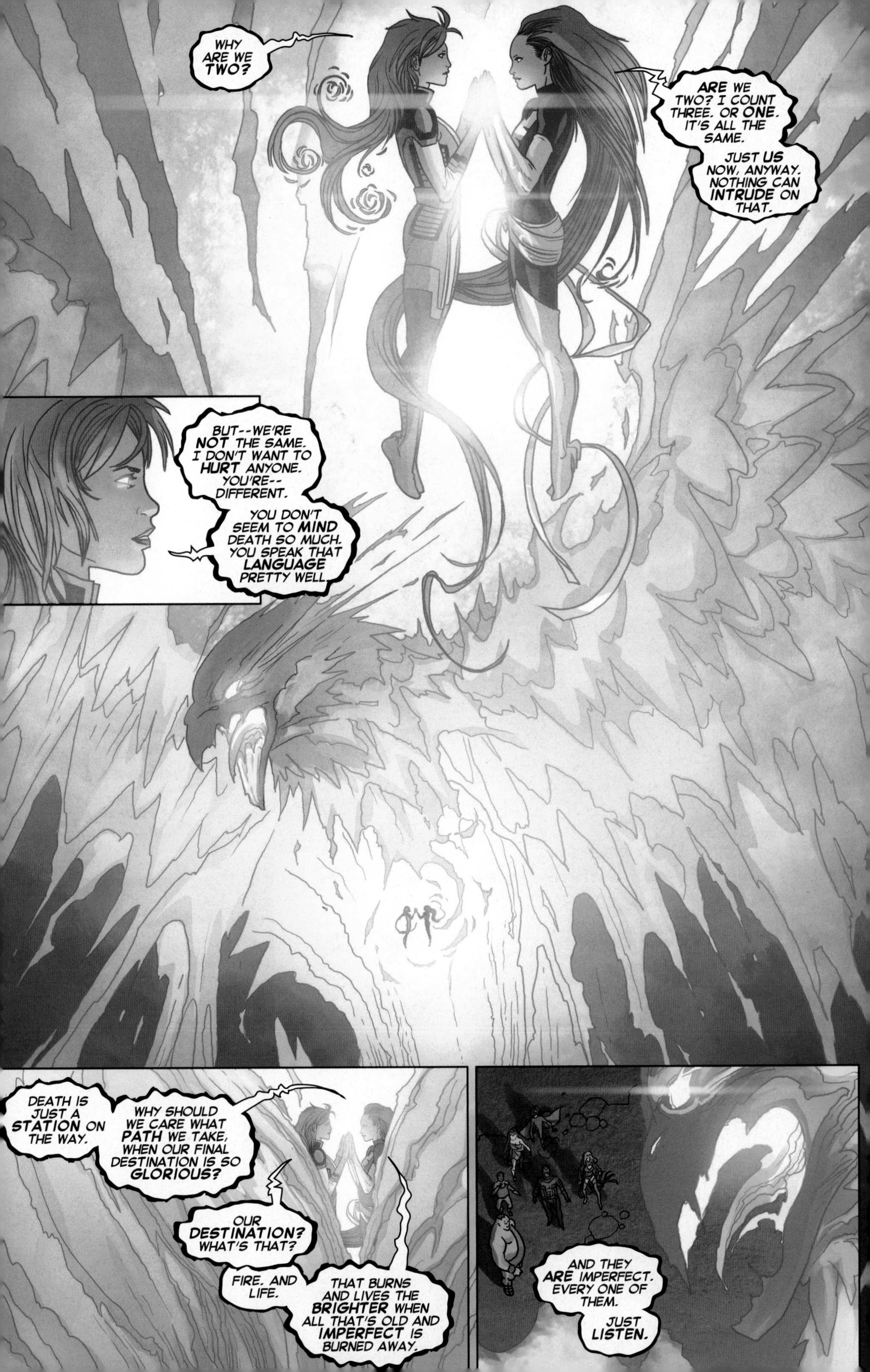

WHY ARE WE TWO?
ARE WE TWO? I COUNT THREE. OR ONE. IT'S ALL THE SAME.
JUST US NOW, ANYWAY. NOTHING CAN INTRUDE ON THAT.
BUT--WE'RE NOT THE SAME. I DON'T WANT TO HURT ANYONE. YOU'RE--DIFFERENT.
YOU DON'T SEEM TO MIND DEATH SO MUCH. YOU SPEAK THAT LANGUAGE PRETTY WELL.
DEATH IS JUST A STATION ON THE WAY.
WHY SHOULD WE CARE WHAT PATH WE TAKE, WHEN OUR FINAL DESTINATION IS SO GLORIOUS?
OUR DESTINATION? WHAT'S THAT?
FIRE. AND LIFE.
THAT BURNS AND LIVES THE BRIGHTER WHEN ALL THAT'S OLD AND IMPERFECT IS BURNED AWAY.
AND THEY ARE IMPERFECT. EVERY ONE OF THEM.
JUST LISTEN.

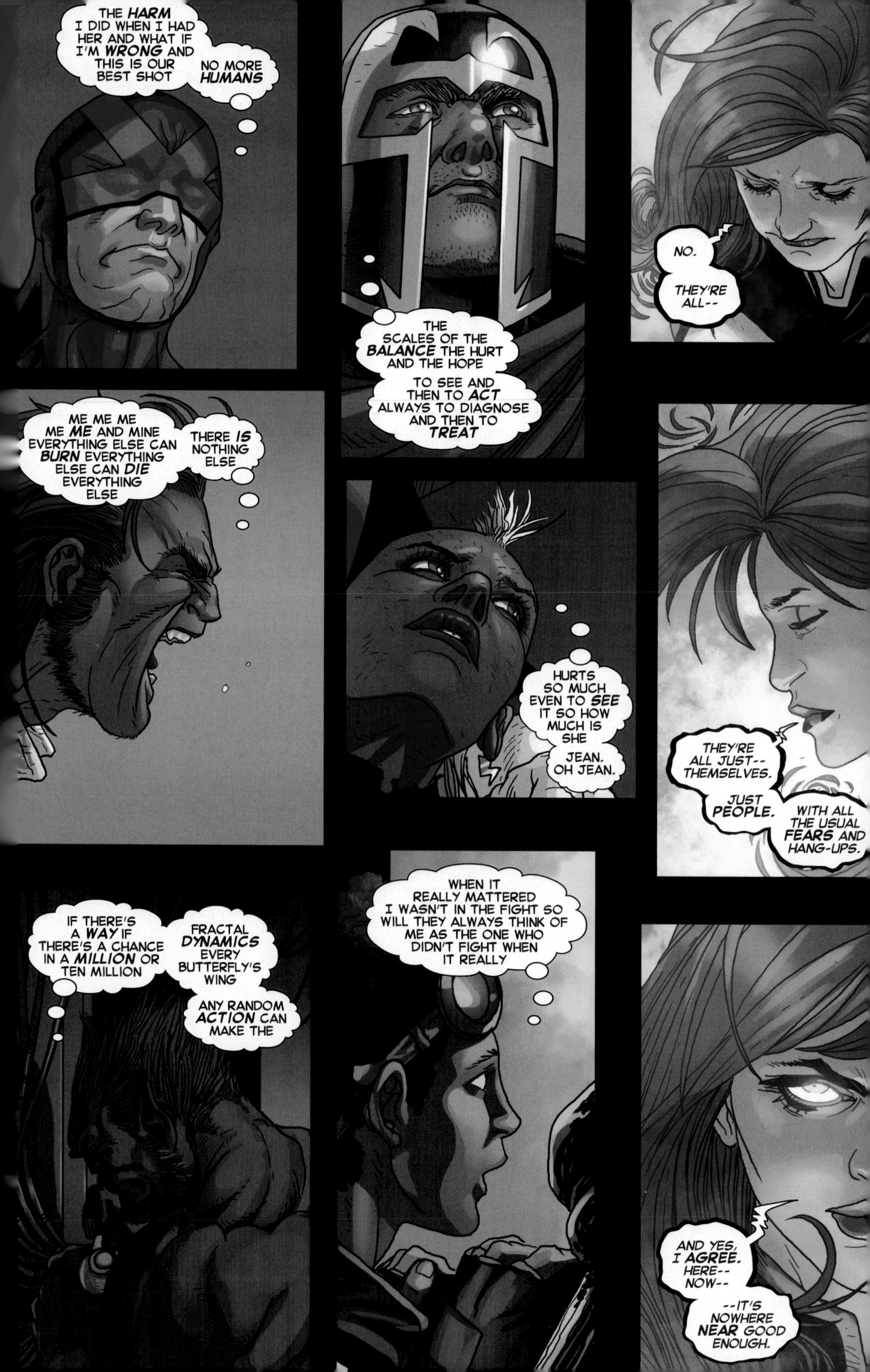
THE HARM I DID WHEN I HAD HER AND WHAT IF I'M WRONG AND THIS IS OUR BEST SHOT
NO MORE HUMANS
THE SCALES OF THE BALANCE THE HURT AND THE HOPE
TO SEE AND THEN TO ACT ALWAYS TO DIAGNOSE AND THEN TO TREAT
NO.
THEY'RE ALL--
ME ME ME ME ME AND MINE EVERYTHING ELSE CAN BURN EVERYTHING ELSE CAN DIE EVERYTHING ELSE
THERE IS NOTHING ELSE
HURTS SO MUCH EVEN TO SEE IT SO HOW MUCH IS SHE
JEAN. OH JEAN.
THEY'RE ALL JUST-- THEMSELVES.
JUST PEOPLE.
WITH ALL THE USUAL FEARS AND HANG-UPS.
IF THERE'S A WAY IF THERE'S A CHANCE IN A MILLION OR TEN MILLION
FRACTAL DYNAMICS EVERY BUTTERFLY'S WING
ANY RANDOM ACTION CAN MAKE THE
WHEN IT REALLY MATTERED I WASN'T IN THE FIGHT SO WILL THEY ALWAYS THINK OF ME AS THE ONE WHO DIDN'T FIGHT WHEN IT REALLY
AND YES, I AGREE. HERE-- NOW--
--IT'S NOWHERE NEAR GOOD ENOUGH.

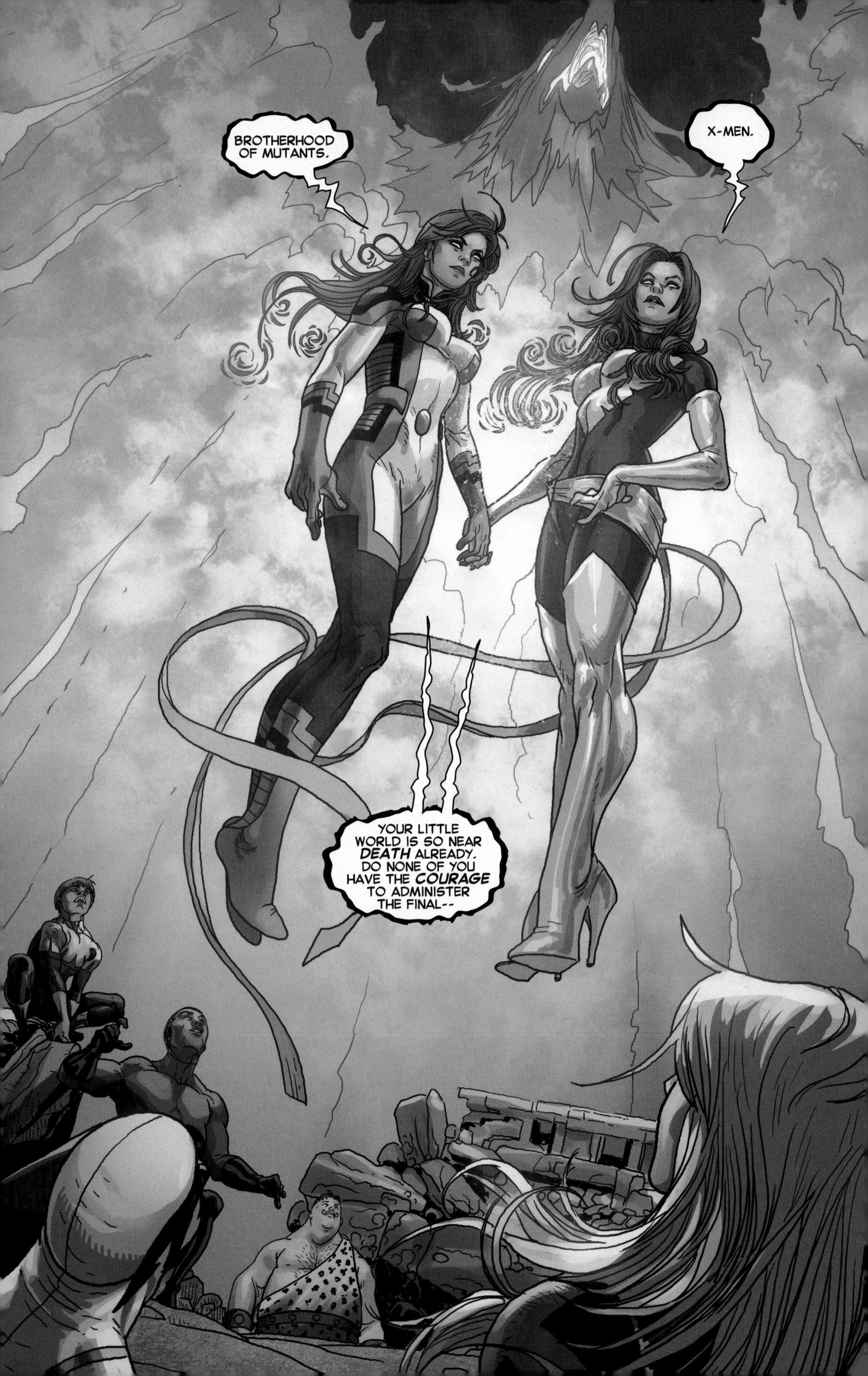
BROTHERHOOD OF MUTANTS.
X-MEN.
YOUR LITTLE WORLD IS SO NEAR DEATH ALREADY. DO NONE OF YOU HAVE THE COURAGE TO ADMINISTER THE FINAL--

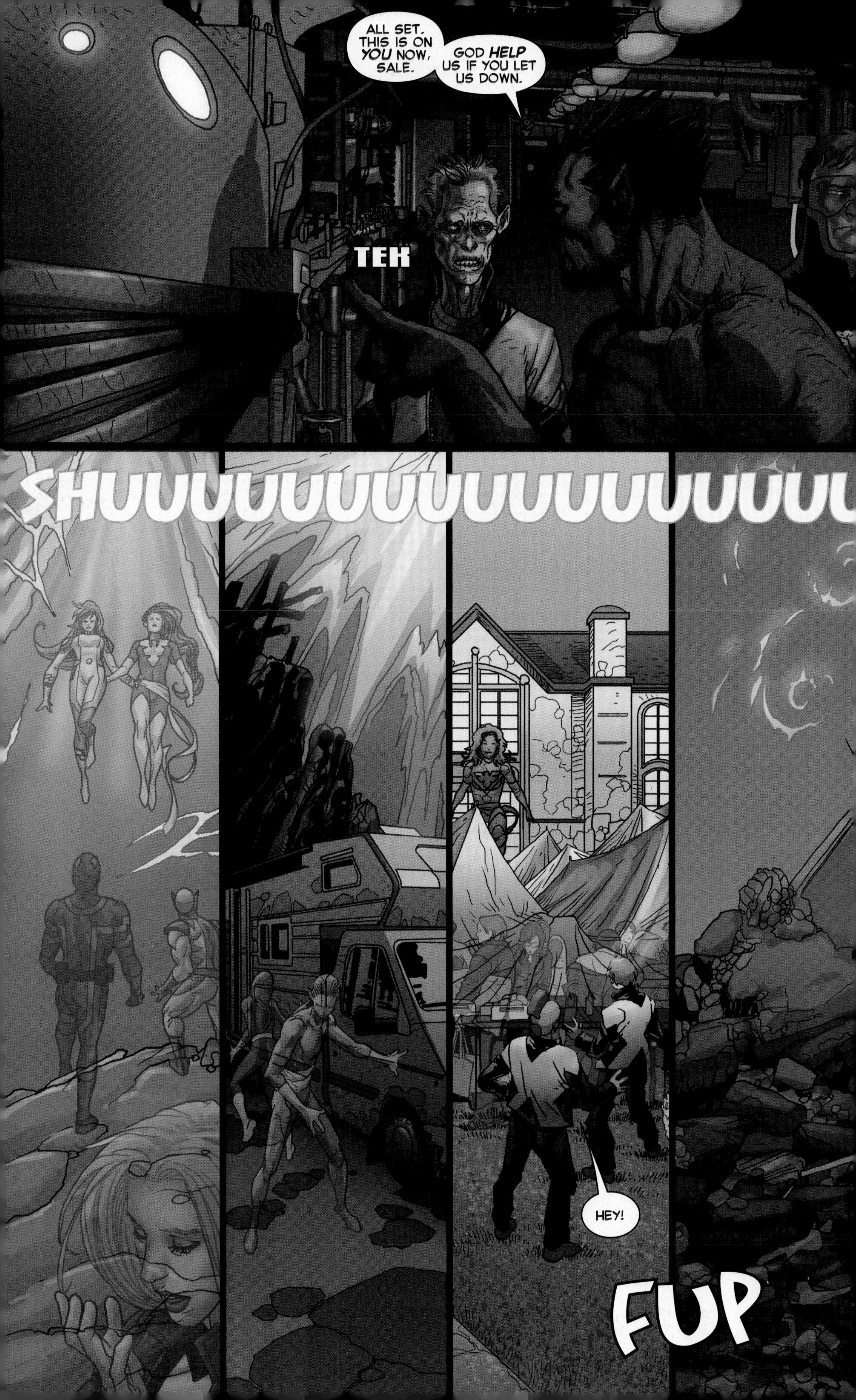
ALL SET. THIS IS ON YOU NOW, SALE.
GOD HELP US IF YOU LET US DOWN.
TEK
SHUUUUUUUUUUUUUUU
HEY!
FUP

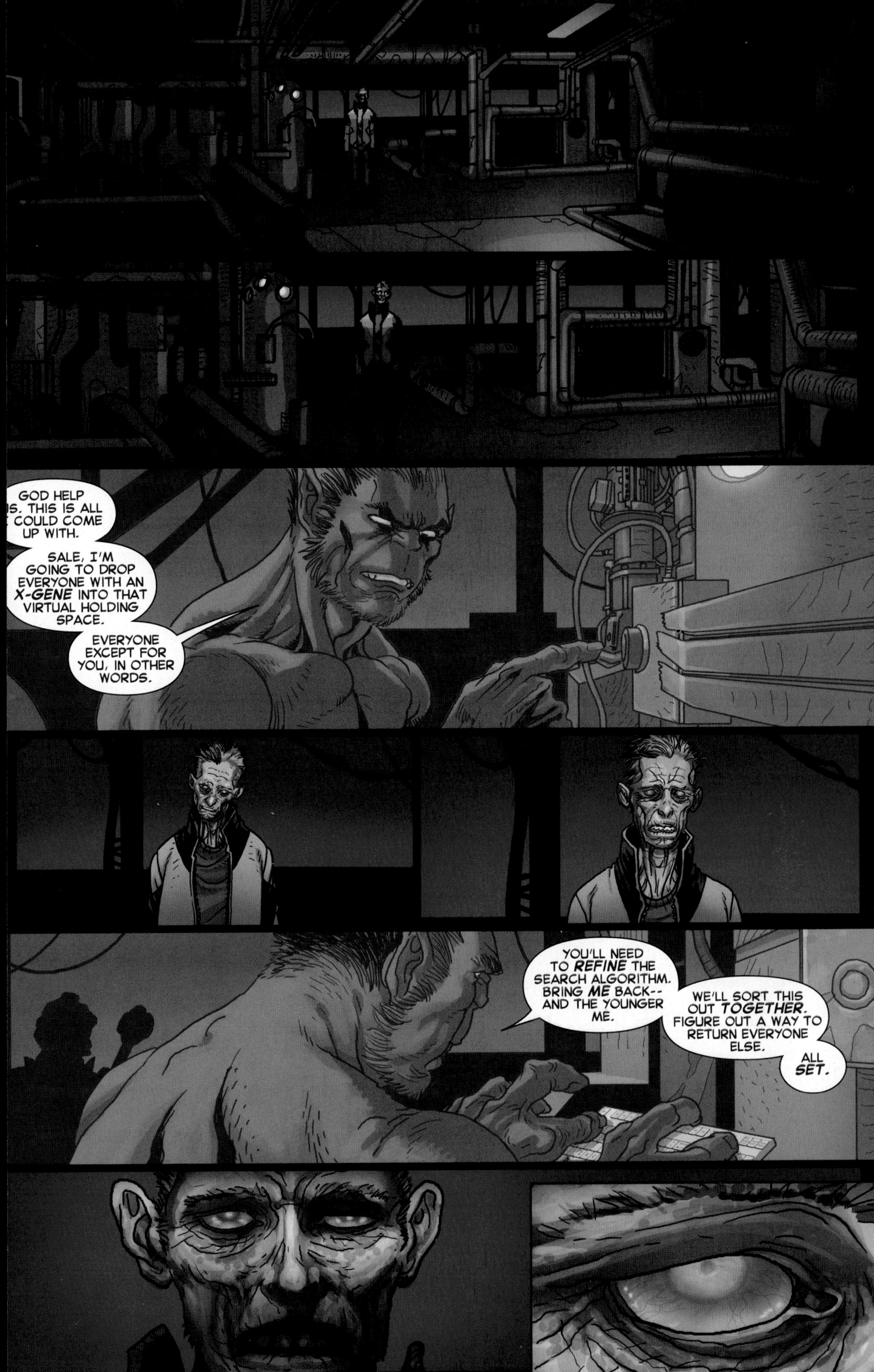
GOD HELP S. THIS IS ALL COULD COME UP WITH.
SALE, I'M GOING TO DROP EVERYONE WITH AN X-GENE INTO THAT VIRTUAL HOLDING SPACE.
EVERYONE EXCEPT FOR YOU, IN OTHER WORDS.
YOU'LL NEED TO REFINE THE SEARCH ALGORITHM. BRING ME BACK-- AND THE YOUNGER ME.
WE'LL SORT THIS OUT TOGETHER. FIGURE OUT A WAY TO RETURN EVERYONE ELSE.
ALL SET.

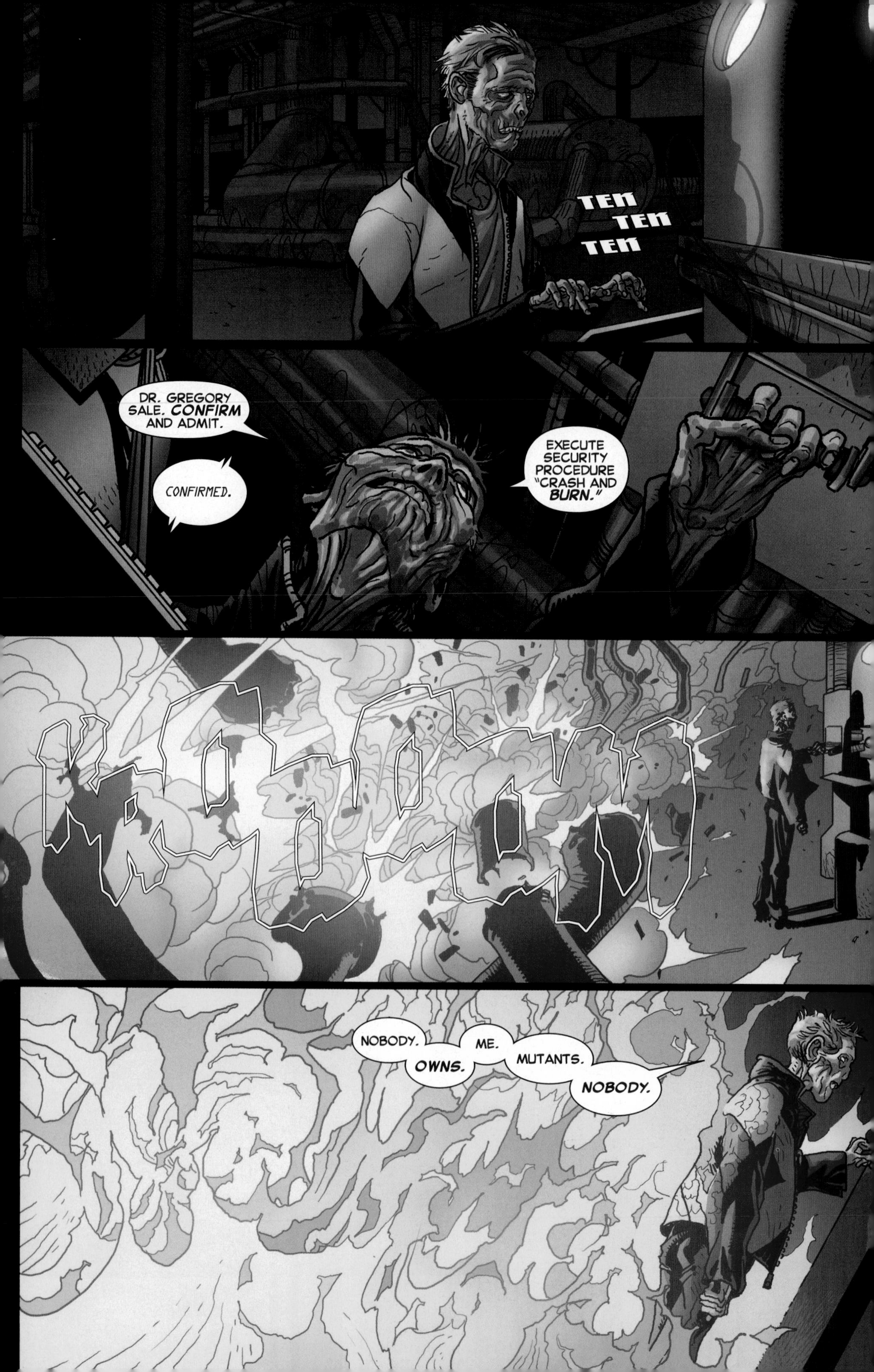
TEK
TEK
TEK
DR. GREGORY SALE. **CONFIRM** AND ADMIT.
CONFIRMED.
EXECUTE SECURITY PROCEDURE "CRASH AND **BURN.**"
KRA-BOOOOM
NOBODY.
OWNS.
ME.
MUTANTS.
NOBODY.

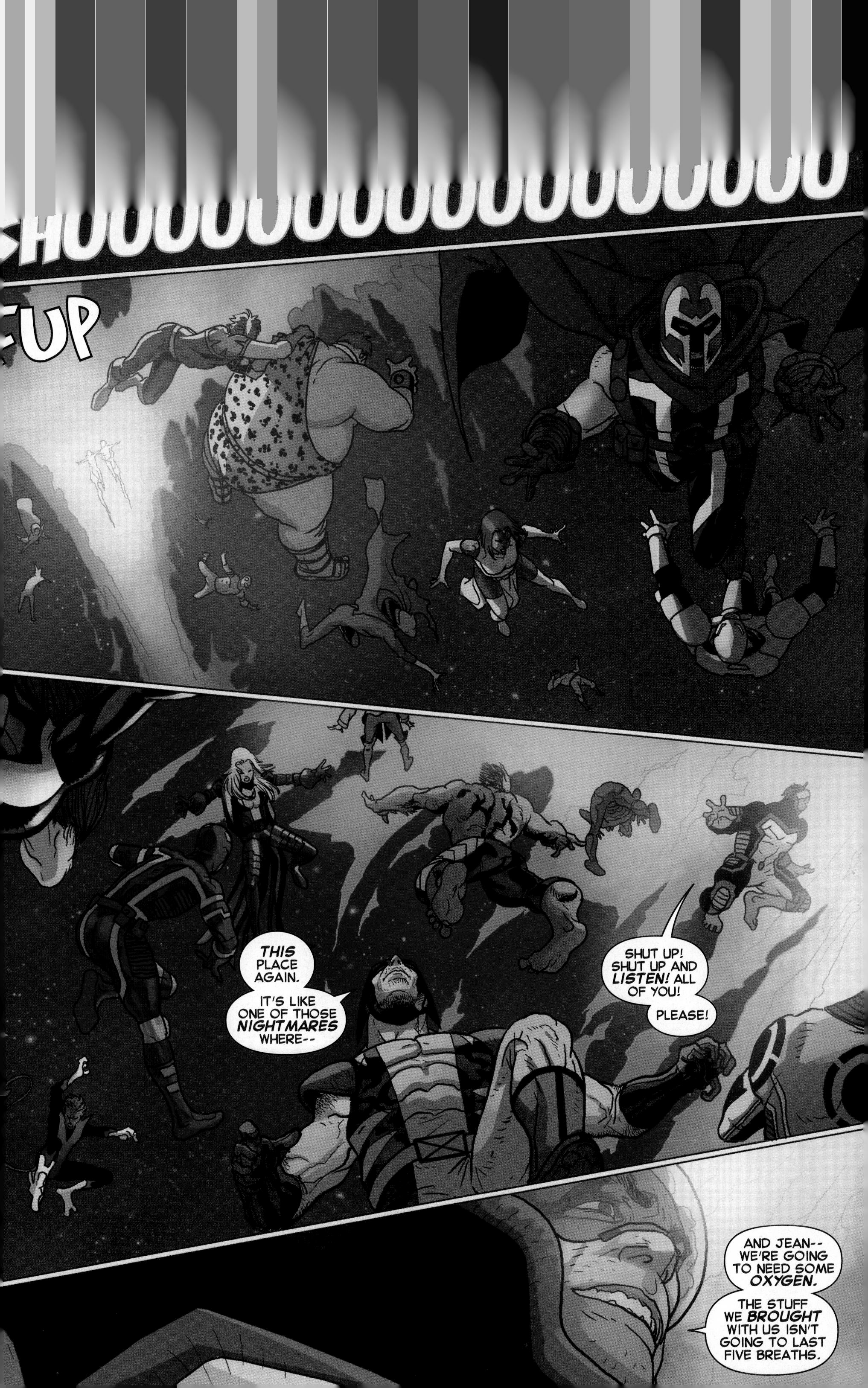
CHOUUUUUUUUUUUUUUUUU
FUP
THIS PLACE AGAIN.
IT'S LIKE ONE OF THOSE NIGHTMARES WHERE--
SHUT UP! SHUT UP AND LISTEN! ALL OF YOU!
PLEASE!
AND JEAN--WE'RE GOING TO NEED SOME OXYGEN.
THE STUFF WE BROUGHT WITH US ISN'T GOING TO LAST FIVE BREATHS.

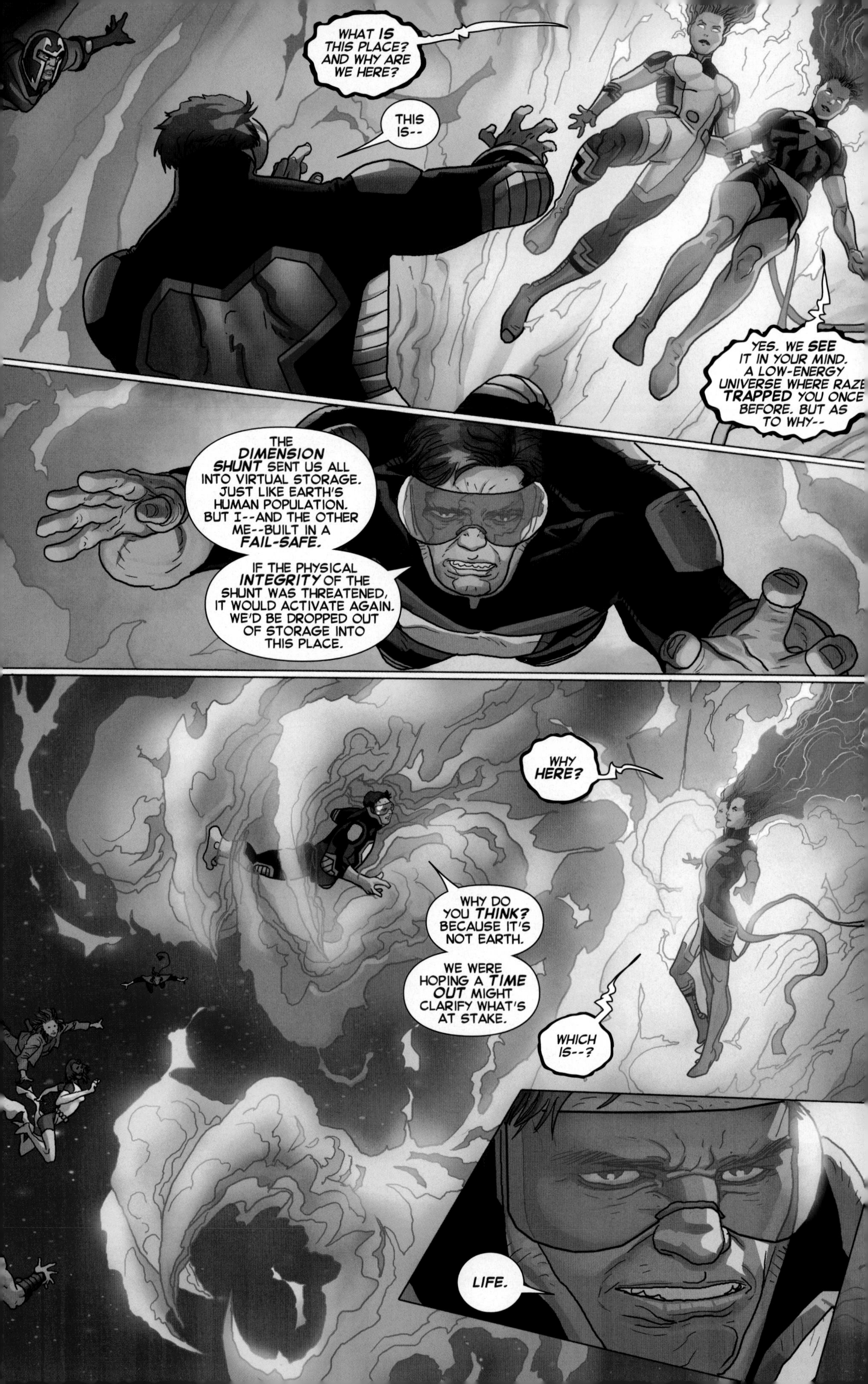
WHAT IS THIS PLACE? AND WHY ARE WE HERE?
THIS IS--
YES. WE SEE IT IN YOUR MIND. A LOW-ENERGY UNIVERSE WHERE RAZE TRAPPED YOU ONCE BEFORE. BUT AS TO WHY--
THE DIMENSION SHUNT SENT US ALL INTO VIRTUAL STORAGE. JUST LIKE EARTH'S HUMAN POPULATION. BUT I--AND THE OTHER ME--BUILT IN A FAIL-SAFE.
IF THE PHYSICAL INTEGRITY OF THE SHUNT WAS THREATENED, IT WOULD ACTIVATE AGAIN. WE'D BE DROPPED OUT OF STORAGE INTO THIS PLACE.
WHY HERE?
WHY DO YOU THINK? BECAUSE IT'S NOT EARTH.
WE WERE HOPING A TIME OUT MIGHT CLARIFY WHAT'S AT STAKE.
WHICH IS--?
LIFE.

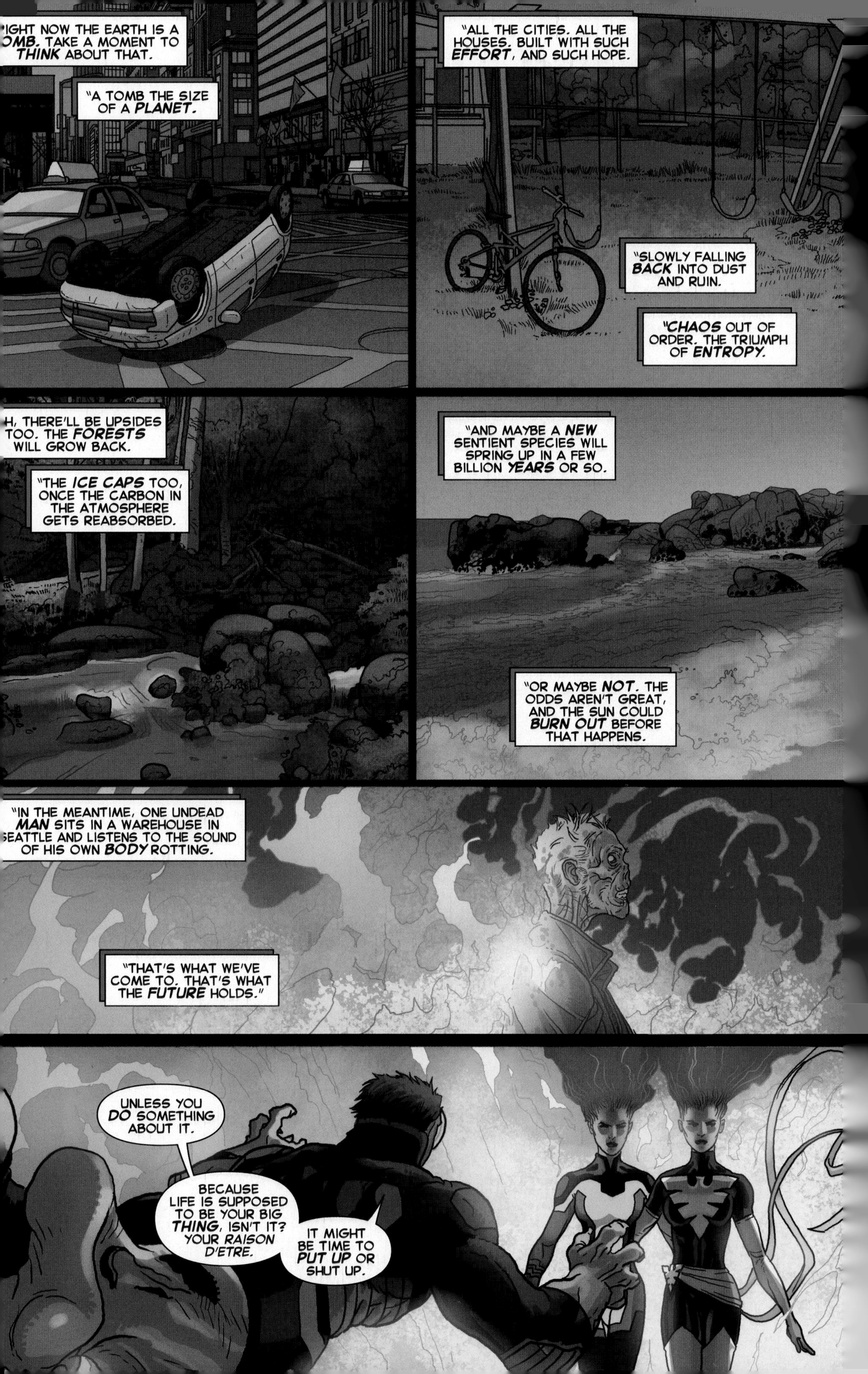
"IGHT NOW THE EARTH IS A OMB. TAKE A MOMENT TO THINK ABOUT THAT.
"A TOMB THE SIZE OF A PLANET.
"ALL THE CITIES. ALL THE HOUSES. BUILT WITH SUCH EFFORT, AND SUCH HOPE.
"SLOWLY FALLING BACK INTO DUST AND RUIN.
"CHAOS OUT OF ORDER. THE TRIUMPH OF ENTROPY.
H, THERE'LL BE UPSIDES TOO. THE FORESTS WILL GROW BACK.
"THE ICE CAPS TOO, ONCE THE CARBON IN THE ATMOSPHERE GETS REABSORBED.
"AND MAYBE A NEW SENTIENT SPECIES WILL SPRING UP IN A FEW BILLION YEARS OR SO.
"OR MAYBE NOT. THE ODDS AREN'T GREAT, AND THE SUN COULD BURN OUT BEFORE THAT HAPPENS.
"IN THE MEANTIME, ONE UNDEAD MAN SITS IN A WAREHOUSE IN EATTLE AND LISTENS TO THE SOUND OF HIS OWN BODY ROTTING.
"THAT'S WHAT WE'VE COME TO. THAT'S WHAT THE FUTURE HOLDS."
UNLESS YOU DO SOMETHING ABOUT IT.
BECAUSE LIFE IS SUPPOSED TO BE YOUR BIG THING, ISN'T IT? YOUR RAISON D'ETRE.
IT MIGHT BE TIME TO PUT UP OR SHUT UP.

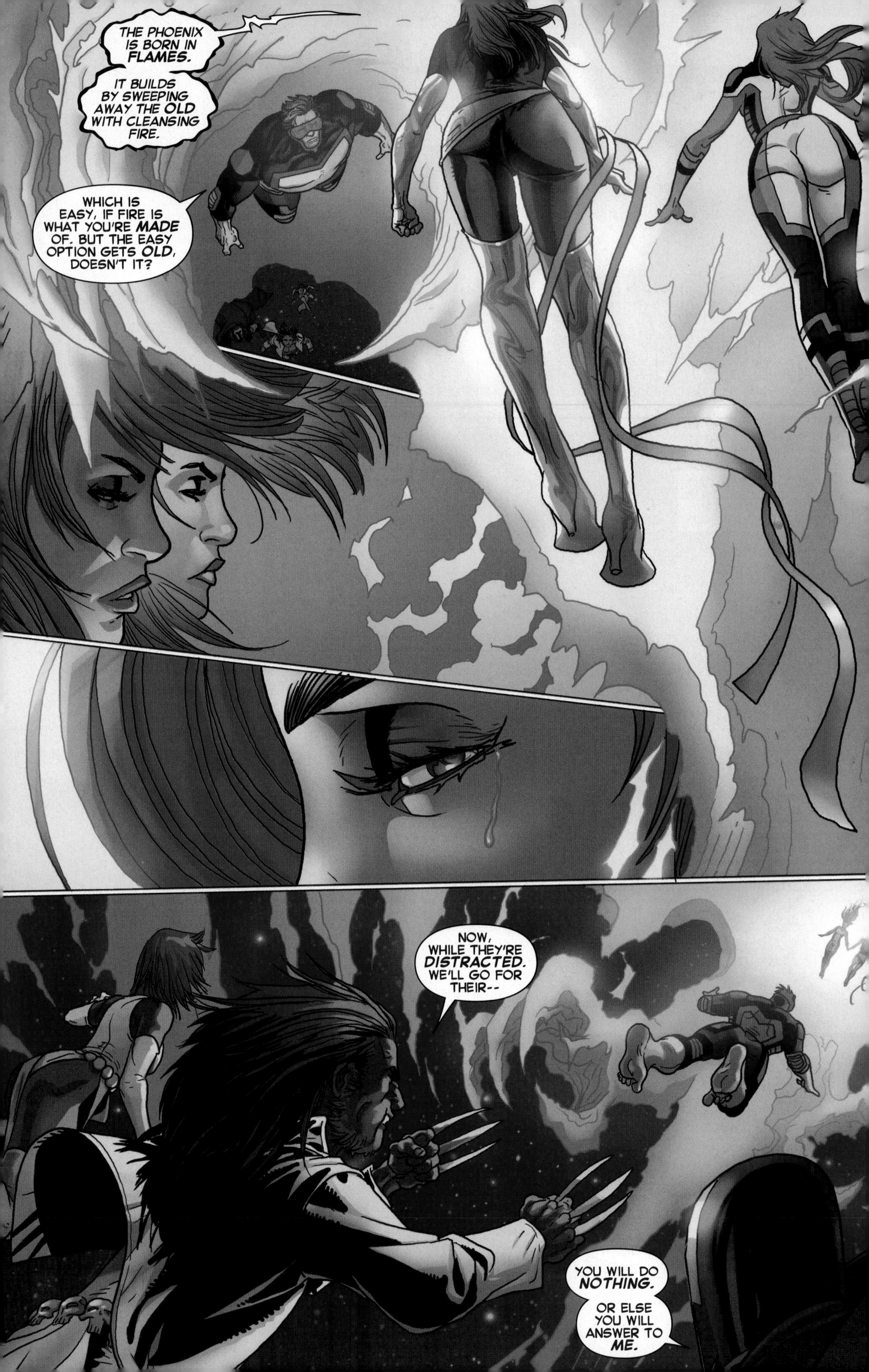
THE PHOENIX IS BORN IN FLAMES.
IT BUILDS BY SWEEPING AWAY THE OLD WITH CLEANSING FIRE.
WHICH IS EASY, IF FIRE IS WHAT YOU'RE MADE OF. BUT THE EASY OPTION GETS OLD, DOESN'T IT?
NOW, WHILE THEY'RE DISTRACTED. WE'LL GO FOR THEIR--
YOU WILL DO NOTHING.
OR ELSE YOU WILL ANSWER TO ME.

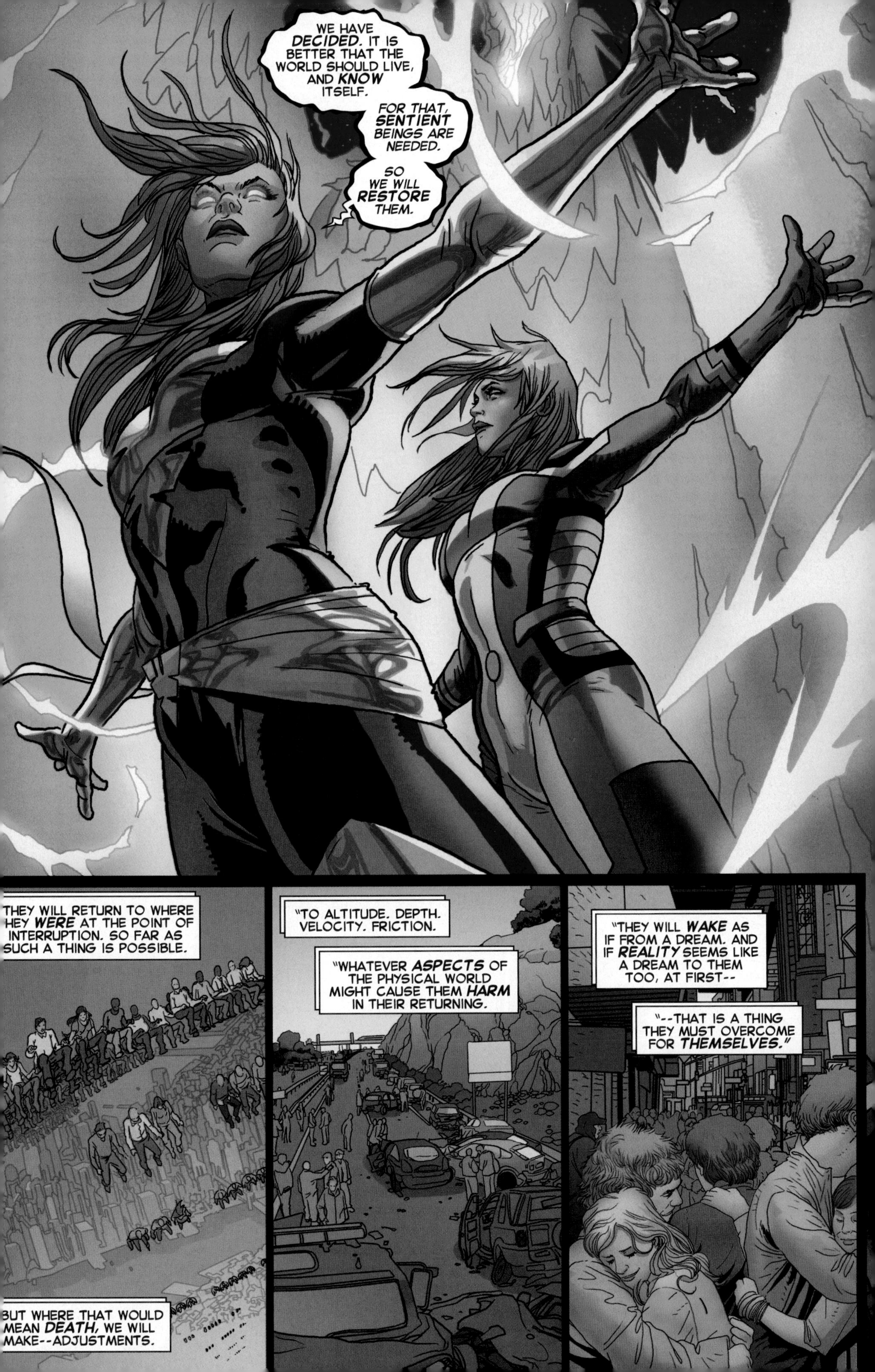
WE HAVE DECIDED. IT IS BETTER THAT THE WORLD SHOULD LIVE, AND KNOW ITSELF.
FOR THAT, SENTIENT BEINGS ARE NEEDED.
SO WE WILL RESTORE THEM.
THEY WILL RETURN TO WHERE HEY WERE AT THE POINT OF INTERRUPTION. SO FAR AS SUCH A THING IS POSSIBLE.
BUT WHERE THAT WOULD MEAN DEATH, WE WILL MAKE--ADJUSTMENTS.
"TO ALTITUDE. DEPTH. VELOCITY. FRICTION.
"WHATEVER ASPECTS OF THE PHYSICAL WORLD MIGHT CAUSE THEM HARM IN THEIR RETURNING.
"THEY WILL WAKE AS IF FROM A DREAM. AND IF REALITY SEEMS LIKE A DREAM TO THEM TOO, AT FIRST--
"--THAT IS A THING THEY MUST OVERCOME FOR THEMSELVES."

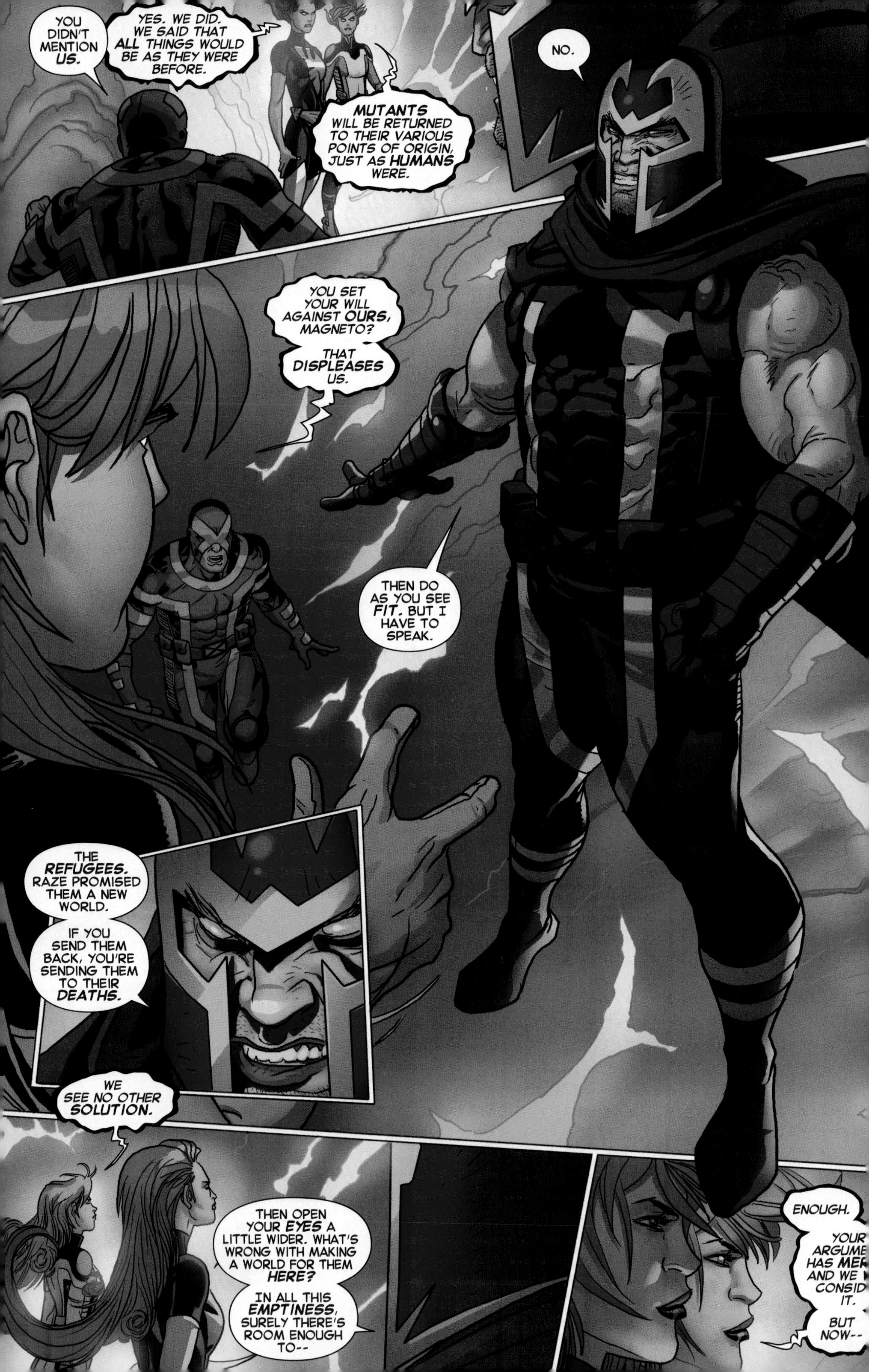
YOU DIDN'T MENTION US.
YES. WE DID. WE SAID THAT ALL THINGS WOULD BE AS THEY WERE BEFORE.
MUTANTS WILL BE RETURNED TO THEIR VARIOUS POINTS OF ORIGIN, JUST AS HUMANS WERE.
NO.
YOU SET YOUR WILL AGAINST OURS, MAGNETO?
THAT DISPLEASES US.
THEN DO AS YOU SEE FIT. BUT I HAVE TO SPEAK.
THE REFUGEES. RAZE PROMISED THEM A NEW WORLD.
IF YOU SEND THEM BACK, YOU'RE SENDING THEM TO THEIR DEATHS.
WE SEE NO OTHER SOLUTION.
THEN OPEN YOUR EYES A LITTLE WIDER. WHAT'S WRONG WITH MAKING A WORLD FOR THEM HERE?
IN ALL THIS EMPTINESS, SURELY THERE'S ROOM ENOUGH TO--
ENOUGH.
BUT NOW--

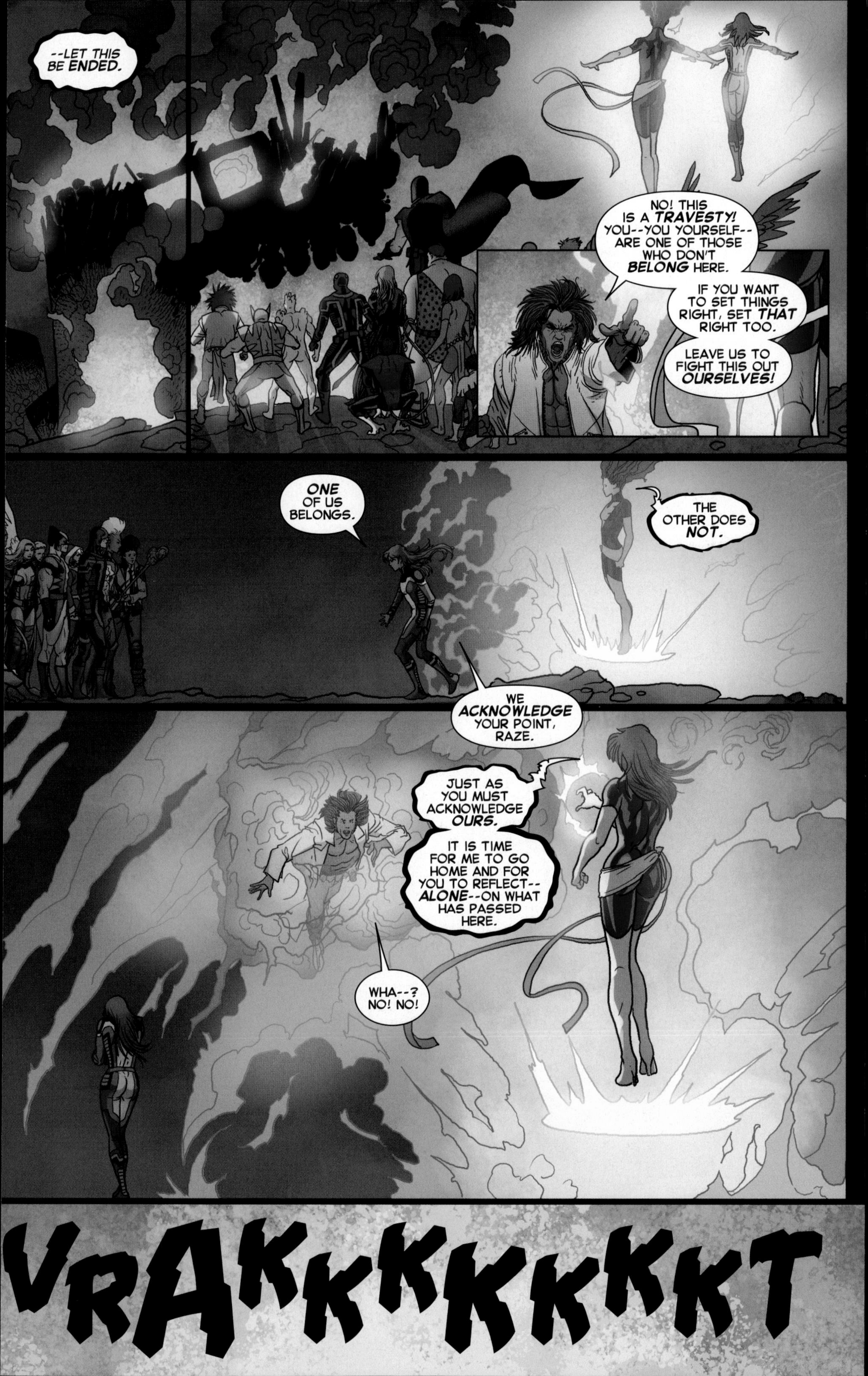

--LET THIS BE ENDED.
NO! THIS IS A TRAVESTY! YOU--YOU YOURSELF--ARE ONE OF THOSE WHO DON'T BELONG HERE.
IF YOU WANT TO SET THINGS RIGHT, SET THAT RIGHT TOO.
LEAVE US TO FIGHT THIS OUT OURSELVES!
ONE OF US BELONGS.
THE OTHER DOES NOT.
WE ACKNOWLEDGE YOUR POINT, RAZE.
JUST AS YOU MUST ACKNOWLEDGE OURS.
IT IS TIME FOR ME TO GO HOME AND FOR YOU TO REFLECT--ALONE--ON WHAT HAS PASSED HERE.
WHA--? NO! NO!
VRAKKKKKKKT

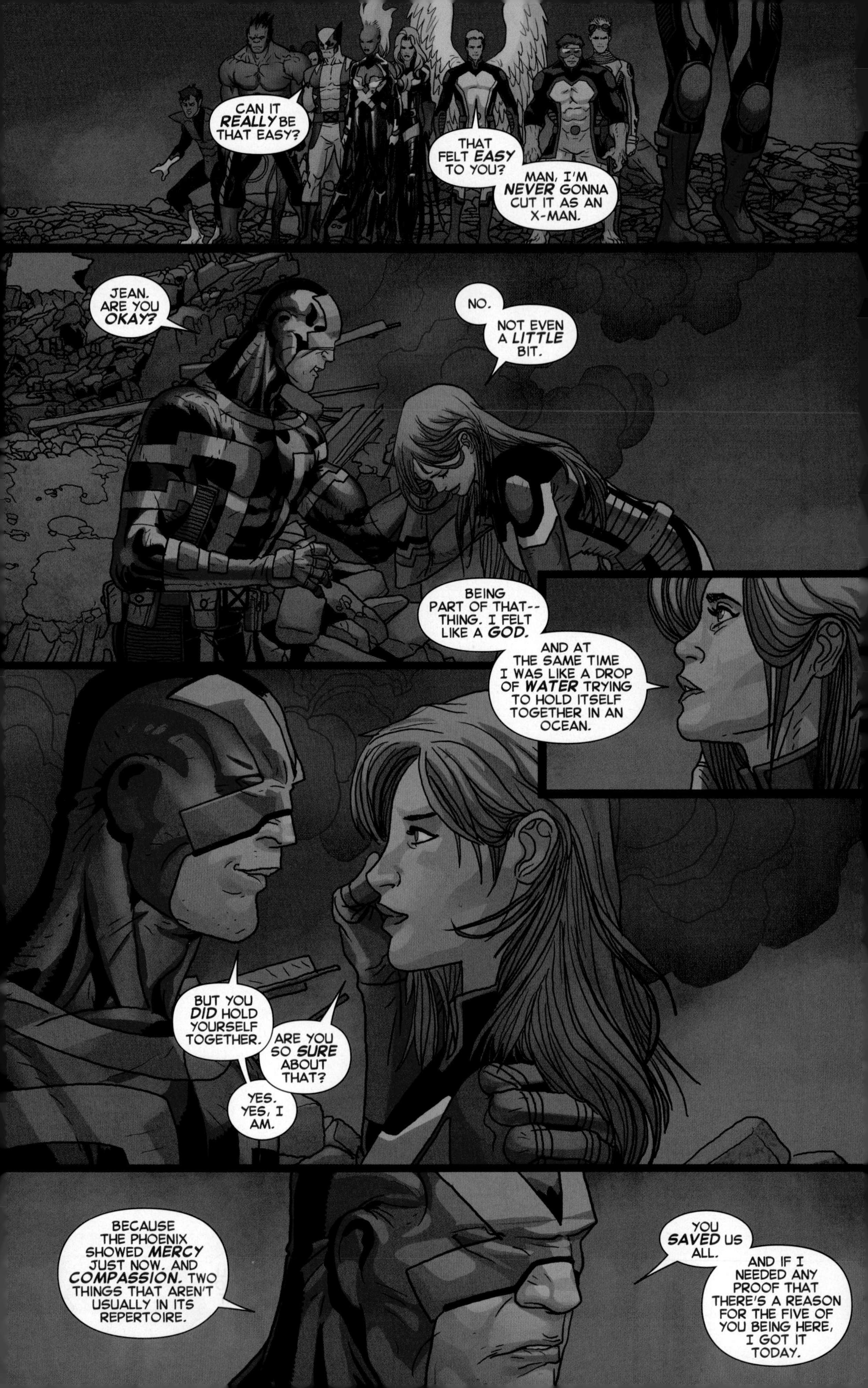
CAN IT REALLY BE THAT EASY?
THAT FELT EASY TO YOU?
MAN, I'M NEVER GONNA CUT IT AS AN X-MAN.
JEAN. ARE YOU OKAY?
NO.
NOT EVEN A LITTLE BIT.
BEING PART OF THAT-- THING. I FELT LIKE A GOD.
AND AT THE SAME TIME I WAS LIKE A DROP OF WATER TRYING TO HOLD ITSELF TOGETHER IN AN OCEAN.
BUT YOU DID HOLD YOURSELF TOGETHER.
ARE YOU SO SURE ABOUT THAT?
YES. YES, I AM.
BECAUSE THE PHOENIX SHOWED MERCY JUST NOW. AND COMPASSION. TWO THINGS THAT AREN'T USUALLY IN ITS REPERTOIRE.
YOU SAVED US ALL.
AND IF I NEEDED ANY PROOF THAT THERE'S A REASON FOR THE FIVE OF YOU BEING HERE, I GOT IT TODAY.

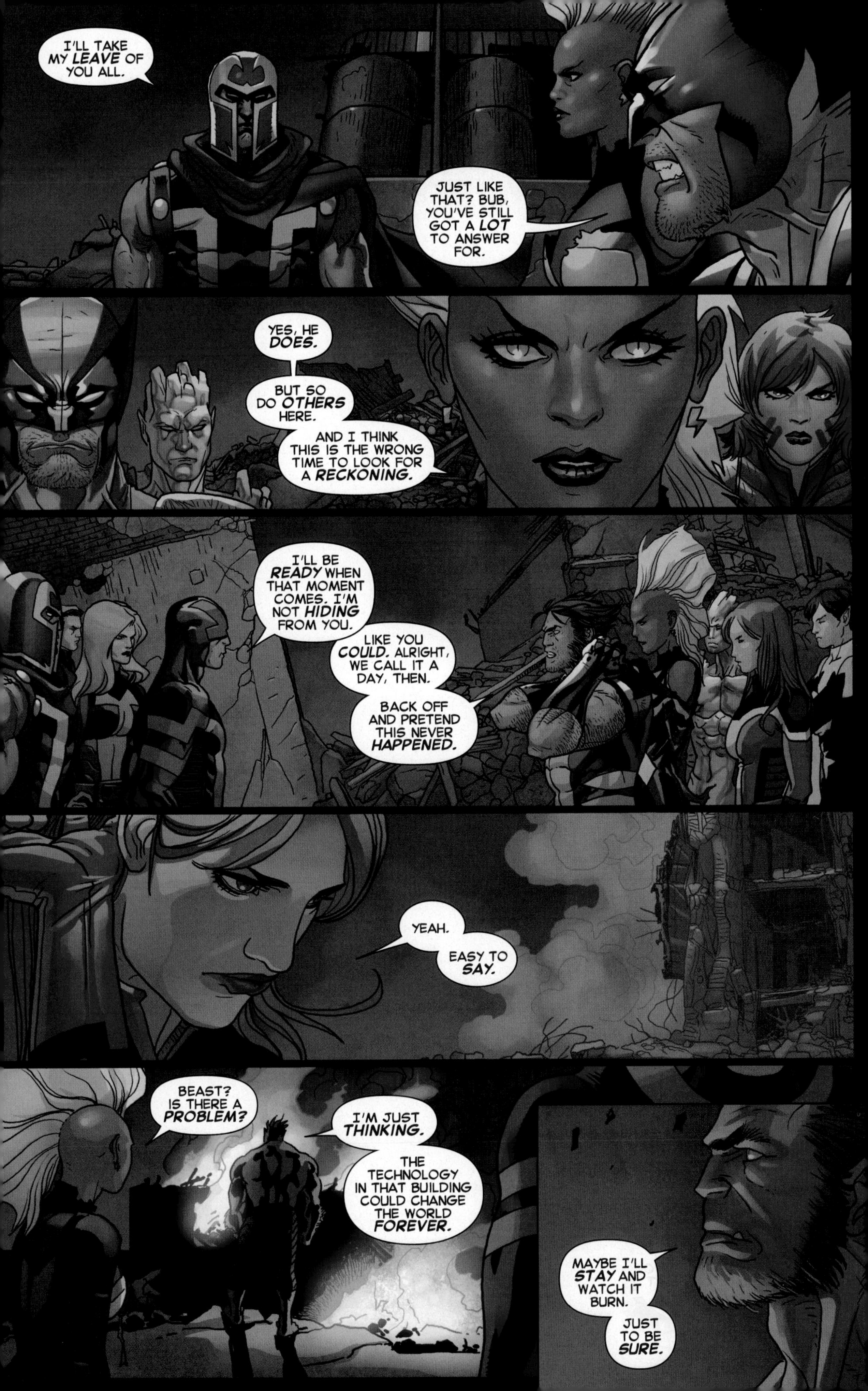
I'LL TAKE MY LEAVE OF YOU ALL.
JUST LIKE THAT? BUB, YOU'VE STILL GOT A LOT TO ANSWER FOR.
YES, HE DOES.
BUT SO DO OTHERS HERE.
AND I THINK THIS IS THE WRONG TIME TO LOOK FOR A RECKONING.
I'LL BE READY WHEN THAT MOMENT COMES. I'M NOT HIDING FROM YOU.
LIKE YOU COULD. ALRIGHT, WE CALL IT A DAY, THEN.
BACK OFF AND PRETEND THIS NEVER HAPPENED.
YEAH.
EASY TO SAY.
BEAST? IS THERE A PROBLEM?
I'M JUST THINKING.
THE TECHNOLOGY IN THAT BUILDING COULD CHANGE THE WORLD FOREVER.
MAYBE I'LL STAY AND WATCH IT BURN.
JUST TO BE SURE.

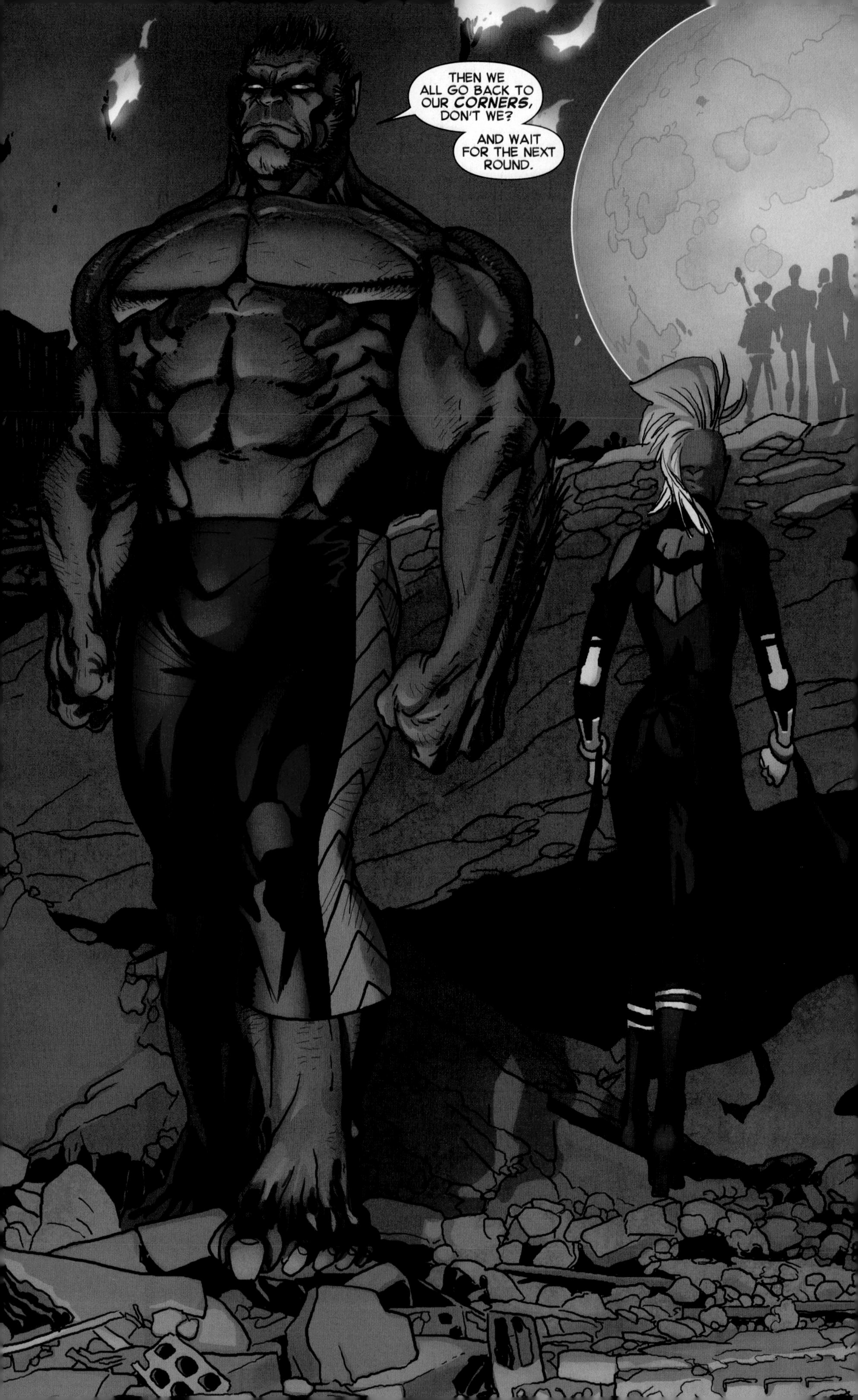
THEN WE ALL GO BACK TO OUR **CORNERS,** DON'T WE?
AND WAIT FOR THE NEXT ROUND.

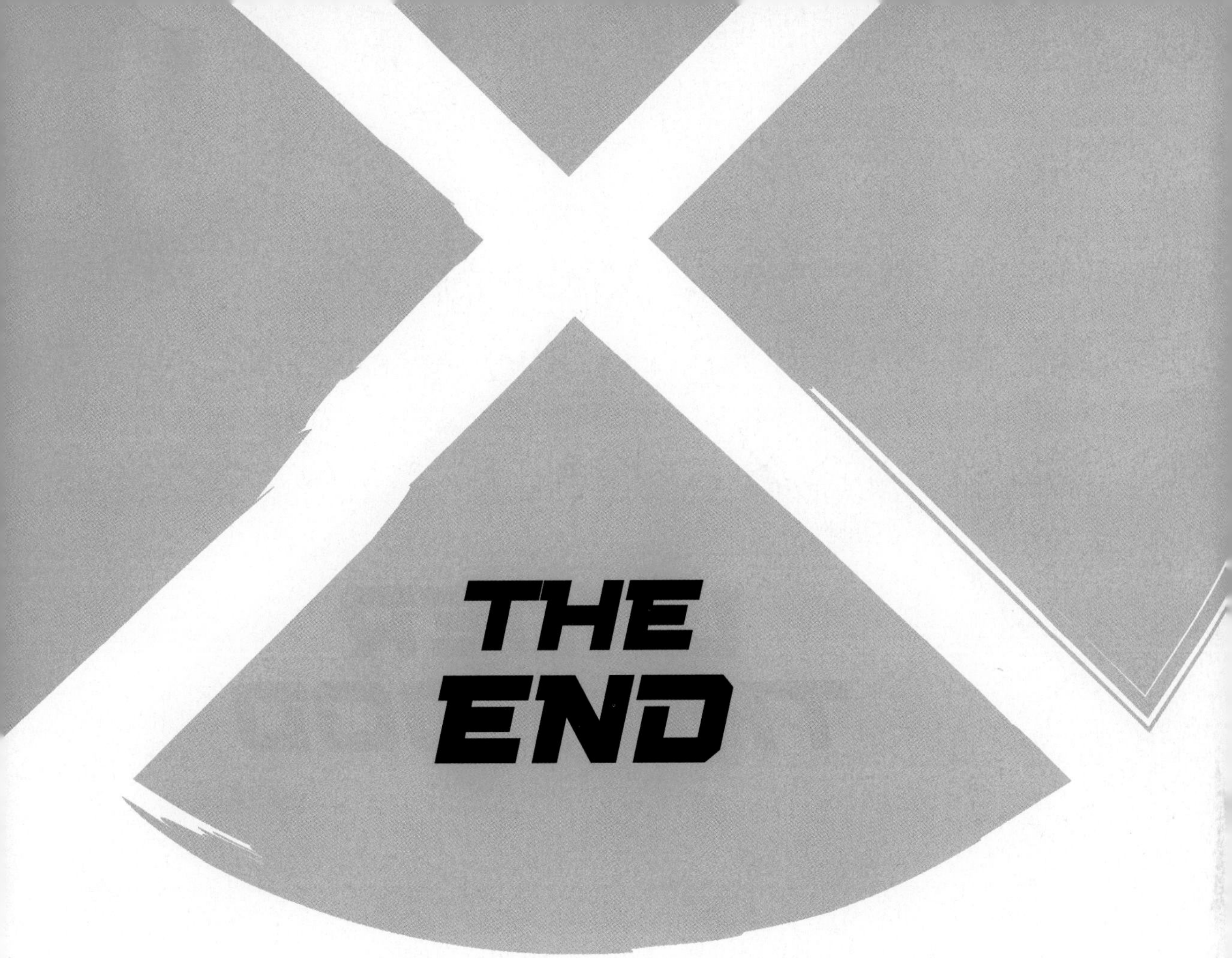
THE END

UNDER THE HOOD

PANEL 1

TWO-SHOT ON WOLVERINE AND NIGHTCRAWLER – NIGHTCRAWLER GRIPS WOLVERINE'S SHOULDER, PREPARING TO TELEPORT.

WOLVERINE: OFFHAND, GLADIATOR, I CAN THINK OF ABOUT A HUNDRED THINGS.

WOLVERINE: ELF, YOU WANNA RULE SOME OF THEM OUT?

NIGHTCRAWLER: BUT OF COURSE.

PANEL 2

WIDE. NIGHTCRAWLER AND WOLVERINE TELEPORT OUT. STORM TAKES TO THE AIR.

FX: BAMF

STORM: RACHEL, LINK OUR MINDS.

RACHEL: [PSI] PARTY LINE. YOU GOT IT, 'RORO.

STORM: WE HAVE SECONDS HERE. LET'S USE THEM.

PANEL 3

INSIDE THE PLANE'S COCKPIT. NIGHTCRAWLER AND WOLVERINE APPEAR IN A ROILING CLOUD OF SMOKE. THEY STARE AT THE EMPTY CONSOLE.

FX: BAMF

NIGHTCRAWLER: *UNGLAUBLICH!*

WOLVERINE: RACHEL, SHOW ORORO WHAT WE'RE SEEING.

WOLVERINE: YOU EVER PILOT A 747 OUT OF A SPIN, ELF?

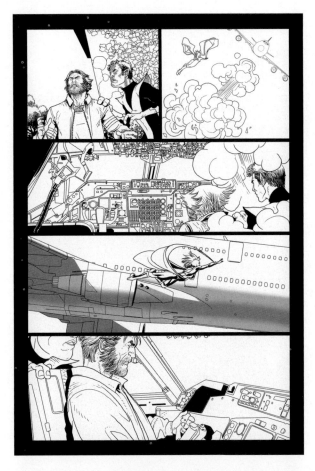

PANEL 4

WIDE, HIGH ANGLE. STORM SOARS ALONGSIDE THE PLANE, WHICH IS STILL AT A CRAZY ANGLE, FALLING RATHER THAN FLYING.

STORM: THE CABIN IS - - EMPTY?

RACHEL: [PSI] NO SIGN OF A PILOT OR A CO-PILOT. PRESSURE'S INTACT, THOUGH. NOBODY BAILED OUT OF THERE.

STORM: CAN LOGAN STEER HER?

PANEL 5

TIGHT ON WOLVERINE. HE'S AT THE CONTROLS OF THE PLANE. HE YELLS ALOUD.

WOLVERINE: THE ENGINES ARE DEAD. I CAN'T DO SQUAT UNLESS WE GET THIS THING'S NOSE UP AND BUILD SOME VELOCITY.

RACHEL: [PSI] OKAY. MESSAGE FROM STORM. "GET READY."

PAGE 17

SPLASH.
A SPECTACULAR PIN-UP SHOT OF CYCLOPS AND
HIS TEAM (MAGIK, EMMA, YOUNG JEAN, YOUNG ICE-
MAN, YOUNG BEAST, YOUNG ANGEL, X-23, TRIAGE)
MATERALISING VIA ONE OF MAGIK'S STEPPING DISKS.
THEY'RE IN GRIM MOOD AND BAD-ASS POSES.

BEAST: [OVERLAPPING] - - IS PROBABLY TO **ASK**
THEM.

PAGE 27

PANEL 1
WIDE. THE X-MEN REACT IN SURPRISE AS THE
TRAP IS SPRUNG. A STEEL CYLINDER ABOUT EIGHT
FEET HIGH AND THREE OR FOUR FEET IN DIAMETER
ERUPTS OUT OF THE SAND, SHOOTING UP TO THE
X-MEN'S HEAD HEIGHT. IT'S SURFACE IS COVERED
WITH SENSORS, TELL-TALES AND HIGH-TECH EXTRU-
SIONS.

WOLVERINE: **RAZE.**

FX: VEEEEEEEEEEE

WOLVERINE: DAMN!

BEAST: PERHAPS WE SHOULD JUST HAVE **AS-
SUMED** THIS WAS A TRAP AND
PROCEEDED FROM THERE.

PANEL 2
TWO-SHOT. MAGNETO SHOUTS OUT TO CYCLOPS,
STARING HARD AT THE DEVICE AS HE BRINGS HIS
POWER TO BEAR ON IT. STANDING BEHIND AND TO
THE RIGHT OF HIM, CYCLOPS ADJUSTS HIS VISOR.

MAGNETO: THIS DEVICE IS EMITTING ENERGY ON
THE SAME **FREQUENCIES** I SENSED
THIS MORNING.

MAGNETO: CYCLOPS?

CYCLOPS: READY WHEN **YOU** ARE.

PANEL 3
WIDE. CYCLOPS AND MAGNETO BLAST THE DEVICE
AT THE SAME TIME, CYKE WITH HIS NEW TYPE OF
EYE BEAM, MAGNETO WITH A RIPPLING BURST OF
ELECTRO-MAGNETIC FORCE. IT'S NOT HARMED IN
THE SLIGHTEST.

FX: VRAKKKKKKT

PANEL 4
STRIPPED ACROSS THE BOTTOM OF THE PAGE, OR
AT BOTTOM RIGHT. A ROW OF DIAGNOSTIC LIGHTS
IN THE DEVICE'S CASING LIGHTS UP.
RED
RED
RED
RED
RED
GREEN

FX: BIP

PAGE 50

PANEL 1
ANGLE, STAYING WIDE. WOLVERINE HAS CUT NIGHT-CRAWLER DOWN, AND NOW DRAPES HIM OVER HIS SHOULDER, PUSHING THE EXPLOSIVE VEST INTO MYSTIQUE'S HANDS.

WOLVERINE: HERE. THIS IS **YOURS.**

MYSTIQUE: I WOULDN'T HAVE **CONSENTED** TO HIS DEATH. JUST SO YOU KNOW.

WOLVERINE: YOU **TALK** TO ME RIGHT NOW, MYS-TIQUE, YOU'RE GONNA START A **WAR.**

WOLVERINE: IF THAT'S WHAT YOU WANT, KEEP RIGHT ON GOING.

PANEL 2
WIDE. ILLYANA SUMMONS A STEPPING DISK AND THE X-MEN START TO PHASE OUT. WOLVERINE STILL CARRYING NIGHTCRAWLER.

STORM: THIS ISN'T **OVER,** RAZE.

RAZE: I'VE GOT **FAITH** IN YOU, CYCLOPS. IN **ALL** OF YOU.

RAZE: THE X-MEN **ALWAYS** DO THE RIGHT THING.

PANEL 3
CLOSE-UP ON RAZE'S FACE. HE'S SMILING.

RAZE: AFTER THEY'VE RUN THROUGH ALL THE **OTHER** OPTIONS.

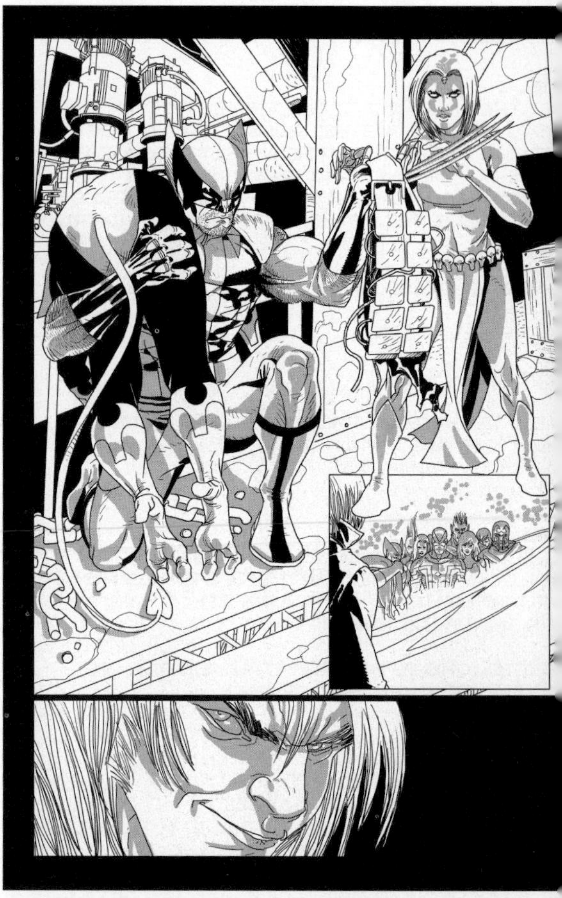

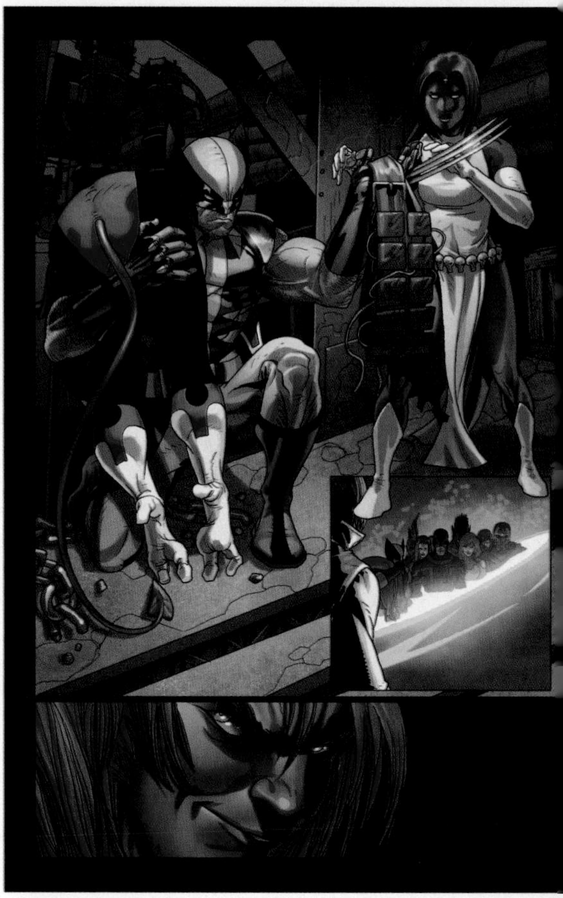

PANEL 1
THE CORRIDOR OUTSIDE THE MED ROOM. CYKE, STORM AND WOLVERINE GOING OVER WHAT THEY'VE JUST HEARD.

CYCLOPS: SENDING IN SPIES WAS A GOOD **CALL**, ORORO.

STORM: WITH SO MANY **STRANGE** MUTANTS TURNING UP, IT SEEMED THAT THE **RISK** WOULD BE MINIMAL.

STORM: BUT WHAT ARE WE TO **MAKE** OF THIS?

PANEL 2
TWO-SHOT ON CYCLOPS AND WOLVERINE. GRIM, INTENSE.

CYCLOPS: I'D SAY IT CHANGES **EVERYTHING**. IF THE HUMAN RACE IS IN SOME SORT OF VIRTUAL **STORAGE**, WE'VE GOT TO RETRIEVE THEM.

CYCLOPS: EVEN IF THAT MEANS GOING TO **WAR** WITH RAZE AND HIS BROTHERHOOD.

WOLVERINE: **ESPECIALLY** IF IT MEANS THAT. BLUE BOY'S **ASKED** FOR IT ONCE TOO OFTEN.

PANEL 3
TIGHT ON STORM. CALM AND SERIOUS.

STORM: SALE'S TECHNOLOGY IS THE **KEY** TO ALL THIS.

STORM: BUT IF **RAZE** COULDN'T MASTER IT EVEN WITH SALE'S HELP, I DOUBT WE'LL DO MUCH **BETTER**.

PANEL 4
WIDE. CYCLOPS THOUGHTFUL – WORKING SOMETHING OUT. STORM STARES AT HIM, CONCERNED.

WOLVERINE: WHAT ABOUT THE CONTRAPTION WE BROUGHT BACK FROM NEW MEXICO? CAN'T WE **RETRO-ENGINEER** IT?

STORM: HANK SAYS NO. THE **LIGHTNING** MELTED HALF ITS CIRCUITS.

STORM: CYCLOPS, WHAT'S WRONG?

CYCLOPS: NOTHING. I'M JUST **THINKING**.

PANEL 5
CLOSE-UP ON CYCLOPS'S FACE. THE MOMENT OF DECISION.

CYCLOPS: YOU SAID WE COULDN'T DO MUCH WITHOUT SALE'S **HELP**.

CYCLOPS: WHAT IF THERE WAS A WAY WE COULD **TALK** TO SALE DIRECTLY?

PANEL 6
WIDE. CYCLOPS WALKS AWAY – TOWARDS US. STORM AND WOLVERINE STARE AFTER HIM.

STORM: BUT - - SALE IS **DEAD**.

CYCLOPS: I KNOW.

CYCLOPS: THAT DOESN'T HAVE TO BE A **DEAL-BREAKER**.

CREATOR BIOGRAPHIES

MIKE CAREY

MIKE CAREY IS A BRITISH WRITER WHOSE WORK SPANS COMICS, NOVELS, RADIO, FILM AND TV. HIS COMIC WORK FOR MARVEL INCLUDES LONG RUNS ON *X-MEN LEGACY* AND *ULTIMATE FANTASTIC FOUR*, AS WELL AS THE *SPELLBINDERS* AND *SIGIL* MINISERIES. HAVING WRITTEN FIVE FELIX CASTOR NOVELS AND (AS ADAM BLAKE) TWO MAINSTREAM THRILLERS, HIS MOST RECENT BOOK IS THE POST-APOCALYPTIC COMING OF AGE STORY *THE GIRL WITH ALL THE GIFTS*. HE IS CURRENTLY WORKING ON SEVERAL FEATURE FILMS AND TELEVISION SERIES INCLUDING A MOVIE ADAPTATION OF JONATHAN TRIGELL'S NOVEL *GENUS*.

SALVADOR LARROCA

AFTER ILLUSTRATING *DEATH'S HEAD II* AND *DARK ANGEL* FOR THE MARVEL UK IMPRINT, **SALVADOR LARROCA** SCORED A REGULAR GIG ON *GHOST RIDER*. HE GRADUATED TO *FANTASTIC FOUR*, WORKING ALONGSIDE ONE OF HIS FAVORITE WRITERS, CHRIS CLAREMONT. FROM 2000 TO 2006, LARROCA DEPICTED MARVEL'S MUTANTS ACROSS *UNCANNY X-MEN*, *X-MEN* AND *X-TREME X-MEN*. HIS POPULARITY CONTINUED TO BUILD AS HE CROSSED OVER TO *NEWUNIVERSAL*, A STRIKING TAKE ON THE NEW UNIVERSE BY WRITER WARREN ELLIS. FOLLOWING A STINT ON *AMAZING SPIDER-MAN*, LARROCA BEGAN WORKING ON ONE OF MARVEL'S BIGGEST HITS, *INVINCIBLE IRON MAN*, WITH WRITER MATT FRACTION.

JUSTIN PONSOR

JUSTIN PONSOR HAS SPENT NEARLY TWO DECADES IN COMICS, HONING HIS CRAFT IN THE STUDIOS OF DC/WILDSTORM, AVALON AND CROSSGEN. EXCLUSIVE TO MARVEL SINCE 2005, HE IS CONSISTENTLY PAIRED WITH THE TOP NAMES IN THE INDUSTRY. NOTABLE AMONG THE MANY TITLES TO WHICH HE'S CONTRIBUTED ARE *AVENGERS*, *INFINITY*, *UNCANNY X-MEN* AND *YOUNG AVENGERS*. CURRENTLY, HE COLORS *GUARDIANS OF THE GALAXY* AND *ULTIMATE COMICS SPIDER-MAN* FROM HIS HOME OFFICE IN FLORIDA.

CORY PETIT

CORY PETIT HAS BEEN LETTERING COMICS SINCE 2002. HE'S WORKED ON *AVENGERS*, *X-FACTOR*, *ALIAS*, *ULTIMATE SPIDER-MAN* AND MANY MORE.

JARED K. FLETCHER

A FEW MONTHS AFTER GRADUATING FROM THE KUBERT SCHOOL, **JARED K. FLETCHER** STARTED WORKING AT DC COMICS AS PART OF THEIR NEW IN-HOUSE LETTERING DEPARTMENT WORKING ON COMICS LIKE *EX MACHINA*, *THE NEW FRONTIER*, AND *BATMAN: YEAR 100*. FOUR YEARS LATER, HE LEFT DC TO PURSUE HIS FREELANCE CAREER AND BEGAN **STUDIO FANTABULOUS**. HE SPENDS LONG DAYS IN HIS UNDERGROUND STUDIO DESIGNING LOGOS AND TYPE TREATMENTS, ART DIRECTING COVERS, CARTOONING, DESIGNING T-SHIRTS, AND BOOKS LIKE THIS ONE. HE LIVES AND WORKS IN BROOKLYN, NY.

ALSO BY

MIKE CAREY

MARVEL
X-MEN
SUPERNOVAS
CAREY•BACHALO•RAMOS•BROOKS

X-MEN: SUPERNOVAS
978-0-7851-2319-4

MARVEL
X-MEN
LEGACY
DIVIDED HE STANDS
CAREY • EATON
ROMITA JR. • TAN • LAND • PETERSON • DEODATO

X-MEN LEGACY: DIVIDED HE STANDS
978-0-7851-3001-7

MARVEL
X-MEN
LEGACY
SINS OF THE FATHER
CAREY • EATON • BRIONES

X-MEN LEGACY: SINS OF THE FATHER
978-0-7851-3003-1

MARVEL
X-MEN
LEGACY
EMPLATE
CAREY • ACUÑA

X-MEN LEGACY: EMPLATE
978-0-7851-4115-0

MARVEL
X-MEN
ORIGINAL SIN
WAY • DEODATO • CAREY • EATON

X-MEN: ORIGINAL SIN
*AVAILABLE DIGITALLY

X-MEN
MARVEL
AGE OF X

X-MEN: AGE OF X
978-0-78515290-3

CROSSGEN
SIGIL
CAREY • KIRK • OLLIFFE
MARVEL
OUT OF TIME

SIGIL
978-0-7851-5622-2

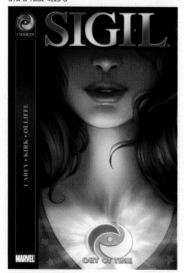

ALSO BY
SALVADOR LARROCA

"Mad Max meets Ocean's 11." —SuperHeroHype.com
CABLE AND X-FORCE
WANTED
HOPELESS
MARVEL NOW!
LARROCA

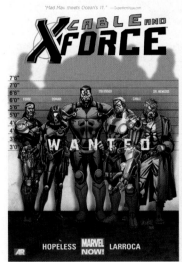

CABLE AND X-FORCE VOL. 1: WANTED
978-0-7851-6699-0

X-MEN
MARVEL
ENDANGERED SPECIES

UNCANNY X-MEN: ENDANGERED SPECIES
978-0-7851-2820-5

MARVEL
X-TREME X-MEN
destiny
CLAREMONT • LARROCA

X-TREME X-MEN
*AVAILABLE DIGITALLY

THE INVINCIBLE
IRON MAN
MARVEL
THE FIVE NIGHTMARES
MATT FRACTION • SALVADOR LARROCA

INVINCIBLE IRON MAN
VOL. 1: THE FIVE NIGHTMARES
978-0-7851-3412-1

*AVAILABLE ON THE **MARVEL COMICS APP**
(FOR IPHONE®, IPAD®, IPOD TOUCH® & ANDROIDTM DEVICES)
AND ONLINE IN THE ***MARVEL DIGITAL COMICS SHOP!***

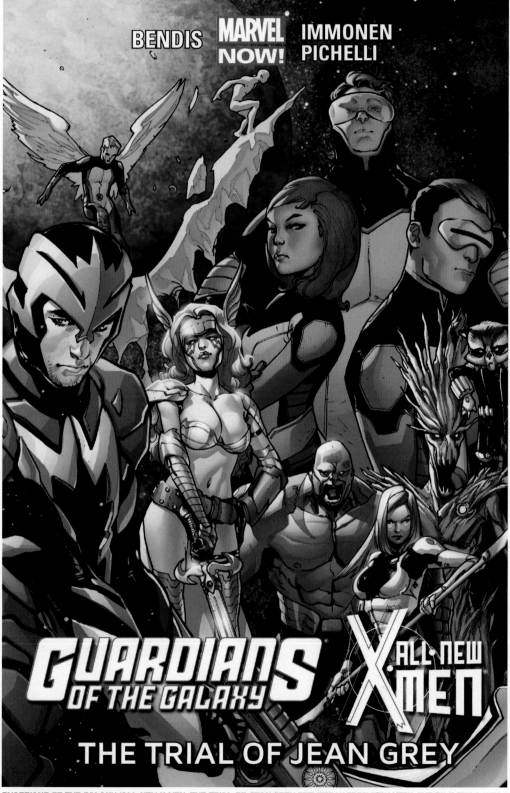

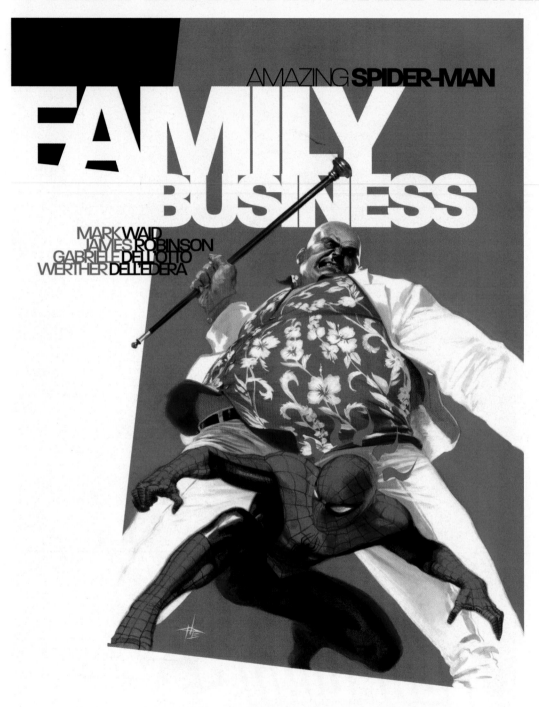

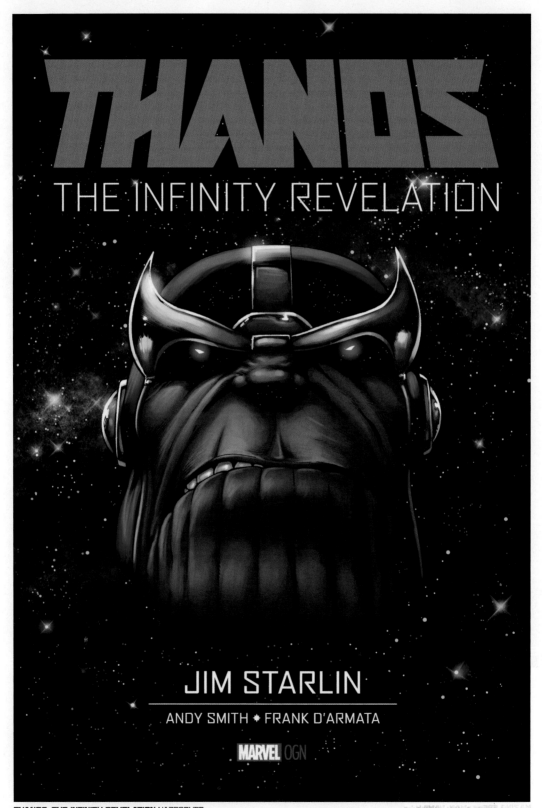

FREE
DIGITAL COPY

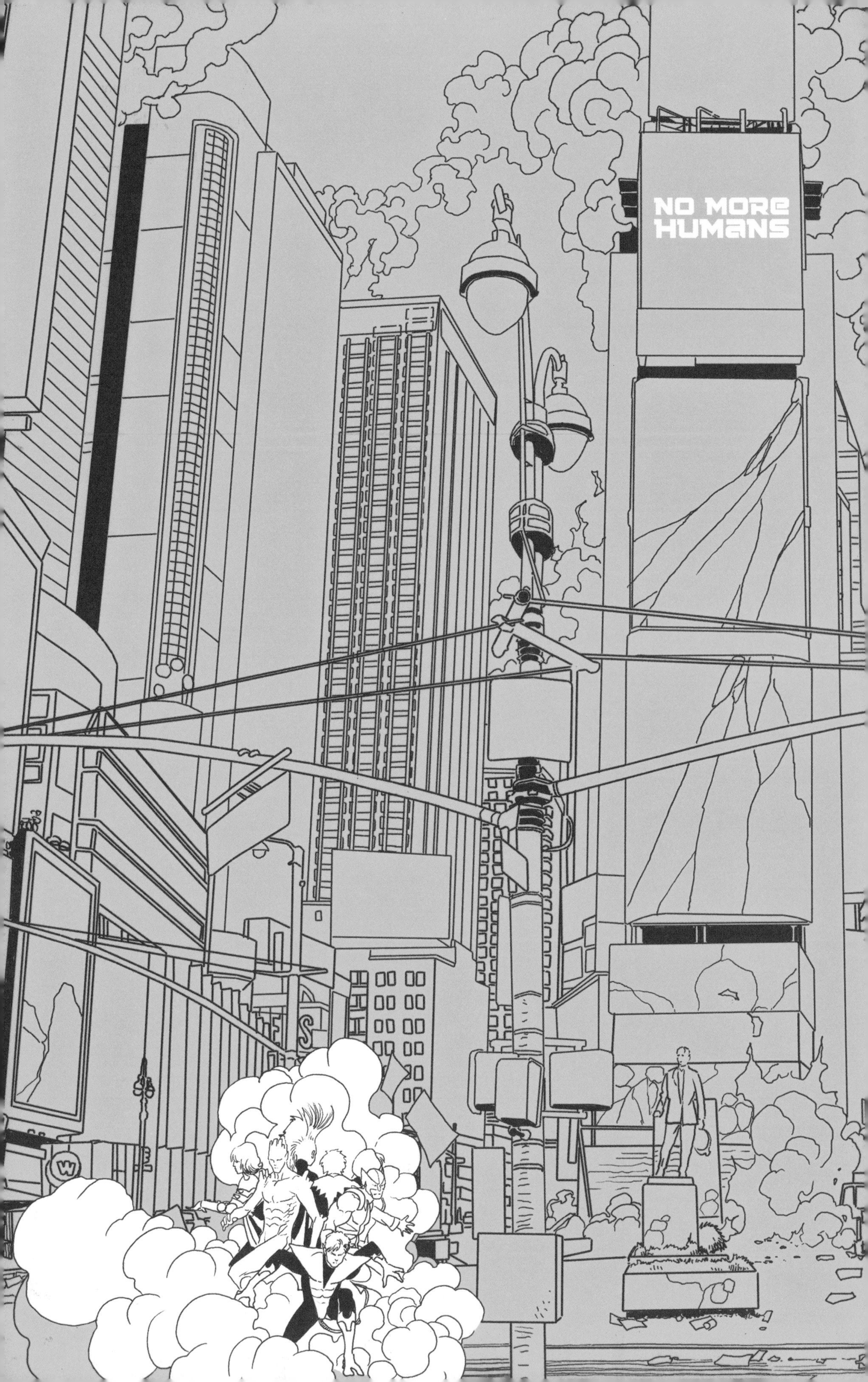
NO MORE HUMANS